A field guide to the
Larger Mammals
of Tanzania

Charles Foley, Lara Foley, Alex Lobora
Maurus Msuha, Tim R.B. Davenport

WILD*Guides*

PRINCETON
press.pri

Published by Princeton University Press,
41 William Street, Princeton, New Jersey 08540
In the United Kingdom: Princeton University Press, 6 Oxford Street,
Woodstock, Oxfordshire OX20 1TW
nathist.press.princeton.edu

British Library Cataloging-in-Publication Data is available

Library of Congress Control Number 2013950246
ISBN 978-0-691-16117-4

Production and design by **WILD**Guides Ltd., Old Basing, Hampshire UK.
Printed in Singapore

10 9 8 7 6 5 4 3 2 1

Contents

THE SPECIES ACCOUNTS

Terrestrial mammals

Wildebeest crossing the Mara River, Serengeti National Park

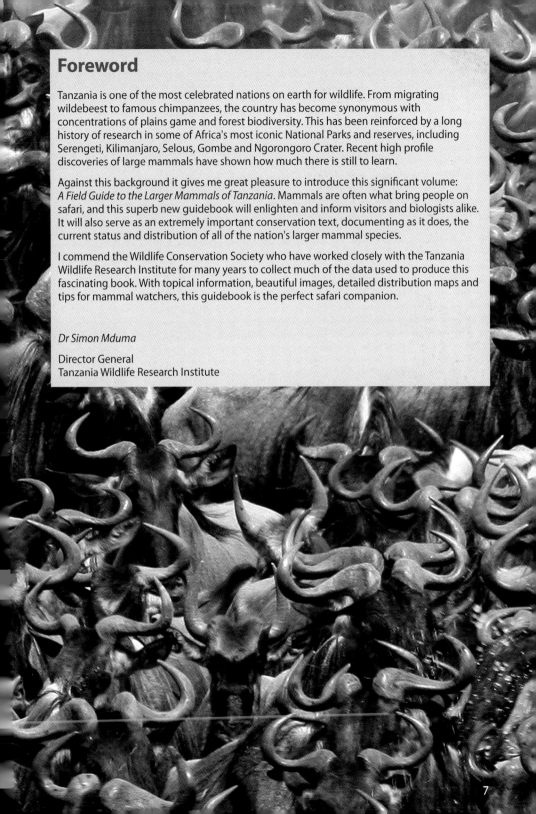

Foreword

Tanzania is one of the most celebrated nations on earth for wildlife. From migrating wildebeest to famous chimpanzees, the country has become synonymous with concentrations of plains game and forest biodiversity. This has been reinforced by a long history of research in some of Africa's most iconic National Parks and reserves, including Serengeti, Kilimanjaro, Selous, Gombe and Ngorongoro Crater. Recent high profile discoveries of large mammals have shown how much there is still to learn.

Against this background it gives me great pleasure to introduce this significant volume: *A Field Guide to the Larger Mammals of Tanzania*. Mammals are often what bring people on safari, and this superb new guidebook will enlighten and inform visitors and biologists alike. It will also serve as an extremely important conservation text, documenting as it does, the current status and distribution of all of the nation's larger mammal species.

I commend the Wildlife Conservation Society who have worked closely with the Tanzania Wildlife Research Institute for many years to collect much of the data used to produce this fascinating book. With topical information, beautiful images, detailed distribution maps and tips for mammal watchers, this guidebook is the perfect safari companion.

Dr Simon Mduma

Director General
Tanzania Wildlife Research Institute

Preface

Tanzania offers outstanding opportunities for some of the most spectacular wildlife watching in the world, and is justifiably famous as an African safari destination. We have written this book to help people visiting or living in Tanzania to find and identify mammals in the country. Our goal is to stimulate a passion for watching wildlife, as well as to encourage an interest in the conservation of these species and their habitats. This is the second book in the Wildlife Conservation Society (WCS)–Tanzania Programme field guide series, following the *Orchids and Wild Flowers of Kitulo Plateau*, also published by Princeton **WILD***Guides*.

This book covers over 135 species of 'larger' mammal: anything from approximately the size of a hedgehog to the Humpback Whale. Although over 340 species of mammal have been recorded in Tanzania, nearly 60% of these are rodents, bats and shrews. With the exception of three of the larger rodents (Cape and Crested Porcupines and Springhare), which a visitor may encounter on safari, we have not included rodents, bats or shrews in this book as data were not sufficient to cover them to the same level of detail. For information on small mammal species in Tanzania, we encourage you to visit the website of The Field Museum, Chicago (see below), which includes a useful identification guide and distribution maps. Whales, dolphins and other marine mammals are included in this book, although we add the caveat that very little is known about these species in Tanzanian waters; the information presented is therefore almost certainly an under-representation of the diversity of marine mammals in this country.

The majority of the distribution data included in this book were collected by the Tanzania Carnivore Project and Tanzania Mammal Atlas Project, which received substantial funding from the British Government's Darwin Initiative and was a collaboration between the Tanzania Wildlife Research Institute (TAWIRI), the Zoological Society of London (ZSL) and the Wildlife Conservation Society (WCS). The mammal distribution database created by these projects now has over 50,000 records, including 15,000 camera trap photographs. WCS has also provided extensive information from its long-term conservation programme in the Southern Highlands and from its other four programmes across the country. There are still many gaps in our knowledge on the distribution of mammals in Tanzania, and we encourage readers to submit any interesting sighting records to **info@tanzaniamammals.org**

All author royalties received from sales of this book will be donated to the Wildlife Conservation Society and used to support the Tanzania Carnivore Project or other wildlife conservation projects in Tanzania. For more information about the work of WCS, ZSL or TAWIRI, please visit the websites listed below.

www.wcstanzania.org

www.wcs.org

www.zsl.org

www.tawiri.or.tz

archive.fieldmuseum.org/tanzania/index.html

darwin.defra.gov.uk

Quick Response (QR) code. Scan the code with a QR reader on a smart phone, computer tablet or other similar device to go to the WCS Tanzania website.

Acknowledgements

A great number of people helped in the creation of this book. We have attempted to list of all of the contributors but if we have inadvertently missed anyone we sincerely apologize.

We extend special thanks to our field teams for their tireless efforts to set camera traps and collect data in the field, often in difficult conditions: Paul Baran, Claire Bracebridge, Emmanuel Lalashe, Ayubu Kajigili, Buto Kalasa, Chediel Kazael, Sylvanos Kimiti, Sophy Machaga, Zawadi Mbwambo, Ramadhani Mduruma, Allen Mmbaga, Noah Mpunga, Michael Munisi, Atupakisye Mwaibanje, Obadia Mwaipungu, Lusajo Mwakalinga, Rajabu Makwiro, Willie Mwalwengwele, Jumanne Ramadhani and Mwemezi Rwiza.

David Moyer greatly assisted with the distribution maps, especially for southern Tanzania. Kenneth K. Coe and Jason Woolgar generously donated many of the photographs. Numerous other photographers also contributed images and are credited on *pages 309–310*. *The IUCN Red List for Threatened Species*™ provided valuable data for the species' pan-African range maps. Andy and Gill Swash and Robert Still at **WILD***Guides* made this book possible with their expertise, infinite patience, keen eye for detail, and good humour. Ellesmere and Sierra Foley contributed in kind with their curiosity and patience during the writing of this book.

Our appreciation goes out to the following people for their valuable contributions:

Michel Allard
Jo Anderson
Mike Angelides
Liz & Neil Baker
Marc Baker
Rachel Balum
Rob Barbour
Sultana Bashir
Colin Beale
Simon Bearder
Richard Bonham
Andrew Bowkett
Gillian Braulik
Doug Braum
Henry Brink
Sjouke & Yoka Bruinsma
Michael Bucknall
Tom Butynski
David Bygott
Tim Caro
Arturo Caso
Silvia Ceppi
Peter Chibwaye
Leah Collett
Anthony Collins
Nobby Cordeiro
Jim Cox
Scott Creel
David Danford
Yvonne de Jong
Glen Dennis
Amy Dickman
Jean Du Plessis
Ron Eggert
Kerstin Erler
Brechtje Eshuis

Anna Estes
Richard Estes
Squack Evans
John & Teresa Foley
Geoff Fox
Chris Fox
Ignas Gara
Philippe Gaubert
Aadje Geertsema
Alex Gerard
Rob Glen
Eliamani Godwin
John Grimshaw
David Guthrie
George Gwaltu
Brian Harris
Mustafa Hassanali
Yves Hausser
Wayne Hendry
Anne Hilborn
Richard Hoare
Hendrick Hoeck
Gary Hoops
Louise Horsfall
Kim Howell
Luke Hunter
Derek Hurt
Eddy Husslage
Denis Ikanda
Ingela Jansson
Peggy Johnson
Peter Jones
Trevor Jones
Walter Jubber
Shadrack Kamenya
Amos Kapama

Adam Scott Kennedy
Vicki Kennedy
Julius Kibebe
Emilian Kihwele
Hamza Kija
Leonard Kileo
Jonathan Kingdon
Ethan Kinsey
Bernard Kissui
Jules Knocker
Richard Knocker
Edwin Konzo
Davin Korda
Hadas Kushnir
Inyasi Lejora
Sophia Lenferna
Jeff Lewis
Laly Lichtenfeld
Martin Loibooki
Novatus Magoma
Honori Maliti
Halima Mangi
John Martins
Danny McCallum
Simon Mduma
Britta Meyer
David Mills
Dennis Minja
Augustine Minja
Deus Mjungu
John Mkindi
Patricia Moehlman
Julius Mollel
Rose Mosha
Pauline Mpuya
Paschal Mrina

John Mshana
Charles Msilanga
Henock Msocha
Linus Munishi
Sixtus Mushi
Frederick Mushi
Peter Mvungi
Nebbo Mwina
Ali Mwinyi
Gilles Nicolet
James Njau
Goodluck Nnko
Guy Norton
Janemary Ntalwila
David O'Bryan
Lisa O'Bryan
Helen O'Neill
Karen Oakes
G. Ole Meing'ataki
Paul Oliver
Boniface Osujaki
Anne Outwater
John Pallangyo
Philip Pendael
Andrew Perkin
Daudi & Trude Peterson
Mike & Lisa Peterson
Thad & Robin Peterson
Guy Picton Phillipps
Alex Piel
Andy Plumptre
Emmanuel Rafael
Galen Rathbun
Keith Roberts
Robert Ross
Francesco Rovero

Victor Runyoro
Edward Salali
Dalili Salum
Gian Schachenmann
Nani Schmeling
Mshujaa Senge
Thomas Shabani
Ryan Shallom
Gemes Shayo
John Shemkunde
Richard Shilunga
Kirstin Siex
Sammy Sikombe
Annette Simonson
Brenden Simonson
Jon Simonson
Laura Simpson
Tony Sinclair
Antonio Sirolli
Bill Stanley
Sue Stolberger
Mary Strauss
Tom Struhsaker
Samwel Sudi
Glory Summay
Jonathan Taylor
Rehema Tibanyenda
Charles Trout
Kikoti Twaha
Ifura Ukio
Wim van den Bergh
John van der Loon
Karine van der Vurst
Andries van der Walt
James Wakibara
Ryan Wienand

Finally, we would like to thank the Tanzania Wildlife Research Institute, Tanzania National Parks, Tanzania Wildlife Division, Commission for Science and Technology, the Tanzania Forest Service, and District Councils across Tanzania for their invaluable assistance, support, and collaboration over the years.

Conservation in Tanzania

Tanzania is one of the most important nations for wildlife conservation in mainland Africa, boasting an extraordinary wealth of flora and fauna, including many endemic species and subspecies. To date, over 10,000 species of trees and plants, 1,100 species of birds and at least 340 species of mammals have been recorded. Tanzania is a particularly important country for large mammals and supports the highest diversity of both ungulates and primates in continental Africa. It also hosts the largest numbers of many iconic African mammals, including Common Wildebeest, Plains Zebra, Giraffe, African Buffalo, Hippopotamus, Lion and African Wild Dog. The nutrient-rich plains of the Serengeti ecosystem (most of which lies in Tanzania) sustain the largest migration of ungulates on the planet, a spectacular annual movement of over one-and-a-half million animals. Additionally, Tanzanian waters support the annual migration of thousands of Humpback Whales.

The philosophy of wildlife and land conservation was enshrined at the beginning of Tanzania's foundation as an independent nation in a speech given by Tanzania's first President, the late Julius Nyerere, in 1961, in what became known as the Arusha Manifesto:

> 'The survival of our wildlife is a matter of grave concern to all of us in Africa. These wild creatures amid the wild places they inhabit are not only important as a source of wonder and inspiration, but are an integral part of our natural resources and our future livelihood and well being.'

At independence in 1961, Tanzania had only one National Park (Serengeti), but the number has since grown to 17 and now represents one of the most extensive and diverse protected area networks in Africa. Today, nearly 20% of Tanzania's land is protected solely for wildlife-related activities as National Parks and Game Reserves, although the degree of conservation management at different sites varies significantly. Some of these protected areas are vast: for example, the Selous Game Reserve and Ruaha National Park, combined, encompass over 70,000 km^2 (over 27,000 mi^2), an area twice the size of The Netherlands.

Despite the network of protected areas, most large mammal species in Tanzania have experienced substantial range reductions and density declines in recent decades, as rapid human population growth and economic development has placed increasing demands on natural resources. Agricultural expansion, illegal timber extraction and tree felling for charcoal production have led to large-scale loss of natural habitat. Coastal and montane forests have been severely affected and continue to suffer extensive degradation.

Of particular importance for nature conservation in Tanzania are the evergreen forests of the Eastern Arc Mountains, the Southern Highlands and the Albertine Rift. These mountains support remnant patches of species-rich forests that several million years ago stretched from central Africa to the Tanzanian coast. These relict forests are now major biodiversity hotspots, supporting large numbers of endemic plant and animal species, including eight of the ten larger mammals

that are endemic to Tanzania. All of these forests continue to suffer substantial habitat loss, with approximately two-thirds of the afromontane forests being lost in the last century. The human population's continued reliance upon wood and charcoal for fuel in Tanzania has resulted in the devastation of swathes of miombo woodland in the south, centre and west of the country and these losses continue unabated.

Agricultural expansion also poses a threat to wildlife migration corridors and seasonal dispersal areas, with many protected areas becoming increasingly isolated. In some areas, such as Tarangire National Park, where the majority of large mammal species migrate seasonally to village land, loss of these corridors could lead to a collapse of the large mammal population of the National Park. The long-term viability of these Parks depends upon neighbouring communities having sufficient incentive to keep their village land accessible to wildlife, by limiting agricultural development and the establishment of permanent settlements in important wildlife areas. Other National Parks, such as Manyara, Ruaha and Serengeti, are threatened by declines in water levels in the main rivers and lakes due to extensive extraction for agricultural irrigation upstream.

Poaching of wildlife for bushmeat and animal parts, such as tusks, skin or scales, has had a major impact on wildlife populations in Tanzania. Demand for bushmeat, both within Tanzania and some neighbouring countries, has increased significantly in recent years. Soaring demand for wildlife products in Asia, notably elephant tusks and rhinoceros horns, has precipitated a poaching crisis for both these species. Elephant populations in Tanzania have suffered heavily, declining by approximately 50% between 2009 and 2013, while the few remaining Black Rhinoceroses in Tanzania require 24-hour protection by armed guards. Tanzania's protected areas are vast and difficult to protect, and law enforcement capacity is very limited in many areas, particularly Game Reserves and Forest Reserves, and wildlife populations have suffered as a result.

Despite these challenges, Tanzania has taken significant measures to improve the conservation of its natural resources. Since 2000, a network of Marine Parks and Reserves has been established in order to protect important coastal and marine habitats. Four new National Parks have been created, including one established primarily to protect wild flowers (Kitulo), and two to protect important areas of coastal forest (Sadaani and Jozani Chwaka Bay). Critically, new Wildlife Management Areas (WMAs) are being established in buffer zones and wildlife corridors in order to enable rural communities to benefit from wildlife on their lands. Activities such as safari tourism can generate significant revenue, encouraging these communities to consider wildlife on their land as an asset rather than a hindrance.

In spite of Tanzania's commitment to wildlife conservation, resources for conservation have to compete with educational, health and infrastructure improvements for its citizens. However, wildlife contributes significantly to Tanzania's economic development through tourism, which is now one of the largest earners of foreign revenue in the country. Tourism is therefore integrally linked with wildlife conservation in Tanzania, although balancing that relationship to minimize the impact of tourism while encouraging revenue flow to protected areas is a key challenge for both the wildlife and the tourism authorities.

The Wildlife Conservation Society (WCS), which has its headquarters at the Bronx Zoo in New York (USA), has been working in Tanzania for over 50 years to help safeguard its unique global heritage. More than 150 projects have been supported through WCS, which uses sound science to inform conservation practice, supports rural communities to better manage their natural resources and receive benefits from conservation, and supports government and non-government institutions to manage and monitor key landscapes and species. WCS continues to support Tanzania in its conservation efforts from a local, grassroots level to national policies, with the goal of helping Tanzania conserve its extraordinary wildlife and environment. See **www.wcstanzania.org** and **www.wcs.org** for more information.

Wildlife habitat being converted to agriculture.

How to use this book

The bulk of this book is dedicated to detailed species accounts covering the larger mammal species found in Tanzania. These accounts aim to help the reader identify an animal seen in the wild and provide an overview of the species' ecology and behaviour. The accounts also include up-to-date information on distribution, including detailed maps, a summary of the population status in Tanzania, and an indication of where best to look for the species.

The taxonomic classification of an organism is not static, and ongoing research on evolutionary relationships, as well as new discoveries, can lead to name changes and species being split or otherwise re-classified. To ensure consistency and clarity, the taxonomy and nomenclature used in this book for terrestrial species and subspecies follows *Mammals of Africa* (Kingdon *et al.*, 2013), with a few exceptions. The marine mammal taxonomy follows *Whales, Dolphins and other Marine Mammals of the World* (Shirihai and Jarrett, 2006).

For each species, the common name (and other common name synonyms), its scientific name, and its name in Swahili, the official language of Tanzania, are provided.

E is used to denote those species that are endemic to Tanzania

A coloured box indicates the species' International Union for Conservation of Nature (IUCN) Red List conservation status. *The IUCN Red List of Threatened Species*™ conservation assessments are developed at a global scale, and occasionally also at a regional or national level. However, since the national conservation status has yet to be assessed for many species in Tanzania, this book gives the species' global Red List conservation status. IUCN Red List status categories (see **www.iucnredlist.org** for more information) may be summarized as follows:

Critically Endangered	faces an extremely high risk of extinction in the wild.
Endangered	faces a very high risk of extinction in the wild.
Vulnerable	considered to be facing a high risk of extinction in the wild.
Near Threatened	likely to qualify for a threatened category (Vulnerable and above) in the near future.
Least Concern	does not qualify for any of the above categories; the species is widespread and/or abundant.

Measurements (box)
HB Head and Body is the length of the body from the tip of the nose to the base of the tail, with the head extended. Where male and female measurements differ significantly, they are given separately (**M** = male, **F** = female).

Ht Height at shoulder (provided for some species) is the measurement from the foot to the top of the shoulder blade in a standing animal.

Tail The length of the tail from the base to the tip.

Wt The weight range of the animal.

Species description
This section provides a brief description of what the species looks like: its general size, body shape, colour and any distinctive characteristics. Horn length is measured along the curve, with the upper figure representing the maximum length recorded in Tanzania.

Subspecies

Subspecies, sometimes referred to as geographic races, are one or more populations of a species that are different in a detectable manner from other populations of the species. These differences are often a variation in colour or size, although they are not sufficiently different for the populations to be considered separate species. Subspecies can be useful in biodiversity mapping and in identifying populations that, with further research, may prove to be full species. In cases where some authorities suggest a subspecies may merit full species status, their distribution range is shown on the map. Where there are reported to be two or more valid subspecies in Tanzania, their approximate geographical ranges and key distinguishing characteristics (where available) are described. If there are no known subspecies, or the validity of the subspecies in Tanzania is doubtful, then no subspecies are listed.

Similar species

This section highlights species that look similar to the one described and details the differences between them to aid identification. Comparative photographic spreads (*pages 262–268*) are provided for species that look alike, displaying side-by-side photographs of the species, scaled to size for easy comparison. Readers are encouraged to check the distribution map and/or habitat preferences to help with differentiation.

Ecology and social behaviour

This section provides a brief description of the species' preferred habitat, diet, group size, territory size and mating strategies, where known. Common behaviours that are likely to be observed, and the time(s) of activity peaks, are also indicated. The information presented aims to assist with species identification. More complete accounts of behaviour and ecology can be found in the *Behavior Guide to African Mammals* by Richard Estes.

Distribution in Tanzania

This section summarizes the areas where the species is known to occur and also details the protected areas in which they are found. Most of the place names referred to are included on the maps of Tanzania (inside front and back covers). Note that the islands of Zanzibar and Pemba are referred to separately throughout the text, although Zanzibar is in fact the name of a semi-autonomous archipelago, which includes two main islands: Unguja and Pemba. It does not include Mafia Island. Unguja is the largest island which hosts the capital, Stone Town; Unguja is widely known as Zanzibar, and that is the name used in this book.

Distribution map

The distribution maps included in this book provide the most accurate information currently available for the range of each species in Tanzania. **Known range** is indicated in dark orange. Light orange is used, where appropriate, to indicate the species' **possible range**. Where more than one species (or subspecies) is included on a map, the distribution of each species (or subspecies) is shown in a different colour as indicated in an accompanying key. Overlapping ranges are shown as hatched lines. Significant geographic features, such as protected area boundaries and major cities, are included as points of reference (see the maps on the inside front and back covers for additional reference). The pan-African distribution is shown as a small inset map (see *page 14* for details).

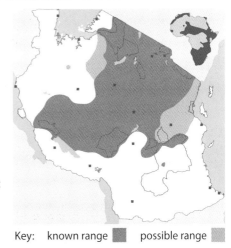

Key: known range ▨   possible range ▨

Where maps use additional colours these are indicated in an accompanying key

13

The data used to create the distribution maps came from a wide variety of sources: camera trap surveys, aerial counts, direct observations, historical and current literature records, and interviews with a large number of tour operators, field guides, professional hunters, community members, National Park personnel and Tanzania Wildlife Division field officers. Most of these data are stored in the Tanzania Mammal Atlas Project database, which is hosted at the Tanzania Wildlife Research Institute (TAWIRI) and currently includes over 50,000 data entries.

Known range was determined by delineating the areas with current records for the species. For large species, including most of the larger antelopes and carnivores (which are vulnerable to hunting or persecution outside protected areas), the distribution range corresponds directly, or very closely, to the actual records. For other species that are less vulnerable (*i.e.* some smaller antelopes, small carnivores, and certain primates) the range has been extrapolated to include areas with historical records and suitable habitat (using *The Vegetation of Africa* (White 1983)); some of these species are also likely to persist in and around cultivated land or areas of human settlement, which now occur in their range.

Possible range includes areas with historical records (pre-1982), unconfirmed recent sightings, or areas of suitable habitat and low human influence (as determined by the 2005 *Last of the Wild* data (Human Footprint v2) from the Wildlife Conservation Society).

It is likely that there are gaps in our distribution maps, as even large mammals still occasionally migrate to or through areas of high human density. However, records from such areas are usually of young animals that are dispersing, or of temporary migrations, and do not indicate permanent populations of the species concerned.

A large amount of the information used in compiling the distribution and status of smaller, nocturnal, or cryptic species, such as many of the carnivores, comes from camera trapping surveys. Camera traps are remotely activated cameras that are triggered by heat or motion of a passing animal – most camera trap models 'capture' animals the size of a rat or larger. The cameras are protected in small, waterproof boxes, and are typically positioned along animal trails. The advantage of camera traps is that they can take pictures both during the day and at night, and can be left in the field for weeks at a time, which reduces disturbance caused by researchers repeatedly visiting a site. The catalogue of pictures also forms a permanent record of the sightings, which can be verified by other scientists.

A note about whales and dolphins: Distribution maps are not included in this book for any of the whales or dolphins found in Tanzanian waters. Most of what is known about cetaceans in the country derives from studies in and around Zanzibar and Dar es Salaam, and there are virtually no published records from elsewhere on the coast. Only species for which there are confirmed records within Tanzania are listed. There are several migratory species that have been reported from neighbouring Kenya, including Blue Whale *Balaenoptera musculus* and Fin Whale *Balaenoptera physalus* that are not currently on the Tanzanian list, although further research may well reveal their presence in Tanzanian waters. The status and distribution of cetaceans in Tanzania is the focus of an ongoing study by the Wildlife Conservation Society.

Pan-African distribution

The species' African distribution is shown as a small inset map of Africa on the species' Tanzania distribution map. These data were provided courtesy of *The IUCN Red List of Threatened Species*™ (**www.iucnredlist.org**). The colour of the pan-African range matches the colour of the species' IUCN Red List status. In the few cases where more than one species is included on a map, the distribution of each species is shown in different colours (as indicated in an accompanying key).

Where to look

This box suggests some of the best places to look for the species in Tanzania. For animals that are diurnal and ubiquitous, several key National Parks or protected areas are listed. For species that are less easily seen, more detailed information on where and when to go is provided. This information should be used in conjunction with the mammal lists for the National Parks and major protected areas (*pages 269–305*), which indicate the likelihood of seeing any particular species.

Population size and conservation status

Most of the population figures for large ungulates presented in this book come from the reports of the Conservation Information Monitoring Unit (CIMU) based at the Tanzania Wildlife Research Institute (TAWIRI), which conducts regular aerial counts in the National Parks and some of the Game Reserves. The methods commonly used in these aerial surveys involve counting animals in a portion of the protected area and then extrapolating those figures to the whole protected area. These counts result in an estimated population size range, which varies depending on the intensity of the survey and the distribution of the animals in the area surveyed, and with the actual number of animals falling somewhere within that range. Combining a number of counts increases the accuracy of the information and provides valuable data on wildlife population trends. For the purposes of this book, either an average or the range of the most recent counts is provided, although if a single count has been used, the date of the count is mentioned.

When no population estimates are available for a species, an indication as to whether it is common, uncommon or rare is provided. Clearly these are subjective terms; a small antelope that is common is likely to occur in much higher numbers than a carnivore that is described as common in the same area. The key threats to each species are also described in this section and, where possible, population trends are indicated.

Photographs

The photographs included in this book were carefully selected to best illustrate a species' shape, colour, and any key distinguishing characteristics – this is typically a side-profile of the animal. While every effort was made to include high quality photographs, occasionally lower quality camera trap photographs were used when other suitable photographs were not available. In some cases these might be the only known photograph of a species, or the best photograph available to highlight key characteristics. Photo captions indicate where in Tanzania a photo was taken (if known), the relevant subspecies, and if the image is from a camera trap or of a captive animal. The country is also listed if the photo was not taken in Tanzania.

National Park and major protected area descriptions and mammal lists

Following the species accounts is a section on the National Parks and major protected areas in Tanzania (*pages 269–305*). This section provides mammal lists for each area, and is coded to indicate the population status of each species and the likelihood of seeing it. The population status for diurnal species was derived from a combination of sighting information and camera trap data. Data for nocturnal species come primarily from camera trap surveys, supplemented by local knowledge.

Mammal Highlights: Many large savanna species, Honey Badger

Aardvark	U	Black-backed Jackal	C	Dwarf Mongoose	C
Chequered Elephant-shrew	U	African Wild Dog	R	Black Rhinoceros	E
Four-toed Elephant-shrew	C	Zorilla	P	Plains Zebra	C
Southern Tree Hyrax	P	African Clawless Otter	C	Bushpig	C
Eastern Tree Hyrax	P	Honey Badger	C	Common Warthog	C
Savanna Elephant	C	African Palm Civet	R	Common Hippopotamus	C
Angola Black-and-white Colobus	C	Cheetah	P	Giraffe	C
Yellow Baboon	C	Serval	U	African Buffalo	C
Vervet Monkey	C	Wild Cat	P	Greater Kudu	U
Mitis Monkey	C	Lion	C	Common Eland	C
Large-eared Greater Galago	C	Leopard	C	Bushbuck	C
Small-eared Greater Galago	C	Large-spotted Genet	C	Suni	U
Senegal Lesser Galago	C	Miombo Genet	P	Bush Duiker	C
Zanzibar Dwarf Galago	C	African Civet	C	Natal Red Duiker	U
East African Springhare	R	Spotted Hyaena	C	Sharpe's Grysbok	P
Crested Porcupine	C	Marsh Mongoose	U	Bohor Reedbuck	C
Cape Porcupine	P	Bushy-tailed Mongoose	U	Waterbuck (Common)	U
African Savanna Hare	C	Slender Mongoose	C	Impala	C
White-bellied Hedgehog	P	White-tailed Mongoose	U	Lichtenstein's Hartebeest	U
Ground Pangolin	R	Banded Mongoose	C	Common Wildebeest	C
Side-striped Jackal	P	Meller's Mongoose	P	Sable Antelope	U

Watching mammals in Tanzania

Organizing your trip

The vast majority of people visiting Tanzania on safari use the services of a safari company or tour operator. This approach is highly recommended since these businesses are well placed to manage everything for you, including providing a vehicle with a driver-guide, booking accommodation and organizing entry permits for all the National Parks. The driver-guides tend to be very good at spotting wildlife, know the best places to go, and can obtain information about interesting mammal sightings from other guides. There are many different companies covering a wide price range. It is strongly recommended that your selected company is registered with TATO, the Tanzania Association of Tour Operators, as this means the company is properly licensed and has the required insurance. See **www.tatotz.org** for a list of registered companies.

Most companies can arrange a tour of the northern parks using lodges or camps, although fewer have experience with the southern circuit. If you are searching for some of the rarer mammal species with restricted ranges outside the National Parks (some of the primates, for instance), then your options narrow considerably. Perhaps the best approach is to use a company that caters for birding clients, since they are more likely to be familiar with requests to access some of the more remote Forest Reserves, and will be able to organize the logistics for you, saving you a great deal of time.

Where to go

The **National Parks** and the **Ngorongoro Conservation Area** attract the great majority of safari visitors to Tanzania, and offer the best facilities for tourism and watching wildlife. Any visit to Tanzania should include at least a few of the National Parks on the itinerary. There are also many **Game Reserves** around the country, although with the exception of the northern portion of the Selous Game Reserve, these are generally restricted for sport hunting and are not accessible to the average photographic tourist. **Forest Reserves** and recently created **Nature Reserves** also provide good habitat for some cryptic forest species, although their densities are usually low and finding them requires a good deal more patience than in savanna habitats. It is worth noting that arranging access to most of the Forest Reserves can be complicated – permits are often available only at the District headquarters, sometimes far from the Forest Reserve itself. **Wildlife Management Areas** (**WMAs**) are new, multi-use areas established on village land, typically located close to a National Park or Game Reserve. Visitor infrastructure in most WMAs is currently poorly developed, but in the future many are likely to offer bush walks and night drives. **Private concessions** or **game ranches** are rare in Tanzania, but the few that exist offer good opportunities for mammal watching. Additional activities such as night drives and bush walks, and facilities such as wildlife hides are often available and significantly increase your chances of seeing rare or nocturnal mammals.

Mammal watching tips

Many of the larger mammals in Tanzania are fairly easy to see. On a 10-day visit to the parks in northern Tanzania, which typically includes a selection of Ngorongoro Conservation Area and Arusha, Tarangire, Manyara and Serengeti NPs, you can expect to see over 35 species of larger mammal. The following tips should help to improve your chances of finding and watching the species that you hope to see.

Use binoculars. Good binoculars are an essential piece of equipment that everyone on safari should carry – and should be the third item on any packing list, after your passport and plane ticket. Binoculars will significantly improve the quality of your wildlife viewing, and this is particularly the case in most of the National Parks where off-road driving to get closer to the animals is prohibited. There are many websites providing excellent information on binoculars, and you should buy the best model that you can afford. It is a purchase that very few people will ever regret. Many people prefer 10× magnification binoculars because they effectively bring the animals closer, although others use 8× magnification models, which often have the advantage of a larger field of vision.

Tourists watching Savanna Elephants in Tarangire National Park.

Talk to your driver at the start of the trip about certain species that you would like to see; tracking down some species may require dedicated searching in specific areas.

Go out early and stay until dusk. Many of the nocturnal animals are active at dawn and dusk and can sometimes be seen on early morning or evening drives.

View of a lodge in Tarangire National Park. Lodge grounds can often be good places to look for mammals, particularly some of the small nocturnal species, such as genets, that may become habituated to human presence.

Be aware of your profile in your safari vehicle. Most animals will ignore you if you are standing still in roof hatch of your vehicle, perceiving you to be part of the vehicle. While some shyer species, such as Leopard, may tolerate a vehicle approaching them, they might bolt if they see abrupt movement, such as a person suddenly appearing in the roof hatch. Your driver should be able to advise you, but if the animal looks wary, stay seated until it has relaxed and then slowly stand up. Try to keep your movements and noise to a minimum.

Look around. Most safari drivers and guides have amazing, trained eyes and are extremely good at finding animals. However, you can help them by looking around, ideally standing up to improve visibility. Being a good mammal observer requires concentration and patience. A good method is to scan in a 90 to 180 degree arc around you so that you cover a large area – and preferably have someone else do the same on the other side of the vehicle. Finding the large cats is something of an art. Some guides have a real talent for this, and they generally look for something that seems out of place or unusual: a Sausage Tree fruit that hangs down too low might be a Leopard's tail, or an oddly shaped termite mound might have a Cheetah on it. The behaviour of other animals can also be used to your advantage: the alarm call of a Vervet Monkey or Impala might tell you that there is a predator in the vicinity, or if all individuals in a herd of zebra or buffalo are looking in one direction, you can be pretty sure they are watching a large carnivore.

Get local advice. Camps often attract small species of nocturnal carnivore such as genets or Honey Badgers that can otherwise be difficult to see on a game drive, or may have unusual species that visit for short periods. It is therefore always worth asking staff what species are currently present. Be prepared to question them using a book that includes identification pictures, as they might think that a particular species is commonplace and not worth mentioning, although it may be of great interest to you. The night watchmen are usually good sources of information for nocturnal species (ask the barman to translate for you, if necessary), and are often happy to knock on your door if the animal shows up in the middle of the night.

Walk slowly in forests. Forest animals can be very shy and will usually see you long before you see them, often providing just a glimpse as they run off through the undergrowth. A good approach is to walk alone and very quietly along paths, stopping frequently to scan for animals. Alternatively, sit and watch an area where you see animal tracks. Just be aware that many forests in Tanzania are home to African Buffalo, so it is advisable to get local advice on which areas are safe for walking. It is important to note that walking without a guide is prohibited in most protected areas.

Safari-goers watching and photographing the wildebeest migration on the Serengeti Plains.

Watch wildlife responsibly. Some species, such as Cheetah, are particularly vulnerable to disturbance. Please be sensitive to their needs; do not approach too close; avoid driving between mothers and offspring, or separating a herd or group; and allow the animal space to forage or hunt.

Go on a night drive. Nearly 40% of Tanzania's larger mammals are either strictly or mostly nocturnal. In order to see these species, you will likely need to do a night walk or, more commonly, a night drive, which involves driving at night looking for animals with a spotlight. Unfortunately these opportunities are presently limited in Tanzania, and the few that are available tend to be quite costly.

Going on a night drive can be very rewarding.

Nevertheless, you are recommended to try at least one night drive while on safari if this is an option in the area in which you are staying. The National Parks that currently allow night drives from selected camps and lodges are Tarangire, Manyara, Ruaha, Mikumi, Saadani and Katavi. There are several lodges and camps in areas outside the National Parks that also offer night drive opportunities, such as in West Kilimanjaro, Ikoma in western Serengeti, Manyara Ranch and camps bordering Tarangire National Park.

There are several important things to remember about night drives:

1) Once the sun is down at the end of a long day's safari, the idea of heading out again at night often deters people – but it is worth persevering as you might see some very interesting creatures.
2) It can get fairly cold on a night drive, particularly in an open vehicle, so bring some warm clothes with you.
3) As with all wildlife watching, there are no guarantees with night drives – on some nights there will be a lot of activity, while on others you might see very little. Do not expect to see as much as you would on a daytime game drive, but there is always the potential reward of seeing something unique.
4) When spotlighting, ensure that the light is not directed at an animal's eyes as this may temporarily impair its vision. Red-colour filters are less obtrusive for watching an animal once it has been located.

Tanzania's major vegetation types

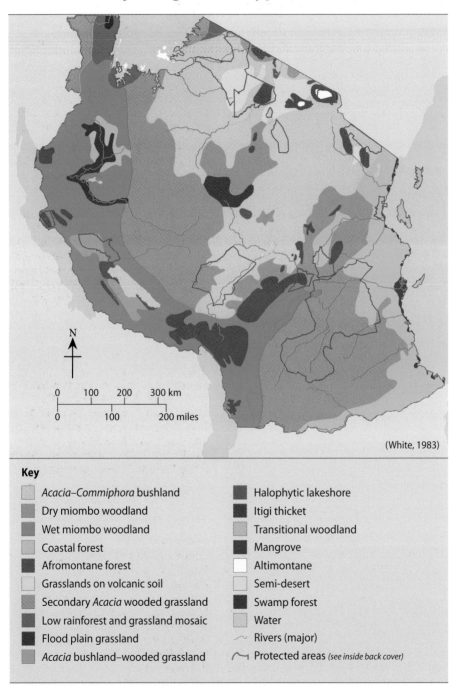

(White, 1983)

Key

	Acacia–Commiphora bushland		Halophytic lakeshore
	Dry miombo woodland		Itigi thicket
	Wet miombo woodland		Transitional woodland
	Coastal forest		Mangrove
	Afromontane forest		Altimontane
	Grasslands on volcanic soil		Semi-desert
	Secondary *Acacia* wooded grassland		Swamp forest
	Low rainforest and grassland mosaic		Water
	Flood plain grassland		Rivers (major)
	Acacia bushland–wooded grassland		Protected areas *(see inside back cover)*

Tanzania can be divided into 18 major vegetation zones, as described in *The Vegetation of Africa* (White, 1983).

Acacia–Commiphora bushland

Acacia–Commiphora bushland

Deciduous bushland and thicket of *Acacia* and/or *Commiphora* trees typically 3–5 m (10–16 ft) tall, the majority of which are bushy with branches near the base, interspersed with wooded grassland. Occasional tall trees such as *Acacia tortilis* and Baobabs may also occur throughout.

Note: The genus *Acacia* has recently been renamed *Vachellia*, however we continue to use *Acacia* throughout this text.

Dry miombo woodland

Dry miombo woodland

Semi-deciduous miombo woodland with annual rainfall less than 1,000 mm (39"). Canopy typically less than 15m (50 ft). *Brachystegia* and *Julbernardia* dominate on soils that are leached and acidic and often shallow and stony. Tree trunks are short and slender with the canopy ascending to a flat-topped crown.

Wet miombo Woodland

Wet miombo woodland

Semi-deciduous miombo woodland with annual rainfall above 1,000 mm (39"). Canopy height is typically more than 15m (50 ft). Rich plant diversity occurs where *Brachystegia* and *Maquesia* are typically associated with evergreen forest and thicket, swamp forest and riparian wetlands.

Coastal forest

Coastal forest

Evergreen forest with trees 15–20 m (50–65 ft) tall in the wet, humid belt along the coastline. High floral diversity with many endemic plant species, although the diversity decreases towards southern Tanzania where it mixes with miombo woodland. Most areas have been highly modified by humans for agriculture and cash crops.

Afromontane forest

Afromontane forest

Multi-layered, typically evergreen forest occurring between 1,200–2,500 m (3,935–8,200 ft) altitude with an annual rainfall of 1,250–2,500 mm (49–98"). The canopy is between 25–45 m (80–150 ft) high, with high plant diversity, especially in forests with higher rainfall. May contain open grassland glades on waterlogged soils.

Grasslands on volcanic soil

Grasslands on volcanic soil

Highly nutritious grasslands created by volcanic soils rich in calcium carbonate (from the dormant volcano Kerimasi in northern Ngorongoro and the active volcano Oldonyo Lengai). More than fifty species of grasses occur here, with the short-grass plains containing the highest amounts of calcium, which is important for lactating ungulates.

Halophytic lakeshore

Halophytic lakeshore

A succession of grassland–swamp–lakeshore vegetation that tolerates saline and alkaline soils found near lake basins in the East African Rift. Often dominated by a single grass species (*Diplachne fusca*) that forms a dense mat up to 2 m (7 ft) tall.

Itigi thicket

Itigi thicket

Deciduous thicket of 3–5 m (10–16 ft) tall shrubs that are almost impenetrable. The sandy soil is soft and wet in the rainy season but dries and hardens in the dry season. The dense canopy prevents light from reaching the understorey, so grasses are virtually absent. The specialized soil limits this area to only 620 km^2 (240 mi^2) in Tanzania.

Mangrove

Mangrove
Found along the deltas of large rivers but also near sheltered ocean shorelines and bays. Trees and shrubs are medium height (2–5m | 7–16 ft) and tolerate saltwater and brackish water. The specialized roots grow above water to absorb air through pores in the bark, but they are also highly impermeable to salt intake.

Altimontane (Afroalpine)

Altimontane (Afroalpine)
High altitude (above 3,800 m | 12,460 ft) dwarf shrubland on shallow, rocky soils with Ericaceae (heathers) dominating. Endemic Giant Lobelias and Giant Senecios (groudsels) are also found here. Floral diversity is relatively low, with approximately 280 plant species occurring throughout this alpine belt.

Other vegetation types:

Low rainforest–grassland mosaic	Areas destroyed by cultivation and fire, replaced with tall (2 m | 6·5 ft) grasslands in a mixed mosaic of small, degraded forest patches.
Secondary *Acacia* wooded grassland	*Acacia* bushland heavily influenced by humans, domestic livestock, elephants and other large animals.
***Acacia* bushland–wooded grassland**	Woodland and wooded grassland dominated by *Acacia* and broad-leaved trees, greatly modified by fire.
Swamp forest	Forest of continuous stand of trees at least 10 m (33 ft) tall in areas with permanent or seasonal floodwaters.
Transitional woodland	Undifferentiated, diverse woodland defined by the absence of miombo in an otherwise miombo-dominated area.
Cultivation replacing montane forest	Natural afromontane vegetation is replaced with cultivation and secondary grasslands.
Semi-desert	Grassland and shrubland with annual rainfall between 100–200 mm (4–8") occurring on deep sand or stony soils.
Floodplain grassland	A mosaic of shifting grassland on seasonally waterlogged soils in the valleys of major rivers. Permanent woodland typically grows along the banks of the river, whereas permanent swamp vegetation fills the river channels.

Overview of mammalian families included in the book

The taxonomic order of the species included in this book follows that of *Mammals of Africa* (Kingdon *et al.*, 2013) and *Mammal Species of the World* (Wilson and Reeder, 2005). The two exceptions are the Dugong (*page 246*), belonging to the Superorder Afrotheria, and the Subantarctic Fur Seal (*page 261*), belonging to Order Carnivora, which, being predominantly marine mammals, have been placed with the whales and dolphins, Order Cetacea. The figures given for each family inicate the number of species recorded in Tanzania.

SUPERORDER **AFROTHERIA** – *mammals of uniquely African origin and common ancestry.*

ORDER Tubulidentata: FAMILY Orycteropodidae
Aardvark: 1 species; *long nose, body, tail and ears, mostly hairless, nocturnal.*

ORDER Macroscelidea: FAMILY Macroscelididae
Elephant-shrews: 6 species [4 larger species covered]; *rodent-like with long, tubular nose.*

ORDER Hyracoidea: FAMILY Procaviidae
Hyraxes: 5 species; *superficially rabbit-like, no tail.*

ORDER Proboscidea: FAMILY Elephantidae
Elephant: 1 species; *massive animal with large ears, long trunk, and tusks.*

ORDER Sirenia: FAMILY Dugongidae
Dugong: 1 species; *large, grey body, strictly aquatic, mainly marine.*

ORDER **PRIMATES** – Primates

FAMILY Hominidae
Chimpanzee: 1 species;
the only great ape in Tanzania, tail is absent.

FAMILY Cercopithecidae: SUBFAMILY Colobinae
Colobus: 5 species; *arboreal with long tail.*

FAMILY Cercopithecidae: SUBFAMILY Cercopithecinae
Mangabeys, baboons, monkeys: 9 species; *long tail, terrestrial or arboreal, and often quadrupedal.*

FAMILY Galagidae
Galagos: 12 species; *long tail, large eyes, arboreal, nocturnal.*

ORDER **RODENTIA** – Rodents

FAMILY Pedetidae
Springhare: 1 species;
resembles a small kangaroo, nocturnal.

FAMILY Hystricidae
Porcupines: 3 species;
long, protective spines, nocturnal.

ORDER **LAGOMORPHA** – Hares and Rabbits

FAMILY Leporidae
Hares & rabbits: 3 species;
large-eared with long hind legs.

ORDER **ERINACEOMORPHA** – Hedgehogs

FAMILY Erinaceidae
Hedgehog: 1 species; *spiny, nocturnal insectivore.*

ORDER **PHOLIDOTA** – Pangolins

FAMILY Manidae
Pangolins: 3 species;
ant-eater with long tail and thick scales.

ORDER **CARNIVORA** – Carnivores

FAMILY Canidae
Jackals, foxes, dogs: 5 species;
dog-like with long muzzle, legs, and tail.

FAMILY Mustelidae
Weasels, otters, badgers : 5 species;
secrete strong scent, some aquatic (otters).

FAMILY Nandiniidae
Palm Civet: 1 species; *spotted with long tail, arboreal.*

FAMILY Felidae
Cats : 6 species;
long body, legs and tail, small head, short muzzle.

FAMILY Viverridae
Genets & civets: 6 species; *spotted with long tail, arboreal (genets) or terrestrial (civets).*

FAMILY Hyaenidae
Hyaenas: 3 species; *sloping back, long legs, large ears.*

FAMILY Herpestidae
Mongooses: 10 species; *long body and tail, short legs.*

FAMILY Otariidae
Fur Seal: 1 species; *small ears, fin-footed, marine.*

ORDER **PERISSODACTYLA** – Odd-toed Ungulates

FAMILY Rhinocerotidae
Rhinoceros: 1 species; *very large, grey, with horns.*

FAMILY Equidae
Zebra: 1 species;
horse-like body with black and white stripes.

ORDER **ARTIODACTYLA** – Even-toed Ungulates

FAMILY Suidae
Pigs: 2 species; *short legs, stocky body, mane, tusks.*

FAMILY Hippopotamidae
Hippopotamus: 1 species;
massive head and body, mostly aquatic.

FAMILY Giraffidae
Giraffe: 1 species;
very long legs and neck with large, brown spots.

FAMILY Bovidae
SUBFAMILY Bovinae
Buffalo & spiral-horned antelopes: 6 species;
thick- or spiral-horns.
SUBFAMILY Antilopinae
Antelopes: 27 species; *small or large, hoofed, males have horns, females may or may not have horns.*

ORDER **CETACEA** – Cetaceans;
long body, tail with flukes, fins, strictly marine.

FAMILY Balaenopteridae
Baleen whale: 1 species;
very large, baleen plates for feeding.

FAMILIES Physeteridae & Kogiidae
Sperm whales: 2 species; *large, bulbous heads.*

FAMILY Ziphiidae
Beaked whale: 2 species; *medium-sized, males two protruding teeth, females toothless.*

FAMILY Delphinidae
Dolphins and blackfish: 11 species;
small, curved dorsal fins, single notch in fluke.

THE SPECIES ACCOUNTS

Giraffe in Mikumi National Park

Aardvark

Orycteropus afer

SWAHILI: Muhanga

A thickset animal with a rounded body, a long, tapered tail, and a small, pig-like head with a very long nose and ears. The body colour ranges from light brown to pinkish-grey and the legs are black. Young animals are usually quite hairy, while adults may be mostly hairless on the back. There are four large claws on the front foot and five on the hind foot. Males and females are the same size.

Subspecies
Four subspecies are listed for Tanzania: *O. a. lademanni, O. a. matschiei, O. a. observandus* and *O. a. ruvanensis,* although their validity is doubtful due to significant intra-specific variation.

Similar species
Unlikely to be mistaken for any other mammal.

Ecology and social behaviour
Aardvarks are found in a wide variety of habitats, including open grassland, woodland, thicket, lowland and montane forest, montane grassland and agricultural land. They avoid rocky terrain, which is difficult to dig. Their diet consists mainly of ants and termites, as well as beetle pupae and larvae. Aardvarks dig into termitaria using their powerful front claws, licking up the invertebrates with a long, sticky tongue. They are solitary and exclusively nocturnal: camera trap records from Tanzania show highest peaks of activity between midnight and 5:00 a.m. Recorded home range sizes vary between 2–5 km² (0·8–2·0 mi²) with size probably related to food density. Individuals may travel several kilometres in a night in search of food. They frequently dig large, deep feeding burrows, which will be jarringly familiar to anyone who has driven off-road in East Africa. Burrows used for shelter can be very large, with multiple entrances, and may be occupied over long periods of time. Active burrows may be recognized by the presence of flies and fresh diggings.

Least Concern	
HB:	100–130 cm (39–67")
Ht:	60–65 cm (24–26")
Tail:	44–60 cm (17–24")
Wt:	50–80 kg (110–176 lb)

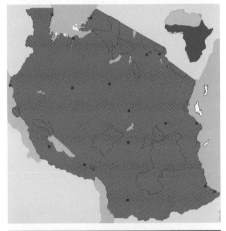

Where to look
Although relatively common in some places, the Aardvark's shy nature and nocturnal habits means it is seldom seen. They are occasionally observed on night drives on Manyara Ranch and Ndarakwai Ranch.

Distribution in Tanzania
Aardvarks are very widespread in Tanzania. They have been recorded in all mainland National Parks, with the exception of Rubondo and Gombe, and they are known from the majority of Game Reserves in the country.

Population size and conservation status
This species probably occurs at low densities across most of its range, although it is likely to be more common where termites are abundant, including much of western Tanzania. It is common in Sumbawanga Rural and Nkasi Districts down to the Zambian border. It frequently inhabits agricultural areas, and is found in coffee plantations on the outskirts of Arusha. Camera trap records for

this species suggests it is relatively common in the lowland forests of Mahale NP and in Ugalla GR. Population trends are unknown, although probably stable in protected areas.

Habitat loss poses the main threat to this species, and it is hunted for food in parts of western Tanzania.

Aardvark
TOP: camera trap photo, Tarangire NP; BOTTOM: captive individual.

Chequered Elephant-shrew   *Rhynchocyon cirnei*

Chequered Sengi

SWAHILI: Njule Madoa

A large elephant-shrew that ranges in colour and pattern from light brown with distinct spots to very dark with no spots. There may be significant variation within a single population. Melanistic individuals have also been recorded.

Subspecies

R. c. reichardi: central montane areas and western Tanzania; light rufous-brown body with six black-and-white bands on the back and sides that run from shoulder to flank.

R. c. macrurus: southeast Tanzania; rump usually dark purple, front light rufous, spots may be absent.

Similar species

Subspecies *macrurus* and the Black-and-rufous Elephant-shrew look very similar but the known ranges of the two do not overlap.

Ecology and social behaviour

The preferred habitat of the Chequered Elephant-shrew is montane, submontane, lowland and coastal forests, and dense to semi-dense miombo woodland. Diurnal and monogamous, pairs defend territories of 1·0–1·7 ha (2·5–4·0 acres). They are strictly insectivorous and usually forage alone. They construct shelters up to 1 m (3 ft) wide from fallen leaves.

Distribution in Tanzania

Found in gallery or riverine forest in the Burigi–Biharamulo GRs, the Rukwa Valley and along the shores of Lake Tanganyika. It occurs in montane forests throughout the Southern Highlands, the Udzungwa, Rubeho and Uvidunda Mountains, Malundwe Mountain in Mikumi NP, and in dense woodland areas at the northwestern edge of Selous GR. Subspecies *macrurus* occurs in dense miombo woodland and coastal forest south of the Rufiji River to the Mozambique border.

Population size and conservation status

Common in Mahale NP, Mount Rungwe and in many of the Eastern Arc Mountains. This species is hunted in many parts of its range.

Near Threatened	
HB:	23–30 cm (9–12")
Tail:	22–26 cm (9–10")
Wt:	320–440 g (11–15·5 oz)

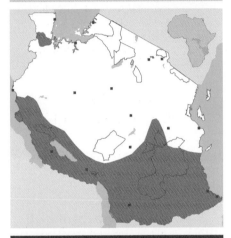

Where to look

Can be seen at Sable Mountain Lodge in Selous GR, in Mahale NP, and also many Forest Reserves across southern Tanzania. A good technique to see them is to sit quietly on forest paths.

Chequered Elephant-shrew
ssp. *reichardi* (Uganda)

Black-and-rufous Elephant-shrew   *Rhynchocyon petersi*

Black-and-rufous Sengi, Zanj Elephant-shrew

SWAHILI: Njule Kinguja, Ngombo Nunga

A large guinea pig-sized animal with very long legs, an extended proboscis, and a long, naked tail. The face and forequarters are orange-rufous, with black extending from the shoulders to the haunches. The tail and legs are orange.

Subspecies
R. p. petersi: Tanzania mainland.
R. p. adersi: Zanzibar and Mafia islands.

Similar species
Separated from Grey-faced Elephant-shrew (*page 30*) and Chequered Elephant-shrew by range.

Ecology and social behaviour
Occurs in coastal and montane forest, coral rag, thick woodland, degraded woodland, agricultural fields and gardens. Diurnal and insectivorous; they are noisy while foraging in dry leaf-litter – a useful clue to their presence.

Distribution in Tanzania
Found in parts of the Eastern Arc Mountains and along the northeast coast of Tanzania. Occurs in the Pare, Usambara, Uluguru and Nguu Mountains and in coastal forest and coral rag forest extending from the Kenya border to the Rufiji River. Also in northern Selous GR and Saadani NP. Present throughout the islands of Mafia and Zanzibar, but absent from Pemba.

Population size and conservation status
Studies of nesting sites in six Eastern Arc Forests have shown that densities range from 19 individuals per km² (50 per mi²) in Chome Forest Reserve (Usambara Mountains) to 79 individuals per km² (200 per mi²) in Pugu Forest Reserve. They are also common in Zoraninge Forest in Saadani NP, and in many of the Forest Reserves on Zanzibar. The main threat facing all elephant-shrews is habitat loss and hunting, and numbers are probably declining throughout their range.

Vulnerable	
HB:	27 cm (11")
Tail:	23 cm (9")
Wt:	400–690 g (14–24 oz)

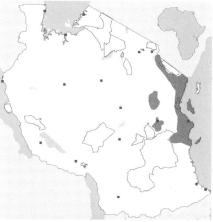

Where to look
Can be reliably seen in several Forest Reserves in Zanzibar, including Mtende Forest, and in the grounds of many lodges on the Island, including Fumba Beach Lodge. Also frequently seen around the Selous Mbega Camp in the Selous GR, particularly during the dry season.

Black-and-rufous Elephant-shrew
ssp. *adersi*, Zanzibar

E Grey-faced Elephant-shrew   *Rhynchocyon udzungwensis*

Grey-faced Sengi, Udzungwa Elephant-shrew

SWAHILI: Njule wa Udzungwa

A large elephant-shrew with a grizzled grey forehead and face, yellow-rufous from the ears to the shoulders, orange sides and black lower rump. The tail is grey-black above and dark brown below, and has a white tip 4–6 cm (1·5–2·0") long.

Similar species
The range of the Grey-faced Elephant-shrew species does not overlap with that of the similar Black-and-rufous Elephant-shrew (*page 29*). Its range does, however, overlap with that of the Chequered Elephant-shrew (*page 28*) in eastern Mwanihana Forest, although that species is smaller and typically has distinct spots on the back.

Ecology and social behaviour
Restricted to montane and submontane forest in the Udzungwa Mountains. It is insectivorous and diurnal and, like other species in this genus, probably forms monogamous pairs, although it typically forages and travels alone. Fallen leaves are used to construct large leaf mounds approximately 1m (3ft) wide, which it uses to shelter at night.

Distribution in Tanzania
This species, which is endemic to Tanzania, was discovered in 2005 during camera trap surveys of the Udzungwa Mountains. Records suggest it is restricted to three forests: Ndundulu, Luhomero and Mwanihana, all within the Udzungwa Mountains, covering an area of 300 km² (120 mi²). All records have come from submontane and montane forest above an altitude of 1,000 m (3,300 ft).

Population size and conservation status
The population density has been estimated from ground surveys to be 50–80 animals per km² (130–210 animals per mi²), providing a total population of 15,000–24,000 within its known range. It is known only from protected areas, and the main threat is habitat loss through forest fires.

Vulnerable	
HB:	30 cm (12")
Tail:	24–26 cm (9–10")
Wt:	655–750 g (23–26 oz)

Where to look
The Grey-faced Elephant-shrew can be seen along trails in the Ndundulu and Luhomero Forests, where walking surveys suggest an encounter rate of approximately one animal every 3·3 hours of walking.

Grey-faced Elephant-shrew
Udzungwa NP

Four-toed Elephant-shrew
Petrodromus tetradactylus

Four-toed Sengi

SWAHILI: Ngombo Panya, Isanje

A mid-sized elephant-shrew with long legs and a conspicuous white ring around the eyes. The back and sides are sandy-brown and the underparts are white. There is a rufous or dark patch on each side of the face, between the eye and the ear.

Subspecies
P. t. sultani: northeast Tanzania.
P. t. rovumae: eastern Tanzania.
P. t. tetradactylus: western Tanzania.
P. t. zanzibaricus: Zanzibar and Mafia islands.

Similar species
The Chequered Elephant-shrew (*page 28*) and Black-and-rufous Elephant-shrew (*page 29*) are both much larger. The Rufous Elephant-shrew *Elephantulus rufescens* and the Short-snouted Elephant-shrew *E. brachyrhynchus* are much smaller and have shorter legs; these two species are both very small and are not covered in this field guide.

Ecology and social behaviour
Found in coastal forest, miombo woodland, and thicket, where they create a wide network of narrow trails that they keep free of leaf-litter. They are solitary or live in pairs, and are mostly nocturnal and crepuscular. Individuals make a characteristic drumming sound by hitting the ground with their feet, usually when alarmed.

Distribution in Tanzania
Widely distributed in Tanzania; known from Katavi, Ruaha, Udzungwa, Mikumi and Sadaani NPs, and the Selous and Burigi–Biharamulo GRs. It is also found on the islands of Zanzibar and Mafia, although not on Pemba. It occurs in the lowland areas of most of the Eastern Arc Mountains, and throughout coastal Tanzania.

Population size and conservation status
Common throughout coastal Tanzania, parts of western Tanzania including Katavi NP, and in Jozani Chwaka Bay NP on Zanzibar. The main threat is habitat loss.

Least Concern	
HB:	16–21 cm (6–8")
Tail:	16–19 cm (6 7.5")
Wt:	130–250 g (4.5–9 oz)

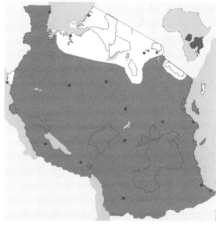

Where to look
Easily seen in the grounds of most lodges in Katavi NP and in Mdonya Old River Camp in Ruaha NP. Occasionally encountered along the edges of riverine forest in Selous GR.

Four-toed Elephant-shrew
ssp. *tetradactylus*, Katavi NP

31

Rock Hyrax

Procavia capensis

Rock Dassie

SWAHILI: Pimbi

A stocky hyrax with short legs, ears and face, giving it a snub-nosed appearance. The dorsal fur is brown and the underparts are cream-coloured in adults, slightly paler in juveniles. There is a patch of erectile hair covering a dorsal gland, which can be yellow, orange or brown. The dense fur is up to 2·5 cm (1") long, and there are long, scattered guard hairs across the body.

Subspecies in Tanzania
P. c. matschiei: only subspecies found in Tanzania.

Similar species
The Bush Hyrax (*page 34*) has a white, rather than yellow, belly and more pronounced white markings above the eyes than adult Rock Hyrax. The Bush Hyrax also has a more slender build and a sharper, more pointed snout. The two species are commonly found on the same kopjes in the Serengeti. The tree hyraxes (*page 36*) are mainly arboreal in areas of overlap and have white running from the lips to the cheeks (see comparative photographs, *page 264*).

Ecology and social behaviour
Rock Hyraxes occupy a wide range of habitats from forests to deserts and high alpine zones. In Tanzania, they are found in rocky outcrops (kopjes) and among boulders with deep rock crevasses in hilly areas in the northern *Acacia–Commiphora* bushland. Rock Hyraxes feed on a variety of grasses, leaves and fruit, and during the wet season are predominantly grazers, although they switch increasingly to browse during the dry season. The animals follow well-worn paths to their grazing areas and feed in groups, usually for short periods during the morning and mid-afternoon, with some individuals acting as sentinels. They are mainly diurnal, though occasionally active during moonlit nights. They live in colonies with as many as 25–35 individuals, consisting of one territorial male and

Least Concern	
HB:	40–58 cm (16–23")
Wt:	2·0–5·4 kg (4·4–12 lb)

Where to look
Rock Hyraxes can be reliably seen on the kopjes at many of the lodges in the Serengeti NP, particularly around Seronera and Lobo, and at the Serengeti entrance gate at Naabi Hill.

several related females and their offspring. There may be several different colonies occupying one rocky outcrop.

Distribution in Tanzania
The Rock Hyrax is restricted to a narrow area of northern Tanzania. It occurs in Serengeti NP, Maswa GR, western Loliondo and the Yaeda Valley. It is not known from Ngorongoro CA although may occur in the Kakesio Hills. There are records from the 1970s from northern Shinyanga and Musoma Districts, although the current status of the species in these areas is not known. Its distribution in the Lake Natron–Kilimanjaro area is unclear, with only one sight record from the lower western slopes of Mount Kilimanjaro. There are also sight records from the Mbono area in western Mkomazi NP, and probable records from around the Minja Forest in the north Pare Mountains.

Population size and conservation status
There are no population estimates for this species in Tanzania. It is very common in the kopjes of central and northern Serengeti, although populations outside the Serengeti ecosystem are mostly small and isolated, and therefore susceptible to local hunting pressure.

The species is rare in West Kilimanjaro, Mkomazi NP and the Parc Mountains, and nothing is known about the status of the populations in northern Shinyanga region and around Lake Victoria. It is hunted by people for food, and also preyed upon by a wide variety of predators. Populations in the Serengeti ecosystem are stable.

Rock Hyrax
TOP: (Kenya); BOTTOM: Serengeti NP (Tanzania)

Bush Hyrax

Heterohyrax brucei

Yellow-spot Dassie

SWAHILI: Pimbi

A small to medium-sized hyrax with a slight build and a pointed face. The body colour is a grizzled grey with a white underside and throat, and there are two distinctive white spots above the eye. The dorsal gland on the back is surrounded by yellow hair, which may be raised when the animal is alarmed or used as a threat, or for courtship display.

Subspecies in Tanzania

Seven subspecies are named for Tanzania: *H. b. dieseneri, H. b. frommi, H. b. lademanni, H. b. munzneri, H. b. prittwitzi, H. b. ssongeae* and *H. b. victoria-njansae*, although their validity is uncertain.

Similar species

Rock Hyraxes (*page 32*) and Bush Hyraxes are commonly seen together in the Serengeti ecosystem. Rock Hyraxes have cream-coloured, rather than white, underparts and duller markings above the eye. They are also larger and have a shorter nose. Tree hyraxes (*page 36*) are larger, typically solitary, and have more white on the cheeks and lower and upper lips (see comparative photographs, *page 264*). They are usually seen sitting in boles or on branches of large trees, and sometimes in the canopy, whereas Bush Hyraxes tend to feed in smaller trees and bushes.

Ecology and social behaviour

Found on rocky outcrops, sheltering in cracks and crevices in the rocks. In Kitulo NP and Mount Rungwe they live amongst rocks in dense montane forest up to up to an altitude of 2,400 m (7,900 ft), forming family groups with one territorial male and up to 30 adult females and young. In the Serengeti NP, Bush Hyraxes and Rock Hyraxes are frequently found on the same rock kopjes where they may share the same sheltering holes. They are diurnal, with activity peaks in the morning and late afternoon.
Bush Hyraxes are primarily browsers and are frequently seen climbing in bushes

Least Concern	
HB:	38–47 cm (15–19")
Wt:	1·3–2·4 kg (3–5 lb)

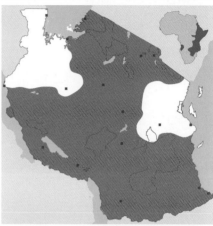

Where to look

Bush Hyraxes are easily seen on the rocks at Naabi Hill at the entrance to Serengeti NP, and at most of the lodges in the National Park. In Manyara NP they are common around the TAHI Lodge on the edge of the escarpment. In Tarangire NP they can be reliably seen on the rocks just south of the main bridge in the north of the National Park. They are also easily seen at the Ruaha River Lodge in Ruaha NP.

where they feed on the leaves and twigs. In the Serengeti, their diet is composed mainly of *Acacia tortilis* and *Allophylus rubifolius*, and grass is seldom, if ever, eaten.

Distribution in Tanzania

The Bush Hyrax is widely distributed across northern, central and southern Tanzania. There are populations in the Serengeti NP, Ngorongoro CA, Tarangire, Manyara, Mkomazi, Ruaha, Udzungwa, Kitulo and Mahale NPs. They are also found in parts of the Selous GR, Mbangala FR, Ugalla GR and in the rocky kopjes in Singida District. There are no records for the far northwest of the country, nor from much of the coastal area between the Kenya border and the Rufiji River.

Population size and conservation status
There are no population estimates for this species in Tanzania. They can be very common in suitable habitat, with densities of up to 75 individuals per hectare (30 per acre) found on some kopjes in the Serengeti.

Bush Hyraxes are widely distributed across protected areas where numbers are generally stable. Outside National Parks and Game Reserves they are heavily hunted for meat, often with bows and arrows or snares, which has led to large declines in some populations – including in Singida Region, as well as to local extinctions – for example around Gombe NP.

Bush Hyrax
TOP: Yaeda Valley; BOTTOM: Tarangire NP

Southern Tree Hyrax
Eastern Tree Hyrax
Western Tree Hyrax

Dendrohyrax arboreus
Dendrohyrax validus
Dendrohyrax dorsalis

Tree Dassie

SWAHILI: Pimbi Mti, Perere

These species are very similar, morphologically and behaviourally, and their species accounts are therefore combined. They are large, arboreal hyraxes with long, soft fur and long sensory guard hairs scattered throughout the pelage. There is a patch of erectile hair covering a dorsal gland.

Southern Tree Hyrax Grizzled grey to brown coat with creamy-white dorsal gland hairs, a cream or white belly, white patches above the eye and white patches stretching from the lower and upper lip to the cheeks.

Eastern Tree Hyrax Dark brown above with yellow-orange belly and russet-brown to yellow dorsal gland hairs. Much darker overall than the Southern Tree Hyrax.

Western Tree Hyrax Dark brown or black coat with yellowish-white dorsal gland hairs. White spot under the chin.

Subspecies in Tanzania

Southern Tree Hyrax *D. a. stuhlmanni*: only subspecies found in Tanzania.

Eastern Tree Hyrax *D. v. validus*: Mount Kilimanjaro, Mount Meru. *D. v. terricola*: Pare and Usambara Mountains. *D. v. schusteri*: Uluguru and Udzungwa Mountains. *D. v. neumanni*: Zanzibar, Pemba. Note: the subspecies are differentiated primarily by call.

Western Tree Hyrax *D. d. marmota*: only subspecies found in Tanzania.

Similar species

Southern Tree Hyrax is most likely to be confused with Bush Hyrax (*page 34*), which is a similar colour. Both species can be found in trees, although the Southern Tree Hyrax usually inhabits larger trees and is mainly solitary. The Bush Hyrax is smaller, has a more elongated, pointed face and much less white on the cheeks (see comparative spread, *page 264*).

Least Concern	
HB:	35–60 cm (14–24")
Wt:	1·2–4·5 kg (2·6–10 lb)

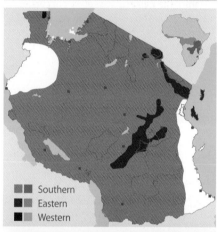

■■ Southern
■■ Eastern
■■ Western

Where to look

The **Southern Tree Hyrax** is frequently seen in large fig trees along the Tarangire River in Tarangire NP, and also on the grounds of Sopa Lodge in Ngorongoro CA. The **Eastern Tree Hyrax** is most easily seen in Jozani Chwaka Bay NP on Zanzibar, where it is sometimes active during the day. The only known place to see the **Western Tree Hyrax** is in Minziro FR.

Ecology and social behaviour

All three species are mostly solitary or found in mother–offspring pairs. They are predominantly arboreal, denning in large, mature trees, although the **Eastern Tree Hyrax** sometimes dens on rocky slopes. Extraordinary calls are made by both sexes, although principally by males. The **Southern Tree Hyrax** starts off with a croaking sound that rises in a crescendo and ends with a series of high-pitched screams. The **Eastern Tree Hyrax** sounds like a hammer hitting a metal post with increasing rapidity before petering out. The **Western Tree Hyrax** makes a long series of climactic high-pitched screams with increasing intensity and gradually decreasing intervals. They are mostly nocturnal, although they can be active throughout the day. They feed mostly on leaves, twigs and fruit.

Distribution in Tanzania
The **Southern Tree Hyrax** occurs in riverine habitat and lowland forests throughout Tanzania. The **Eastern Tree Hyrax** occurs in many montane forests, including Arusha and Kilimanjaro NPs, the Pare Mountains and most of the Eastern Arc Mountains. It is also found on the northeast coast and on Zanzibar

and Pemba, but not Mafia. The **Western Tree Hyrax** is only known from the Minziro FR.

Population size and conservation status
The **Southern Tree Hyrax** is common in many parts of Tanzania, including Tarangire NP and the northern section of the Selous GR. The **Eastern Tree Hyrax** is abundant on the southern and northern slopes of Mount Kilimanjaro and is common in Jozani Chwaka Bay NP on Zanzibar. The population of **Western Tree Hyrax** is restricted to one small corner of Tanzania and thus is likely to be small. All three species are hunted for their meat, and populations are declining.

TOP: **Southern Tree Hyrax:** Tarangire NP (Tanzania);
MIDDLE: **Eastern Tree Hyrax:** camera trap photo, Kilimanjaro NP (Tanzania);
BOTTOM: **Western Tree Hyrax:** (Gabon)

ELEPHANT: Proboscidea

Savanna Elephant   *Loxodonta africana*

SWAHILI: Tembo, Ndovu

The largest living land mammal, Savanna Elephants have huge bodies, a long, highly mobile trunk, and large ears. Their bodies are grey, with little hair, and the tail is long with a black tassel at the tip. Both sexes have tusks, although these are typically much larger in males. The largest pair of tusks ever recorded (103 kg and 97 kg | 227 lb and 213 lb) were from a bull shot on Mount Kilimanjaro at the end of the 19th century. Adult males are significantly larger than females.

Similar species
Unmistakable.

Ecology and social behaviour
Savanna Elephants are highly adaptable animals that live in a wide variety of habitats, including deserts, open savannas, wetlands, bushland, woodland and montane forests, although their distribution is restricted by the availability of water. They feed preferentially on grasses, although will eat a diverse range of vegetation. They have multiple, hierarchical social groupings ranging from mother–infant units, to family groups, bond groups, clans and subpopulations that exhibit varying levels of social interaction. Females live in family groups led by the oldest female, the matriarch, and can vary in size from 2–50 animals, usually comprising several adult females and their offspring. During the wet season, family groups may gather together in large aggregations, which may serve to attract dominant breeding males. In the dry season, when resources are scarce, family groups often move alone, or may split further into mother–infant units. Males leave the family group when they are between the ages eight and 12 to join bachelor groups, which are highly dynamic in composition. Sexually mature bulls enter musth, which is a period of heightened sexual activity akin to rutting behaviour in other ungulates. During musth they usually exhibit aggressive behaviour, will dribble urine continuously (which turns the penis and inner sides of the back legs white or green), and exude thick liquid from their

Vulnerable	
HB:	5·0–7·5 m (16–25 ft)
Ht:	M 3 m (10 ft) | F 2·5 m (8 ft)
Tail:	100 cm (39")
Wt:	M 5,000–6,000 kg (11,000–13,200 lb) F 2,500–3,000 kg (5,500–6,600 lb)

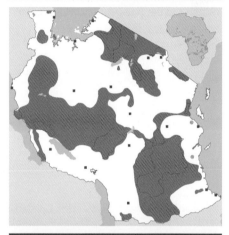

Where to look
Savanna Elephants are easily seen in many of the National Parks with savanna habitat, including Mikumi, Ruaha, Serengeti and Tarangire, as well as the Ngorongoro CA and Selous GR. Tarangire NP is one of the best places in Africa to see large herds of elephants, with many hundreds congregating along the Tarangire River between August and November. The Ngorongoro Crater can be a good place to see mature males with large tusks – a few individuals reside there throughout the year.

temporal glands. The oldest males typically monopolize breeding opportunities.

Distribution in Tanzania
Despite their size and significant food and habitat requirements, Savanna Elephants are still remarkably widely distributed in Tanzania. They are found in every mainland National Park except Kitulo and Gombe and also occur in most Game Reserves (apart from Mpanga–Kipengere and Ibanda GRs), and in a surprising number of Forest Reserves.

Population size and conservation status
The Selous Game Reserve had an estimated population of 39,000 elephants in 2009, although by 2013 this number had plummeted to 13,000 animals as a result of poaching. Other important populations include the Ruaha ecosystem (with approximately 20,000 individuals), Katavi ecosystem (6,000), Serengeti ecosystem (3,100) and the Tarangire ecosystem (2,500).

Ivory poaching represents a significant threat to elephant populations. An upsurge in ivory demand from Asia has led to a significant increase in poaching levels, notably in southern and western Tanzania, and the Tanzanian population is currently declining. Loss of migration corridors between protected areas due to agriculture and the establishment of settlements is another significant threat.

Savanna Elephant
TOP: male, Ngorongoro CA; BOTTOM: females with calves, Tarangire NP

Chimpanzee

Pan troglodytes

SWAHILI: Sokwe Mtu

A large, powerfully built ape with black fur, although older individuals are often partially bald and have white hair on their chin and lower back. The skin on the face and hands is mostly black, but can be pink or mottled. As with all great apes, Chimpanzees have no tail. They are quadrupedal and walk on their knuckles.

Subspecies
P. t. schweinfurthii: the only subspecies found in Tanzania.

Similar species
Unlikely to be mistaken for any other mammal.

Ecology and social behaviour
The preferred habitat of Chimpanzees is forest, forest-woodland mosaic, and occasionally wooded grasslands. They live in multi-male and multi-female groups of 20 to over 100 individuals, typically separating into smaller groups to feed. Home ranges vary from 10–50 km² (4–20 mi²). They are diurnal and both terrestrial and arboreal, sleeping in nests made of leaves that they construct each night. Their omnivorous diet includes fruits, leaves, monkeys and other vertebrates, and occasionally invertebrates.

Distribution in Tanzania
Chimpanzees are restricted to the far west of Tanzania, mainly along the edge of Lake Tanganyika. There are populations in Gombe and Mahale NPs; east of Mahale NP, they occur in the Lubaliti and Ntakata Hills, along the Masito escarpment and extend east as far as the Ugalla Niensi Open Area. They are also distributed between Mahale NP and the Wansisi Hills to the northwest of Katavi NP, including the Mwese and Lugalla Hills. The most southerly population of Chimpanzee in Africa is found on the escarpment above the southwestern shore of Lake Tanganyika at Loasi FR, Tembwa and the Lwafi GR. In the 1960s, seventeen Chimpanzees from European zoos and circuses were released onto Rubondo Island and have now formed a breeding

	Endangered
HB:	70–92 cm (28–36")
Wt:	M 28–56 kg (62–123 lb)
	F 20–46 kg (44–101 lb)

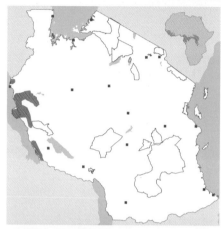

Where to look
The Chimpanzee populations in Gombe and Mahale NPs have both been the focus of long-term research projects that have continued uninterrupted since the 1960s. Both National Parks have habituated groups that are used for Chimpanzee-based tourism, and trips can be organized through a safari company or directly with the National Park. In Mahale NP, sightings are very likely on a 3-day trip between the months of July and April. Sightings in May and June may be less reliable as the Chimpanzee groups are often fragmented at the end of the rainy season when food is abundant throughout the National Park.

population of free-ranging individuals. At least some of these animals are believed to have originated from West Africa and, if this is the case, would be a different subspecies from the other Tanzanian populations.

Population size and conservation status
The total population of Chimpanzees in Tanzania in 2006 was estimated at 2,700–2,800 individuals. The majority of

these (approximately 2,600 animals) are in the Mahale–Ugalla Niensi area. The largest population, approximately 1,500 animals, lives in the Lubaliti and Ntakata hills to the east of Mahale, with a further 600 in Mahale NP, 200 in Masito, and 330 in Ugalla Niensi. There are 100 animals in Gombe NP and an estimated 40 individuals on Rubondo NP. There are probably a further 100 individuals in Loasi FR and Lwafi GR. Nearly 60% of Tanzania's Chimpanzee population occurs outside protected areas. Habitat loss, particularly riverine forest felled for making charcoal, is a major threat to these populations.

Chimpanzee numbers in the Mahale ecosystem have declined since the 1970s, and the Masito area is under increasing threat from an expanding human population from the Malagarasi River to the north and the Lake Tanganyika lakeshore to the west. The corridor of land between Mahale and Wansisi Hills is also experiencing increasing cultivation, particularly around Lubalisi, which threatens to sever the two areas. In Loasi FR, hunting for bushmeat, primarily for sale to markets in the Democratic Republic of Congo, poses a threat to the small population.

Chimpanzee
MAIN PHOTO: male, Mahale NP; INSET: infant, Mahale NP

Angola Black-and-white Colobus   *Colobus angolensis*

SWAHILI: Mbega (Mweupe), Kuluzu

A large monkey with a silky black body, long white hairs forming epaulettes on the shoulders, and long, dense white hairs on the cheeks. The face is black and hairless, with a narrow white band on the forehead separating the face from the black head. The tail is long, with the amount of white on the tip varying by subspecies.

Least Concern	
HB:	50–65 cm (20–26")
Tail:	70–90 cm (28–35")
Wt:	M 7–12 kg (15–26 lb) | F 6–9 kg (13–20 lb)

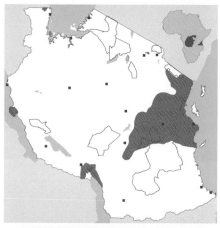

Subspecies
C. a. palliatus: northeast, central, and southern Tanzania; distal one-third of the tail is white.
C. a. ruwenzorii: northwest Tanzania; tip of the tail is white.
C. a. sharpei: Southern Highlands; long epaulettes down to forearms and very bushy white side-whiskers.
C. a. ssp. nov.: western Tanzania; tip of the tail is white, no white pubic band.

Similar species
The Guereza Black-and-white Colobus (*page 44*) is restricted to northern Tanzania and its range does not overlap with the Angola Black-and-white Colobus.

Ecology and social behaviour
Found in a range of forest types, including coastal, riverine, montane, bamboo and seasonally flooded forests. Occasionally found in mangroves and coconut groves. Diurnal and arboreal, Angola Black-and-white Colobuses seldom spend time on the ground, although they will cross montane grassland to pass between forest patches. They live in small groups of 2–20 individuals, usually with one male and two or more females and their young. Males that are not in family groups are usually solitary or occasionally in groups of 2–3 individuals. Group home ranges overlap considerably, and two groups may temporarily aggregate into large groups of 30 or more individuals. In Nyungwe Forest (Rwanda), groups as large as 300 individuals have been recorded. Males perform a characteristic loud, roaring display, often accompanied by branch shaking. Their diet is mostly leaves, seeds and flowers.

Where to look
Readily seen along the riverine forests in Sadaani NP. Also frequently seen along the Rufiji River in the Selous GR, where they are common around the Stiegler's Gorge, and they can be observed daily at Selous Mbega Camp. Other reliable sites are the Livingstone Forest in Kitulo NP and the Mount Rungwe Nature Reserve.

This species often associates with Kipunji (*page 56*) and Mitis Monkeys (*page 68*).

Distribution in Tanzania
The Angola Black-and-white Colobus is widely distributed across eastern Tanzania, with isolated populations in western Tanzania. There are records from all of the Eastern Arc Mountains, with the exception of the Mahenge Mountains, and it also occurs in many forested areas along the coast. It is known from Mkomazi, Sadaani, Mikumi, Udzungwa, Kitulo and Mahale NPs, northern Selous GR and Mount Rungwe Nature Reserve. There is also a population in Minziro FR. There are no substantiated records from south of the Rufiji or Kilombero Rivers.

Population size and conservation status

There are believed to be at least 10,000 Angola Black-and-white Colobuses in the Udzungwa Mountains, which is probably the largest population in the country. The highest densities within this area, based on hourly encounter rates during ground surveys, are in Udzungwa NP, Kilombero Nature Reserve and Uzungwa Scarp FR. This species is also locally common in appropriate habitat in Mikumi, Sadaani and Kitulo NPs, Amani Nature Reserve, northern Selous GR and on Mount Rungwe. It is uncommon in Mahale NP. They are hunted for meat, and increasingly for their pelts, in the Uzungwa Scarp FR and in the forests throughout the Southern Highlands, the pelts being mostly exported to Malawi for use in traditional medicine. Numbers are probably stable in National Parks although declining in Forest Reserves due to illegal hunting and habitat loss resulting from encroachment by local communities.

Angola Black-and-white Colobus
MAIN PHOTO: ssp. *ruwenzorii* (Rwanda); INSET: ssp. *palliatus*, Sadaani NP (Tanzania)

Guereza Black-and-white Colobus · *Colobus guereza*

Guereza Colobus, Abyssinian Black-and-white Colobus

SWAHILI: Mbega Mweupe, Kuluzu

A large monkey with a black body and a mantle of long white hairs around the shoulders, flanks, and lower back. The tail is long and bushy and mostly white with a black base. The chin, cheeks, and a narrow strip across the forehead are white, and the face and top of the head are black. Individuals living at higher altitudes typically have longer and thicker fur.

Subspecies

C. g. caudatus: Mount Kilimanjaro and Mount Meru.

C. g. matschiei: Serengeti ecosystem.

Similar species

Separated by range from the similar Angola Black-and-white Colobus (*page 42*).

Ecology and social behaviour

Guereza Black-and-white Colobuses inhabit montane and riparian forest, evergreen thickets, and occasionally conifer plantations. They are diurnal and arboreal, spending a significant amount of time in the middle to upper canopies, and seldom come to the ground. Their diet consists mostly of leaves and fruits, but they will also consume seeds, arthropods, bark and soil. This species typically lives in small groups of 6–10 individuals, with a single male and several females and their young. Larger groups of 25–30 individuals, often with multiple males, can also occur. Home ranges tend to be small, varying between 1–100 ha (2–250 acres), and are typically around 2 ha (5 acres) or less. Home ranges may overlap with those of neighbouring groups. Males make a distinctive loud croaking call that carries long distances and individuals from different groups will often call synchronously in the early morning, probably to advertise their territories.

Distribution in Tanzania

The Guereza Black-and-white Colobus is restricted to a few populations in Tanzania.

Least Concern	
HB:	M 53–75 cm (21–30")
	F 50–65 cm (20–26")
Tail:	55–90 cm (22–35")
Wt:	M 8–14 kg (18–31 lb) | F 5–10 kg (11–22 lb)

Where to look

Guereza Black-and-white Colobuses are frequently seen in Arusha NP, particularly along the roads between the National Park gate and the Ngurdoto museum, and the road up to the Meru Crater. To find them, stop regularly and scan and listen for them jumping through the trees. They can also be seen on many of the trails up Mount Kilimanjaro, as well as on Simba Farm in West Kilimanjaro. The gardens of Ngare Sero Lodge outside Arusha are also a reliable location for this species.

It is found throughout the forests of Kilimanjaro NP and there are isolated populations in the Rau and Kahe FRs to the southeast of Moshi town and in the North Pare Mountains. In Arusha NP, they are found both on Mount Meru and in the forests surrounding Ngurdoto Crater. There are also small populations on private or community land on the lower slopes of Mount Meru, including at Ngaramtoni and Ngare Sero. There is a separate population in the Serengeti ecosystem, in the western corridor of Serengeti NP, Grumeti GR, and in the Loliondo Forest and the Ng'arwa and Itira Forests bordering Kenya. They are absent from the forests of Ngorongoro and the mountains west of Mount Meru. Guereza Black-and-white Colobuses were introduced onto Rubondo Island during the 1960s and a small breeding population has now become established.

Population size and conservation status
There are no population figures for this species, although it is very common in both Arusha and Kilimanjaro NPs. In the forests of

Mount Kilimanjaro, it is most common on the north and western slopes between altitudes of 1,800–2,300 m (5,900–7,500 ft), but less so on the southern slopes although very common on the Umbwe route. It is locally common in the small forests in Loliondo and uncommon in the riverine forest along the Grumeti River. In past years there was some hunting of this species for skins and this may still occur in unprotected areas. However, it adapts well to degraded habitat and most of the populations in protected areas are probably stable.

Guereza Black-and-white Colobus
ssp. *caudatus*, Arusha NP

E Zanzibar Red Colobus

Procolobus kirkii
(Pilicolobus kirkii)

Kirk's Red Colobus

SWAHILI: Kima Punju

A medium-size monkey with a red back, black shoulders and white underparts. The face is black, with a pink nose and lips, and framed by a striking white crest, while the back of the head and neck is red. The legs are black or grey above and white below and the hands and feet are black. The tail is long, red above and white or pale below. There is significant variation in colour pattern between individuals. Females are slightly larger and more robust than males.

Similar species
Mitis Monkeys (*page 68*) may also have red on the back but have dark sides and legs.

Ecology and social behaviour
Zanzibar Red Colobuses are found in a variety of habitats including evergreen groundwater forest, coral rag thicket, mangrove swamps, secondary forest and agricultural land. They prefer high canopy forest although much of this has now disappeared. Their diet consists of leaves, fruits and herbs, also native and introduced crops, and sometimes charcoal. Individuals living in mangrove forests feed predominantly on mangrove leaves. They live in multi-male and multi-female groups with an average of 2·5 males and 10·6 females in a group. Dominant males may monopolize matings but all males within a group will breed. Group size ranges from 5–85 individuals, with 15–30 individuals being most common; groups are larger in and around Jozani Chwaka Bay NP than in the coral rag thickets. Groups do not display any territoriality and home ranges may overlap completely with one or more other groups.

Distribution in Tanzania
The Zanzibar Red Colobus is endemic to Zanzibar, where it occurs in the northeast and across the south-central parts of the island. It may, however, have formerly occurred on the mainland. A population was introduced into Ngezi–Vumawimbi Forest on Pemba Island in 1973. On Zanzibar, it occurs in Jozani Chwaka Bay NP and the adjacent

Endangered	
HB:	42–56 cm (17–22")
Tail:	55–75 cm (22–30")
Wt:	5·5–9·4 kg (12–21 lb)

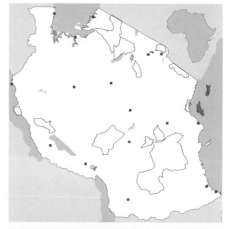

Where to look
Zanzibar Red Colobus sightings are guaranteed at Jozani Chwaka Bay NP, where guides take tourists to see habituated groups in the forest. The income received is shared between the National Park and the adjacent local communities, providing an important incentive for the farmers to protect these endangered animals. They are also frequently seen in Mtende, Kiwengwa and Masingini Forests.

agricultural land, on Uzi Island, and in isolated populations along the eastern coast from Kiwengwa Forest to Mtende Forest in the south. In western Zanzibar, it is found in Maji Mekundu Forest, and a population was introduced to Masingini Forest in 1977–8.

Population size and conservation status
The Zanzibar Red Colobus population has been estimated to be 2,000–3,000 individuals, and it is one of the most threatened primates in Africa. The largest population occurs in and around Jozani Chwaka Bay NP, which may have some 500–750 individuals, with the highest densities found on the agricultural land on the southern border of the National

Park. These high densities are probably due to troops constricting into remaining areas of habitat as a result of extensive habitat loss elsewhere. They occur at lower densities in other parts of the Island, including in the coral rag thicket on the eastern and southern coast. A population of 15 individuals introduced onto Pemba in 1973 had increased to 35–40 animals by 2011. Almost 50% of the Zanzibar Red Colobus population lives in areas where they have little or no official protection, and numbers are continuing to decline. The main threat is habitat loss to agriculture, wood gathering and charcoal production; this loss is significant and likely to lead to severe population declines in the future. They are also killed by farmers, feral dogs and by vehicles on roads.

Zanzibar Red Colobus
TOP: male, Jozani Chwaka Bay NP; BOTTOM: mother and infant, Jozani Chwaka Bay NP

E Udzungwa Red Colobus

Procolobus gordonorum
(Pilicolobus gordonorum)

Iringa Red Colobus, Uhehe Red Colobus

SWAHILI: Mbega Mwekundu

Endangered	
HB:	60–65 cm (24–26")
Tail:	64–69 cm (25–27")
Wt:	not available

A medium-sized monkey with a distinctive bright red cap, white underparts and a dark back – although some individuals have a rufous patch on the lower back. The long limbs have black outer sides and white inner sides. The feet and hands are black. The tail has a black upper side and a bicolored underside, with the basal third white and the rest dark. The nose and lips are pink, and the facial skin is black. Prominent white cheeks are separated from the red crown by a band of black fur. Males and females are similarly patterned, although males are slightly larger.

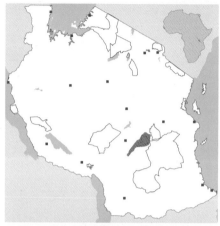

Similar species
The Mitis Monkey (*page 68*), which frequently has a red 'saddle', lacks red on the head.

Ecology and social behaviour
The Udzungwa Red Colobus is diurnal, and highly arboreal, inhabiting a variety of forest habitats, including lowland, montane, groundwater, secondary and riverine, as well as miombo woodland abutting forested areas. It lives in multi-male and multi-female groups that vary considerably in size, from 3–83 individuals, with an average of 27 animals. The quality and size of available habitat influences group size, with larger groups occurring in areas where there are large tracts of intact forest; smaller groups being found in degraded and fragmented forest areas. It feeds predominantly on leaves, although some fruits are also eaten.

Distribution in Tanzania
Udzungwa Red Colobus is a Tanzanian endemic, restricted to the forests of the Udzungwa Mountains and a few small forest blocks and riverine forest areas in the Kilombero Valley. Within the Udzungwa Mountains, it occurs in Udzungwa NP and in the majority of forest blocks except those in the far southwest of the mountain range in the Mufindi area. In the Kilombero Valley it is found in very small patches of forest

Where to look
The Udzungwa Red Colobus is regularly seen on the main Mwanihana trail in Udzungwa NP.

including the Magombera and Kiwanga Forests, and in riverine forest along the Msolwa River. A population that occurred north of the Udzungwa NP in the Vidunda Mountains is believed to have gone extinct.

Population size and conservation status
The total population of Udzungwa Red Colobus was estimated at 25,000–35,000 individuals in 2009. The greatest numbers occur in the Mwanihana Forest in the Udzungwa NP, where it is most common between altitudes of 300–700 m (1,000–2,300 ft). There is an estimated population of roughly 1,000 individuals in the Magombera Forest in the Kilombero Valley, the high population density being due to habitat loss elsewhere. This species is vulnerable to hunting, with dogs being used to isolate the monkeys in trees, where they are then easily shot. In the Uzungwa Scarp FR, the population of Udzungwa Red Colobuses declined almost to extinction between 2004 and 2009, and other populations in the area

may be similarly threatened. Fire and illegal logging also threatens populations in small forest patches. The population is believed to be stable inside Udzungwa NP, and declining in the forests outside the National Park, most of which have little protection.

Udzungwa Red Colobus
Udzungwa Mountains

Eastern Red Colobus

Procolobus rufomitratus
(Pilicolobus rufomitratus)

Central African Red Colobus, Ashy Red Colobus

SWAHILI: Mbega Mwekundu

Least Concern	
HB:	58–63 cm (23–25")
Tail:	69 cm (27")
Wt:	M 10·5 kg (23 lb) | F 6 kg (13 lb)

A medium-sized monkey with a dark brown or black back, brown on the outer sides of the limbs, and black feet. The inner sides of the limbs are light cream or white. The face is greyish, and the crown is black extending as far as the ears and topped with a red cap. There is a white fringe extending from the chin to the ears. The tail is dark brown or black above and white below, with a black tuft at the tip. Adult males are up to 25% larger than females. Populations on the Ufipa Plateau have long hair and frequently have stump tails.

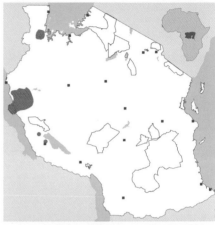

Subspecies

P. r. tephrosceles: only subspecies in Tanzania.

Similar species

Mitis Monkeys (*page 68*) have dark sides and legs, and no red on the head.

Ecology and social behaviour

The Eastern Red Colobus is mostly diurnal and arboreal, inhabiting a variety of forest types including lowland riverine forest, wet miombo, submontane and montane forest up to an altitude of 2,400 m (5,300 ft). It lives in multi-male and female groups, usually, although not always, with a dominant male that monopolizes breeding. Group sizes in Mbizi FR averaged 40 individuals (range 30–56). Groups occupy home ranges of approximately 1 km² (0·4 mi²), although the species is not territorial and there is significant home range overlap with other groups. It feeds almost exclusively on leaves, particularly young leaves, seeds and buds. This species frequently associates with other species of monkey, including Red-tailed Monkey (*page 66*) and Mitis Monkey.

Distribution in Tanzania

The Eastern Red Colobus is known from the forests of Burigi–Biharamulo GRs, along the northeastern edge of Lake Tanganyika, including Gombe and Mahale NPs, and the Mbizi and Mbuzi Forests on the Ufipa Plateau.

Where to look

Eastern Red Colobus is commonly seen in Mahale NP in the lowland forest around many of the lodges and camps. It can also be reliably seen in Gombe NP, as well as in Mbizi FR close to Sumbawanga town.

It has also been recorded in the riverine forests that spread inland from Lake Tanganyika, including Issa, west of Ugalla GR. There is a record of this species from the 1950s from the Moyowosi GR, although there is no recent information on this population. This species is probably more widely distributed in relict forest populations in western Tanzania than previously thought.

Population size and conservation status

There are no accurate numbers for the Eastern Red Colobus in Tanzania. A count in Mbizi Forest in 2006 indicated a population of 1,217 individuals. The population in the nearby Mbuzi Forest, which was estimated at 137 individuals in 2006, had declined by 50% in 2011 due to habitat loss. There are no figures for Gombe and Mahale NPs, although numbers were stable in one part of Mahale Forest between 1996 and 2002, despite high levels of Chimpanzee (*page 40*) predation. This predation can be extreme, killing up to 40% of the entire population in a single year, which has led to a gradual decline of Eastern Red Colobus numbers in Gombe NP.

Habitat loss outside protected areas is also a significant threat. The Mbizi and Mbuzi Forests are now severely degraded and require urgent conservation action, while several small Eastern Red Colobus populations on the Ufipa Plateau, including in Nsangu and Misheta Forests, are now extinct.

Eastern Red Colobus
ssp. *tephrosceles* (Uganda)

E Sanje Mangabey   *Cercocebus sanjei*

SWAHILI: Sanje

A medium-sized monkey with a long tail and long legs. The fur is also long and speckled grey or grey-brown on the back and legs, and pale yellow or cream on the underbelly. There is an erect, double fringe of fur on the forehead. The bare skin on the face is pink or grey and the brow is black. The tail is the same colour as the body and has a white tip, and the bare rump is blue-grey. Males are larger and more thickset than the females.

Ecology and social behaviour
Sanje Mangabeys inhabit the understorey of primary and secondary montane and submontane forest although they will also traverse degraded forest mosaic. Approximately 50–70% of their time is spent travelling and foraging on the ground, searching for fruits and seeds that form a major part of their diet. Other foods include plants, invertebrates and occasionally small mammals and birds. This species lives in large groups of 35–60 individuals, consisting of multiple females and males, which use home ranges that average 4–6 km² (1·5–2·0 mi²) and generally overlap with the ranges of neighbouring groups. It is often found in association with other primates, including Angola Black-and-white Colobuses (*page 42*) and Mitis Monkeys (*page 68*). It has a range of vocalizations including a loud, distinctive "*whoop-gooble*" made by males to advertise the presence of the troop to neighbouring groups.

Similar species
No similar species are found within its range.

Distribution in Tanzania
The Sanje Mangabey is endemic to Tanzania and restricted to only two forests in the Udzungwa Mountains: the Mwanihana Forest in Udzungwa NP and the Uzungwa Scarp FR. Intensive surveys have not revealed any other populations within the Udzungwa Mountains or farther afield.

Endangered	
HB:	approx. 50–65 cm (20–25")
Ht:	approx. 55–65 cm (22–25")
Wt:	approx. M 10 kg (22 lb) | F 6 kg (13 lb)

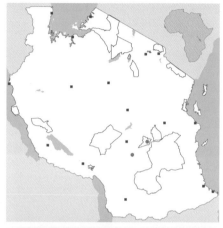

Where to look
There is a habituated group of Sanje Mangabey that can be reliably seen in Udzungwa NP. Trips can be arranged at the National Park headquarters at Mang'ula, where a dedicated guide can lead people to the troop.

Population size and conservation status
Recent surveys suggest that the total population of Sanje Mangabeys is approximately 2,800–3,500 individuals. The larger Mwanihana Forest has an estimated 50–60 groups with a total of 1,750–2,100 individuals, and the Uzungwa Scarp FR has another 30–40 groups with approximately 1,050–1,400 animals. Hourly group encounter rates during ground surveys suggest that densities in the Uzungwa Scarp FR are equivalent to or higher than those in Mwanihana. Population trends are not known. Threats to the population in the Uzungwa Scarp FR, where enforcement of regulations is minimal, include habitat loss and degradation resulting from uncontrolled tree cutting, as well as accidental capture in snares set for

duikers and other ungulates. Hunting of primates occurs in the Forest Reserve, but does not appear to have negatively affected the Sanje Mangabey. The population in Mwanihana Forest within Udzungwa NP is much better protected. Both populations are small and lack interconnectivity, making them susceptible to outbreaks of disease and other stochastic events.

Sanje Mangabey
TOP: adult female, Udzungwa Mountains; BOTTOM: family group grooming, Udzungwa Mountains.

Uganda Grey-cheeked Mangabey   *Lophocebus ugandae*

SWAHILI: Kima Kishungi Kahawia

The Uganda Grey-cheeked Mangabey was, until recently, considered a subspecies of the Grey-cheeked Mangabey *Lophocebus albigena*. It is a medium-sized monkey with a dark, long-haired, brown to black coat, and a cloak of longer hair on the shoulders that ranges in colour from grey to light brown. From a distance, this monkey may appear entirely black. The face is naked with black skin and there is a tufted crown on the head with two prominent spikes of hair above each eye. The tail is long and usually carried upright with the tip pointing forwards towards the head. The skin in the perianal area is usually black, although this turns pink and swells significantly in sexually receptive females.

Not Assessed	
HB:	50–70 cm (20–28")
Tail:	55–75 cm (22–30")
Wt:	M 7–10 kg (15–22 lb) | F 6 kg (13 lb)

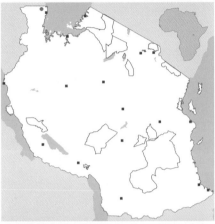

Similar species
The Angola Black-and-white Colobus (*page 42*) has long white hairs on the shoulder, bushy white cheeks and white on the tail and body. The Mitis Monkey (*page 68*) is smaller and the Red-tailed Monkey (*page 66*) has a distinctive red tail and a white nose.

Ecology and social behaviour
In Tanzania the Uganda Grey-cheeked Mangabey is only found in a patch of forest that is contiguous with the Guinea–Congo lowland forests of central Africa. This area is dominated by *Baikiaea–Podocarpus* and flooded seasonally by the Kagera River. This mangabey is a diurnal and arboreal species, seldom venturing to the ground, and feeds mainly on fruit, although it also eats leaves, roots and invertebrates. It has also been recorded feeding on birds' eggs and snakes. It lives in mixed-sex troops of 6–30 individuals, in home ranges of 1·5–2·0 km² (less than one mi²) that overlap considerably with those of neighbouring groups. Different groups occasionally come together for short periods, although they typically avoid each other. Males produce a loud "*whoop-gobble*" call that is used to communicate troop location and movement. This species is gregarious and will frequently

Where to look
Uganda Grey-cheeked Mangabeys can be seen along the main road passing through Minziro FR, particularly in the early morning and late afternoon. Two days is usually sufficient to find this species.

associate with other primates, including Red-tailed Monkeys and Mitis Monkeys.

Distribution in Tanzania
The Uganda Grey-cheeked Mangabey is restricted to the Minziro FR in the far northwest of Tanzania, where it forms a contiguous population with individuals from the Sango Bay Forest in Uganda.

Population size and conservation status
The size of the population of Uganda Grey-cheeked Mangabey in Minziro FR (which is approximately 290 km² \| 112 mi²) is unknown, although it is relatively uncommon and probably numbers less than 500 individuals. It is not known whether this species is actively hunted for food, although it may be vulnerable to illegal logging. Its small population size makes it susceptible to stochastic events.

Uganda Grey-cheeked Mangabey
TOP: (Uganda); BOTTOM: (Uganda)

55

E Kipunji

Rungwecebus kipunji

SWAHILI: Kipunji

A medium sized monkey with a long tail and dense pelage. The back and sides are light brown to rufous-brown and the belly is off-white. The lower limbs are darker brown, and the hands and feet are black. The facial skin is bare and black, and there is a prominent crest of grey-brown hair on the crown and elongated whiskers on the cheeks. The upper half of the tail is dusky-brown and the lower half is off-white, interspersed with darker hairs. This species was initially thought to be a mangabey but subsequent molecular and morphological analyses have shown it to be more closely related to the baboon genus *Papio* and it has been placed in a new, monospecific, genus *Rungwecebus*.

Similar species

From a distance, the Kipunji may be confused with a young or female baboon (*pages 58–60*). As with baboons, the young may be carried on the back of adults, the tail is held out away from the body and some of the calls are similar. However, the Kipunji's muzzle is not extended and it is slighter in build and almost completely arboreal.

Ecology and social behaviour

The Kipunji is restricted to degraded submontane and montane forest at altitudes between 1,500–2,500 m (5,000–8,000 ft) in Rungwe–Kitulo, and submontane forest in Ndundulu at altitudes b§etween 1,300–1,750 m (4,300–5,700 ft). It mostly utilizes tall canopy trees above 10 m (33 ft) and avoids open areas unless raiding crops. Kipunji are diurnal and arboreal, living in multi-male and multi-female groups with 20–39 individuals in Rungwe–Kitulo and 15–25 individuals in Ndundulu. They are non-territorial with overlapping home ranges, although they will perform territorial displays when two groups meet. Average home range size on Mount Rungwe is 3 km² (1 mi²). Kipunji have at least 12 recognized calls, including a dramatic "*honk-bark*" used as a group-spacing mechanism. They have a varied diet

Critically Endangered	
HB:	approx. 85–90 cm (33–35")
Tail:	approx. 90 cm (35")
Wt:	approx. 10–15 kg (22–33 lb)

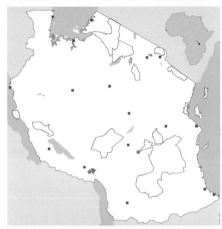

Where to look

Due to their shy nature and isolated distribution, the Kipunji is not easy to observe. This species was only recently discovered, and no official viewing opportunities have yet been developed.

(122 species have been recorded), which includes leaves, fruits, bark and invertebrates, as well as crops (particularly maize).

Distribution in Tanzania

The Kipunji is endemic to Tanzania, and was only discovered by teams working in the Southern Highlands in 2003 and Udzungwa Mountains in 2004. It is restricted to Mount Rungwe and the adjacent Livingstone Forests in Kitulo NP in the Southern Highlands, and the Ndundulu Forest in the recently gazetted Kilombero Nature Reserve in the Udzungwa Mountains. The total known range in Tanzania is less than 50 km² (20 mi²), covering 24 km² (9 mi²) and 18 km² (7 mi²) in Mount Rungwe and Kitulo NP, respectively, and approximately 5 km² (2 mi²) in Ndundulu Forest.

Population size and conservation status

The total population of Kipunji in 2007

was estimated at 1,117 animals living in approximately 38 groups, making it one of the most threatened primates in Africa. The largest numbers are found in the Livingstone Forest in Kitulo NP, which has 541 individuals in 18 groups, and there are a further 501 animals in 16 groups on Mount Rungwe and 75 individuals in four groups in Ndundulu. The forests on Mount Rungwe and Kitulo NP are heavily degraded, and there is poor habitat connectivity between the various groups.

The Livingstone Forest is protected within the Kitulo NP and the other two populations occur in Mount Rungwe Nature Reserve and Kilombero Nature Reserve. Major threats include hunting for meat and as retribution for crop raiding, and habitat loss through illegal charcoal production, logging and agricultural expansion. The only patch of forest connecting the populations in Mount Rungwe to the Kitulo NP, the narrow Bujingijila corridor, has also been severely degraded by agriculture.

Kipunji
MAIN PHOTO: male, Southern Highlands; INSET: female with young, Southern Highlands

Olive Baboon

Papio anubis

SWAHILI: Nyani

An olive-brown or brown baboon with a lightly speckled coat. The tail is kinked close to its base. The muzzle is black and hairless and there is also a hairless patch on the rump, which is typically black although turns red in females when they are sexually receptive. Males are twice the size of females and have a distinct mane around the head and shoulders.

Similar species

The Yellow Baboon (*page 60*) has a paler yellow pelage and longer legs and muzzle than the Olive Baboon and males do not have a distinct mane. The tail is kinked lower down the tail than in Olive Baboons.

Ecology and social behaviour

Olive Baboons are found in a wide range of habitats, from savanna to montane forest as well as agricultural land, where there are both permanent water and suitable nocturnal refugia, including trees, rocky cliffs and caves. They live in multi-male and multi-female groups of 30–200 individuals, although 30–50 individuals is more common. Males have a dominance hierarchy that determines breeding success, with the highest-ranking male securing most matings. Males disperse from their family group at age 7–13 years. Home range size varies from 4–44 km² (1·5–17 mi²) and may overlap substantially with those of other troops. Troops typically avoid each other but may share sleeping sites. Olive Baboons are omnivorous, feeding on a wide assortment of fruits, grasses and leaves, as well as invertebrates, birds and small mammals, including young Impala (*page 230*).

Distribution in Tanzania

The Olive Baboon is restricted to northern and northwestern Tanzania. It is found in Kilimanjaro, Arusha, Tarangire and Serengeti NPs, Ngorongoro CA, Lake Natron, the Yaeda Valley, Moyowosi–Kigosi GRs, Gombe NP, Burigi–Biharamulo GRs, Ibanda–Rumanyika GRs and Minziro FR. There is an extensive hybrid zone where the ranges of the Olive

Least Concern	
HB:	M 55–90 cm (22–35")
	F 50–70 cm (20–28")
Tail:	M 41–60 cm (16–24")
	F 32–54 cm (13–21")
Wt:	M 8–30 kg (18–66 lb) | F 6–17 kg (13–37 lb)

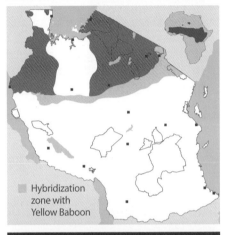

Hybridization zone with Yellow Baboon

Where to look

This species is easily seen in many northern National Parks, including Tarangire, Manyara, Serengeti and Ngorongoro CA.

and Yellow Baboons (*page 60*) overlap and interbreed. This stretches from the Malagarasi River in the west, through Ugalla and Swagaswaga GRs and the southern Maasai Steppe to West Kilimanjaro and Mkomazi NP. In these areas, pure Olive and Yellow Baboons may be found, as well as baboons with traits of both species. The baboons in Swagaswaga GR have stronger Olive than Yellow Baboon features, while this trend is reversed in animals in Mkomazi NP and the lower northern slopes of Mount Kilimanjaro. The exact extent of the hybridization zone is unclear and requires further research.

Population size and conservation status

The Olive Baboon is very common in many protected areas including Arusha, Manyara and northern Tarangire NPs, the Serengeti ecosystem, Moyowosi–Kigosi GRs, Burigi–

Biharamulo GRs and Gombe NP. It occurs at lower densities outside protected areas, although is locally common in the Lake Natron to West Kilimanjaro area.

Baboons are killed for crop raiding and occasionally hunted for meat, but populations are believed to be stable across northern Tanzania.

Olive Baboon
TOP: male, Tarangire NP; BOTTOM: female with infant, Tarangire NP

Yellow Baboon   *Papio cynocephalus*

SWAHILI: Nyani Njano

A long-legged baboon with yellow to yellow-grey upperparts and white underparts. The tail is long and is kinked approximately one-quarter along the length from the base. The muzzle is hairless and grey-black. There is a hairless patch on the rump, which is typically black, although this swells and turns red in females when they are sexually receptive. Males have no mane.

Subspecies
P. c. cynocephalus: throughout Tanzania, except for the southwest; large with a long muzzle.

P. c. kindae: Mahale NP and along the southern lakeshore of Lake Tanganyika; smaller and more slender with shorter muzzle.

Similar species
The Olive Baboon (*page 58*) is darker and has shorter legs and muzzle, and males have a distinct mane. Hybrids between the two species have intermediate traits and occur where the ranges overlap.

Ecology and social behaviour
Although Yellow Baboons are commonly associated with miombo woodland, they are also found in grassland, *Acacia* woodland, agricultural land and the edges of coastal and lowland forest. They use groves of trees as sleeping sites and are seldom found far from such areas. Similarly, they are absent from areas without permanent water. Diurnal and mainly terrestrial, these baboons live in multi-male and multi-female groups of 20–80 individuals, but singles and multi-male groups also occur. Home ranges of different troops overlap greatly, though troops typically avoid one another. Yellow Baboons are omnivorous and have a broad diet that includes grasses, seeds, roots, invertebrates, birds and small mammals, including young dik-diks (*page 208*) and Impalas (*page 230*).

Distribution in Tanzania
Yellow Baboons are found across southern, central, eastern and much of western Tanzania. On the northern boundary, their

Least Concern	
HB:	M 62–85 cm (24–33") F 51–69 cm (20–27")
Tail:	45–66 cm (18–26")
Wt:	M 20–28 kg (44–62 lb) | F 9–17 kg (20–37 lb)

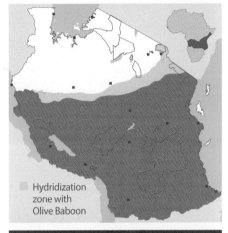

Hydridization zone with Olive Baboon

Where to look
The Yellow Baboon can be seen in many of the National Parks on the southern circuit, including Mikumi, Ruaha and Sadaani NPs. It is also one of the few species that is likely to be seen outside protected areas along the main highways. Subspecies *kindae* is easily seen in Mahale NP in the forests along the edge of Lake Tanganyika, where troops frequently pass through the grounds of the main lodges and camps.

range overlaps with that of the Olive Baboon, with hybrids between the two species known from Swagaswaga GR, where males resemble Olive Baboons and females resemble Yellow Baboons. Hybridization is also common in West Kilimanjaro and Mkomazi NP, where individuals have mostly Yellow Baboon traits. The approximate extent of the hybridization zone is shown on the distribution map, although the limits of this zone may need to be refined based on further research. Yellow Baboons are found in Sadaani, Mikumi and Udzungwa NPs, the Ruaha–Rungwa and Katavi–Rukwa ecosystems and the Selous and

Ugalla GRs. They are also widely distributed outside protected areas, occurring throughout much of the coastal region, southern Singida and Morogoro District.

Population size and conservation status
The Yellow Baboon is locally abundant in Mikumi and Ruaha NPs and parts of the Selous GR, and is generally common across much of its range, particularly in protected areas. There are no population figures or trends for the country, but numbers are likely to be stable in protected areas and probably slowly declining in non-protected areas, mainly as a result of habitat loss and persecution for pest control.

Yellow Baboon
TOP: male ssp. *cynocephalus*, Sadaani NP; BOTTOM: female ssp. *kindae*, Mahale NP

Patas Monkey

Erythrocebus patas

SWAHILI: Kima Mwekundu

A medium-sized monkey with a slender body, small head and very long legs. It is rufous-brown on the back, sides, crown of the head and upper side of the tail, while the legs and shoulders are grey (occasionally black in old males) and the underparts are white. Males are significantly larger than females and have bare red skin around the anus and a blue scrotum. There is bare black skin on the face and white hair on the cheeks. The tail is long with a distinct kink close to the base.

Subspecies
E. p. baumstarki: only subspecies found in Tanzania.

Similar species
This species is unlikely to be confused with any other primate, although at a distance, walking males may be mistaken for Thomson's Gazelles (*page 212*).

Ecology and social behaviour
In Tanzania, Patas Monkeys are very closely associated with *Acacia drepanolobium* woodland, in which they feed and sleep. They are mostly terrestrial and quadrupedal and are capable of running at speeds of up to 55 kph (34 mph). Their diet is varied and includes leaves, fruits and tree gum, as well as invertebrates and small vertebrates. Patas Monkeys live in family groups of 10–40 individuals; smaller groups usually have only one adult male, although there may be several males in larger groups. Males are sometimes solitary or live in all-male groups. Group territories range in size from 23–52 km² (9–20 mi²) and are actively defended against incursions from other groups.

Distribution in Tanzania
The Patas Monkey is at the very southern end of its range in Tanzania, and the population is small and fragmented. There were historically three separate populations in Tanzania: in the western Serengeti, West Kilimanjaro and around the volcanic mountains west of Arusha. In West Kilimanjaro, small groups

Least Concern	
HB:	M 60–87 cm (24–34")
	F 50–60 cm (20–24")
Ht:	M 34–50 cm (13–20")
	F 28–45 cm (11–18")
Tail:	50–74 cm (20–29")
Wt:	M 7·5–13 kg (17–29 lb) | F 4·0–7·5 kg (9–17 lb)

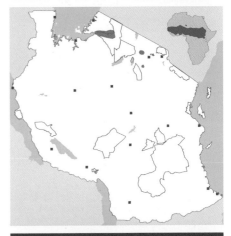

Where to look
Sightings of Patas Monkeys are becoming increasingly infrequent in Tanzania. They are sometimes observed on the Msabi Plains and in the Mbalageti area in the western Serengeti NP, and occasionally in Ikona WMA.

of Patas Monkeys were recorded in the Lerangwa Wildlife Corridor and on Ndarakwai Ranch in 1990, and again near Tinga Tinga in 2001. However, there have been no sightings in this area since then, despite intensive coverage by community game scouts, and there is a good chance that the species is now extinct in West Kilimanjaro. There is a small group of Patas Monkeys in the southern foothills of Burko Mountain, and another around Lolkisale Mountain, although there have been no records from the Lolkisale population since 2005. In the western Serengeti ecosystem, the majority of records have come from outside the National Park in the Ikona WMA, although sightings there have declined significantly since 2008. It is possible that individuals from this population have migrated to the western corridor of the Serengeti NP.

Population size and conservation status
The largest population of Patas Monkeys in Tanzania is in the western Serengeti, with perhaps 200–300 individuals. The population on the slopes of Burko Mountain has approximately 20–30 animals, and it is possible that there are still some 20–30 individuals in the Lolkisale area.

The total Tanzanian population is therefore now likely to number fewer than 400 individuals. The main threat is changing fire régimes and an increase in cattle farming in Ikona WMA, while the very small populations are also vulnerable to stochastic events such as disease. The number of Patas Monkeys is continuing to decline, and, following the likely extinction of the West Kilimanjaro population, the only viable population may now be in the western Serengeti. This population represents an endemic subspecies, which now faces a high risk of extinction.

Patas Monkey
Rare images of ssp. *baumstarki*, which is endemic to Tanzania.
TOP: female and juvenile, Serengeti NP;
RIGHT: male, Serengeti NP

Vervet Monkey

Chlorocebus pygerythrus

SWAHILI: Tumbili, Ngedere

A small monkey with a grizzled, olive-brown, yellow-brown or tan back, grey legs and white underparts. The tail is long, grey above and white beneath with a black tip. The face is black face, surrounded by a white fringe, and the top of the head and neck are olive-brown. The legs and feet are black. The skin at the base of the tail is red and males have a vivid blue scrotum and a bright red penis.

Subspecies

C. p. rufoviridis: western Tanzania; large, the back is yellow or reddish and darker towards the base of the tail.

C. p. nesiotis: Pemba Island; similar to *C. p. rufoviridis* although smaller.

C. p. hilgerti: northern Tanzania; the back is a pale yellow-brown.

C. p. tantalus: central, coastal and western Tanzania; the back is olive-green. The animals on the island of Zanzibar are probably this subspecies, but may be hybrids between different subspecies.

Note: Vervet Monkeys belong to a large species complex comprising different groups or clusters that are treated by some authorities as full species and by others as subspecies.

Similar species

Mitis Monkeys (*page 68*) and Red-tailed Monkeys (*page 66*) are both larger and darker than Vervet Monkeys.

Ecology and social behaviour

Vervet Monkeys use a very wide variety of habitat types including wooded grasslands, woodland, coastal and montane forest edge, scrubland, agricultural land and urban areas. They generally avoid dense forest, using instead the edges of the forest, and are absent from patches of montane grassland, open savanna, grasslands and agricultural land with few trees. Their main habitat requirements are access to water, trees in which to sleep, and cover. Their diet is varied, with fruits and flowers their preferred food sources, although they also eat grasses, leaves, invertebrates,

Least Concern	
HB:	40–70 cm (16–28")
Tail:	40–75 cm (16–30")
Wt:	M 4·0–6·5 kg (9–14 lb) | F 3·5–5·0 kg (8–11 lb)

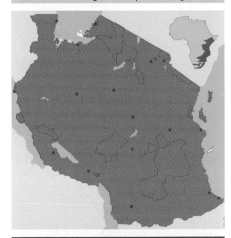

Where to look

This species is commonly seen around many lodges and picnic sites, both on the northern and southern tour circuits. Sightings are almost guaranteed in Ruaha, Mikumi, Manyara, northern Tarangire and central Serengeti NPs.

birds' eggs, small reptiles, birds and mammals. Predominantly terrestrial, Vervet Monkeys are diurnal and live in multi-male, multi-female groups of up to 50 animals, with an average of 25 individuals; a few dominant males monopolize breeding opportunities. Home ranges vary by habitat type and quality, and usually cover 20–100 ha (50–250 acres).

Distribution in Tanzania

The Vervet Monkey is probably the most widely distributed large mammal species in Tanzania, occurring throughout the country. It is found in all National Parks, with the exception of Kitulo NP, where it is known only from lower slopes of the plateau outside the boundaries of the Park. It also occurs in all Game Reserves and in many towns and cities. It is absent from Mafia Island.

Population size and conservation status
There are no population estimates for the Vervet Monkey in Tanzania, but it is locally common or abundant in many parts of the country and frequently seen outside protected areas. They can suffer from heavy predation, which in some areas has caused significant local population declines and occasionally extinctions. Their main predators are Leopards (*page 132*), and to a lesser extent, Yellow Baboons (*page 60*) and large birds of prey, including Martial Eagles *Polemaetus bellicosus*. Population trends are not known.

Vervet Monkey
TOP: female with infant ssp. *hilgerti*, Manyara NP; BOTTOM: male ssp. *hilgerti*, Lake Eyasi

Red-tailed Monkey

Cercopithecus ascanius

SWAHILI: Kima Mkia Mwekundu

A medium-sized monkey with a grizzled brown back, dark or black legs, and white throat and underparts. The upper half of the tail is the same colour as the body, while the lower half is bright red with a black tip. There is a heart-shaped white spot on the nose, with the surrounding facial skin being blue or black, and a black band on the forehead, The ears are white, and there are long white whiskers on the cheeks tipped with black. Males are typically 30% larger than females.

Least Concern	
HB:	35–50 cm (14 20")
Tail:	60–85 cm (24–33")
Wt:	2–5 kg (4–11 lb)

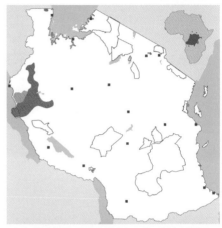

Subspecies
C. a. schmidti: only subspecies found in Tanzania.

Similar species
Although the Mitis Monkey (*page 68*) is a similar size, the Red-tailed Monkey is easily distinguished by its white nose and red tail. Red-tailed Monkey frequently hybridizes with Mitis Monkey in Gombe NP. The offspring, which have intermediate features, may be found in groups of either species.

Ecology and social behaviour
Red-tailed Monkeys inhabit a variety of forest types, including gallery and submontane forests, as well as riverine forests within miombo or *Acacia* woodland. They are diurnal and arboreal, although occasionally seen on the ground, and have a varied diet that includes fruits, seeds, leaves and invertebrates, and, less commonly, reptiles, small mammals and birds. They typically live in single male, multi-female groups of 15–50 individuals, although groups may occasionally have more than one adult male. Bachelor males are either solitary or form loose coalitions. Groups have home ranges of up to 68 ha (170 acres), although there is often considerable overlap between the home ranges of adjacent groups.

Distribution in Tanzania
The Red-tailed Monkey is restricted to a narrow area of western and northwestern Tanzania. It occurs throughout the forests of Mahale and Gombe NPs, and along the

Where to look
Red-tailed Monkeys are easily seen in a day during forest walks in both Mahale and Gombe NPs, where they are common in the lowland forest areas around most of the lodges and bungalows. They can also be seen in Minziro FR during a two-day visit, particularly on the edges of the forest along the main road.

riverine forests in Luganzo Open Area, Issa, western Ugalla GR and Moyowosi GR. There is also a population in Minziro FR in the far north on the border with Uganda.

Population size and conservation status
This species is locally common in both Mahale and Gombe NPs and in the Minziro FR, although the population in Minziro is small. It is uncommon in the riverine forests of Issa, west of Tongwe FR and the Moyowosi GR. The main threats outside protected areas are habitat loss and possibly hunting, although it is a fast-moving species and therefore relatively difficult to hunt. Small, isolated populations, such as those in Ugalla and Moyowosi GRs, will be vulnerable to local extinction due to disease or heavy predation.

Red-tailed Monkey
(Kenya)

Mitis Monkey

Cercopithecus mitis

Blue Monkey, Sykes's Monkey, Gentle Monkey

SWAHILI: Karasinga, Kima

A medium-sized monkey with a long tail and dense fur. The back colour is highly variable, ranging through speckled blue-grey to green, orange, russet or red. The front forelimbs are black and the hind legs are black or dark grey. They typically have long facial hair, a white throat, a white or black brow and a black cap.

Subspecies

C. m. albogularis: northern Tanzania (Mount Kilimanjaro and Mount Meru), Zanzibar; russet or green back, white on throat.

C. m. doggetti: west and northwest Tanzania; grizzled grey or orange back, black legs.

C. m. moloneyi: Southern Highlands to the southern and western Udzungwa Mountains; deep red back, throat pale grey.

C. m. monoides: Saadani NP, Udzungwa Mountains, Selous GR to Mozambique border; russet rump, grey underparts.

Note: The taxonomy of the Mitis Monkey group is complicated and many issues surrounding separation of this group into species are unresolved. This book follows the latest taxonomic thinking and treats the Mitis Monkey group as a species complex, splitting it into different groups or clusters, some of which may warrant being treated as full species in the light of further research.

Similar species

The Vervet Monkey (*page 64*) is smaller with a lighter-coloured body and white underparts. All three species of red colobus (*pages 46–50*) have red caps.

Ecology and social behaviour

Mitis Monkeys inhabit a wide variety of forest types, including montane, riverine, secondary and coniferous forests. They adapt well to human environments and can be found in major towns and cities where there are large trees for cover. They are diurnal and mostly arboreal, spending less than 5% of their time on the ground. The diet comprises mainly fruits, leaves, flowers and invertebrates.

Least Concern	
HB:	M 50–70 cm (20–28")
	F 40–60 cm (16–24")
Tail:	50–90 cm (20–35")
Wt:	M 6–9 kg (13–20 lb) | F 3–5 kg (7–11 lb)

Where to look

Mitis Monkeys are easily seen in the groundwater forest in Manyara NP, and in forested areas in Sadaani, Kitulo, Jozani Chwaka Bay, Arusha, Kilimanjaro and Udzungwa NPs.

Group sizes vary from 2–25 individuals, with multiple females and a single male. Bachelor males are either solitary or live in all-male groups of 2–12 individuals. Home ranges vary from 1–3 km² (0·4–1·0 mi²). They often associate with other primates, including colobuses (*pages 42–50*) and Kipunji (*page 56*).

Distribution in Tanzania

The Mitis Monkey has a patchy distribution, covering much of the coast and parts of the north, west and central areas of the country. It occurs in most of the montane forests in northern Tanzania, including Kilimanjaro, Arusha, and Manyara NPs, Ngorongoro CA, Arusha city and the forests along the East African Rift wall as far south as Babati and the Ufiome FR. There are also populations in forests across the coastal area as far south as the Mozambique border, much of the northern Selous GR, and throughout the Eastern Arc Mountains and Southern Highlands, including Mount Rungwe and Kitulo NP. They are also widespread in forested areas in western Tanzania, including Katavi, Mahale and Gombe NPs, and there are populations in Burigi–Biharamulo GRs, Ibanda–Rumanyika GRs and Minziro FR. They are found in most National Parks, although are absent from Serengeti, Tarangire and Rubondo. An isolated population has been reported close to Nyigoti village, west of the Serengeti NP.

Population size and conservation status
Mitis Monkeys are locally common across many parts of its range, including Kilimanjaro, Arusha, Manyara, Sadaani, Udzungwa and Gombe NPs, and in forests along the Ruvu–Pangani River. Small numbers still occur in many urban or semi-urban areas. The principle threat to the species is habitat loss, which particularly affects small, isolated populations. They are also extensively hunted for meat in the Southern Highlands and southwest Tanzania. Population trends are unknown.

Mitis Monkey
TOP: male ssp. *moloneyi*, Southern Highlands; BOTTOM: male ssp. *albogularis*, Arusha NP

Large-eared Greater Galago

Otolemur crassicaudatus

Thick-tailed Greater Galago / Bushbaby

SWAHILI: Komba Masikio Makubwa

A large galago with big, hairless ears. The species is highly variable, with back colours ranging from light grey to brown or dark brown, and underparts that are usually paler or cream-coloured. Some individuals are melanistic, and some of these may have white markings on the chest. The hair on the tail is long and bushy with varying amounts of black. The call usually comprises 8–10 cries of approximately the same pitch, reminiscent of a human infant crying, made at gradually increasing intervals.

Subspecies

O. c. argentatus: east, southeast, and western shores of Lake Victoria, including Serengeti NP and Minziro FR; the largest subspecies.

O. c. monteiri: rest of Tanzania, including western shores of Lake Victoria; smaller body than *O. c. argentatus*.

Similar species

The Large-eared Greater Galago is very difficult to distinguish in the field from the Small-eared Greater Galago (*page 72*) on the basis of morphological characteristics alone. The Small-eared is generally more rufous-brown and has a different call. It is also more agile, being able to land with its hind feet first when leaping (a feat the Large-eared Greater Galago is unable to accomplish).

Ecology and social behaviour

The Large-eared Greater Galago inhabits forest, forest-agriculture mosaics, and riverine, open and miombo woodlands. It is also found in urban areas where there is suitable tree cover. It is strictly nocturnal and arboreal, retreating to nests built in dense vegetation during the day. This species is the most social of all galagos, the young frequently travelling and feeding with their mother in a cohesive group. Both sexes are territorial. It commonly feeds on tree gum, which it extracts by biting through tree bark, but also consumes invertebrates and fruit.

Least Concern	
HB:	26–40 cm (10–16")
Tail:	30–55 cm (12–22")
Wt:	1·1–1·2 kg (2·4–2·6 lb)

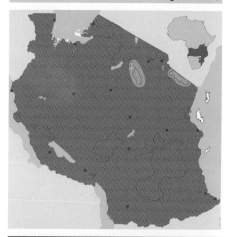

Where to look

The Large-eared Greater Galago is frequently seen in the trees in many of the lodges in Katavi NP, and in the grounds of the Vuma Hills Lodge in Mikumi NP. It can also be seen at night around the lodges and bungalows in Mahale NP.

Distribution in Tanzania

The Large-eared Greater Galago is widespread in Tanzania. It is known from all of the mainland National Parks, with the exception of Mkomazi and Rubondo NPs, and it is unclear whether this species or the Small-eared Greater Galago occurs in the Sangaiwe Hills in Tarangire NP. There are no confirmed records from Manyara NP, although it may occur in the Marang Forest on top of the East African Rift escarpment. The species occurs throughout the miombo woodland in western and southern Tanzania, but is absent from the islands of Zanzibar, Pemba, and Mafia.

Population size and conservation status

There are no abundance figures for the Large-eared Greater Galago in Tanzania. It is common across much of western Tanzania, including Katavi NP, and the lower forests of

Mahale NP, Ugalla GR and Minziro FR. It is also common in Mikumi NP and probably across much of the Selous GR. The main threat to this species is habitat loss, although its wide range of favoured habitats means it is less vulnerable than other species of galago.

Large-eared Greater Galago
TOP: ssp. *monteiri*, Mahale NP (Tanzania); BOTTOM: melanistic individual ssp. *argentatus* (Kenya)

71

Small-eared Greater Galago

Otolemur garnettii

Garnett's Galago / Bushbaby

SWAHILI: Komba Masikio Madogo

Least Concern	
HB:	23–34 cm (9–13")
Tail:	31–44 cm (12–17")
Wt:	0·6–1·0 kg (1·3–2·0 lb)

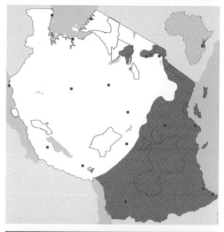

A large galago with a rufous-brown or grey-brown back, and light brown or cream underparts and insides of the legs. The outer side of the legs, head, face and upper half of the tail are usually the same colour as the back, with the lower half of the tail in some cases paler or with a black tip. The ears are large and hairless. The call starts with two low-pitched cries, followed by 7–8 cries that ascend and then descend in pitch, with the last few becoming longer and trailing away.

Subspecies

O. g. garnettii: Islands of Zanzibar, Pemba and Mafia; reddish back.

O. g. panganiensis: northern Tanzania; grey-brown back.

O. g. lasiotis: coastal Tanzania; grey or grey-brown back.

Similar species

Small-eared Greater Galago is very difficult to distinguish with certainty from the Large-eared Greater Galago (*page 70*), except by call, although the Large-eared Greater Galago has very slightly larger ears and is typically greyer.

Ecology and social behaviour

Small-eared Greater Galagos are found in a wide variety of forest types including coastal forest, forest-agriculture mosaics, riverine forest and submontane forest up to an altitude of 2,400 m (7,900 ft). They are nocturnal and arboreal but unlike most galagos are typically solitary and nest alone. They spend the day sleeping in nests in trees, and have not been recorded using tree holes. Their main food sources include invertebrates and fruits, and they will frequently forage in farmland, feeding on fruit crops.

Distribution in Tanzania

The Small-eared Greater Galago is restricted mainly to eastern and southern Tanzania, ranging from the border with Kenya to the border with Mozambique. In the north it is

Where to look

Common in some of the lodges in Stone Town on Zanzibar, where they are fed at night. They also occur in the grounds of many lodges on the outskirts of Arusha, including Arusha Coffee Lodge and the Mount Meru Game Lodge, and are frequently seen on night drives in Manyara NP.

found in Ngorongoro CA and in Manyara, Arusha, Kilimanjaro and Mkomazi NPs. It is unclear whether it is this species or the Large-eared Greater Galago that occurs in the Sangaiwe Hills of Tarangire NP. The species is found in most of the Eastern Arc Mountains including the Pare, Usambara, Nguru, Rubeho and Uluguru Mountains, although in Udzungwa NP it is only known from one record at Mbatwa. It occurs in Mikumi NP and in the Selous GR, and all along the coast including Kilulu Hill FR in the north, Sadaani NP, Dar es Salaam, and Rondo and Ziwani FRs in the far south. There are a few records from the Livingstone Mountains. It also occurs on the islands of Zanzibar, Pemba, and Mafia.

Population size and conservation status
This species is common in many areas, including Manyara NP, Arusha city, much of the coast, and the islands of Zanzibar and Pemba. Densities of up to 38 individuals per km² (100 individuals per mi²) have been recorded in coastal forests in Kenya and similar densities probably occur in coastal forests in Tanzania. This species adapts well to human environments, but habitat loss and hunting for bushmeat (in some areas) are long-term threats. Nothing is known about population size or trends.

Small-eared Greater Galago
TOP: ssp. *lasiotis* (Kenya); BOTTOM: a very furry individual from the Livingstone Mountains, ssp. *panganiensis*

Northern Lesser Galago
Senegal Galago / Bushbaby

Galago senegalensis

Southern Lesser Galago
Mohol Galago / Bushbaby

Galago moholi

SWAHILI: Komba

Small galagos with a soft, woolly pelage
ranging in colour from grey to light brown.
There are often yellowish tints on the limbs.
The tail is long, with short hair at the base
and longer hair at the tip, and ranges in
colour from light brown to black. There is a
narrow white stripe running down the nose.
The Southern Lesser Galago was formerly
considered a subspecies of the Northern
Lesser Galago but is now considered to be a
full species. The two species look very similar
and are best distinguished by their calls:
the **Northern Lesser Galago** call consists of
single low-pitched notes issued at a regular
tempo; the call of the **Southern Lesser Galago**
is more complex and comprises long-lasting,
high-pitched, double-note cries that gradually
increase in intensity.

Suspecies
Northern Lesser Galago
G. s. braccatus: northeast Tanzania;
yellow on front part of limbs.

G. s. sotikae: north, central, western Tanzania;
bright yellow on front and hind limbs.

Similar species
There is little habitat overlap with the
various dwarf galago species (*pages 76–83*),
which typically live in forested areas and are
usually more arboreal; the lesser galagos also
frequently move on the ground, behaviour
that is uncommon in dwarf galagos. The
greater galagos (*pages 70–72*) are much larger.

Ecology and social behaviour
The lesser galagos occur in open *Acacia* and
miombo savanna woodland and in thicket
and scrub. They generally avoid dense forest,
occurring only at the edges. Both species are
strictly nocturnal, with peak activity shortly
after and shortly before sunset and sunrise.
Group sizes are small, up to six animals,
and individuals usually forage alone.

Least Concern	
HB:	14–21 cm (5·5–18")
Tail:	20–25 cm (8–10")
Wt:	150–300 g (5·0–10·5 oz)

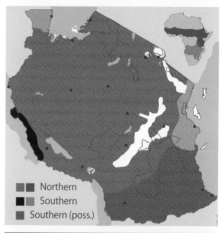

Northern
Southern
Southern (poss.)

Where to look
Northern Lesser Galagos are regularly seen on
night drives in West Kilimanjaro, Ndarakwai
Ranch, and in Manyara and Tarangire NPs. They
can also be seen on the grounds of some of
the tented camps in Katavi NP, including Chada
Camp, and at Kisima Ngeda Camp at Lake Eyasi.

Although lesser galagos are primarily arboreal,
they do forage on the ground, sometimes
leaping large distances on their hind legs.
They nest in holes in trees, in open birds' nests
or in nests of leaves that they have constructed
themselves. The diet consists predominantly
of invertebrates including caterpillars, termites
and spiders, as well as gum from *Acacia* and
other tree species. Home range sizes vary
from 5–20 hectares (12–50 acres).

Distribution in Tanzania
The **Northern Lesser Galago** occurs in
wooded areas throughout central and
northern Tanzania, approximately north of

the Rufiji River. It is found in all mainland National Parks except for Kitulo, Rubondo and Kilimanjaro, although it is present in the foothills of Mount Kilimanjaro. It has not been recorded in Sadaani NP but it may occur in the *Acacia* woodland areas. There is one record of the Northern Lesser Galago from Udzungwa NP in the woodland west of Ndundulu Forest. The **Southern Lesser Galago** may replace the Northern Lesser Galago in southern Tanzania, approximately south of the Rufiji River. To date, the only confirmed records of Southern Lesser Galago in Tanzania are from Lwafi GR and Loasi FR, and more work is needed to establish the status of this species.

Population size and conservation status

There are no population estimates for the **Northern Lesser Galago** in Tanzania, although it is very common in many parts of the country including Serengeti NP, West Kilimanjaro, Yaeda Valley, southern Tarangire NP and Mikumi, Katavi and Manyara NPs. It is, however, typically less common in miombo woodland than in *Acacia* woodland. There are no population estimates for **Southern Lesser Galago** in Tanzania.

TOP: **Southern Lesser Galago:** (Namibia);
BOTTOM: **Northern Lesser Galago:**
ssp. *sotikae* (Kenya)

75

Dwarf Galagos

There are currently eight species of dwarf galago known from Tanzania, and it is likely that new species will be described in the future. The dwarf galagos are very small, arboreal, nocturnal primates with large eyes and ears, long, upturned noses and long tails. All species have a white stripe running from the lower forehead to the nose. The species look very similar and can be very difficult to separate, even by experts. The most reliable identification features are their advertising calls and the shape of the penis, although range and habitat type can also be useful.

Further information, including recordings of the advertising calls of all of the Tanzanian galagos, can be found at:

www.wildsolutions.nl/vocalprofile.htm

This website can also be accessed via the QR code (*right*).

Thomas's Dwarf Galago
Galagoides thomasi

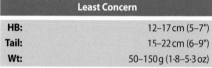

SWAHILI: Komba

A tiny galago with a dark to light brown back and limbs, and paler brown underparts. The tail is long and slender and is the same colour or slightly darker than the body. The call of the Thomas's Dwarf Galago is a short crescendo that rapidly increases in speed and pitch and is delivered a minimum of three times per bout and repeated over several minutes.

Similar species
See Demidoff's Dwarf Galago.

Ecology and social behaviour
Known in Tanzania only from seasonally-flooded swamp forest. They live in groups of 8–12 individuals, although they usually forage alone. Their main diet is invertebrates, and they also eat fruit and tree gum. Thomas's Dwarf Galagos build nests high up in the canopy or utilize tree holes.

Distribution in Tanzania
Known only from the Minziro FR in Tanzania. Thomas's Dwarf Galago was encountered on the edge of the forest and in the forest canopy during a survey of the Forest Reserve.

Population size and conservation status
Thomas's Dwarf Galago is locally common in Minziro FR, although the population is likely to be small.

Least Concern	
HB:	12–17 cm (5–7")
Tail:	15–22 cm (6–9")
Wt:	50–150 g (1·8–5·3 oz)

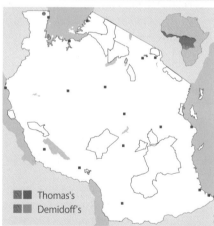

Thomas's
Demidoff's

Note: In Tanzania, both Thomas's and Demidoff's Dwarf Galagos are only found in the Minzoro Forest Reserve

Where to look
Spotlighting at night in Minziro FR offers the only chance of observing this species in Tanzania.

Demidoff's Dwarf Galago

Galagoides demidovii

SWAHILI: Komba

Least Concern	
HB:	12–15 cm (5–6")
Tail:	15–22 cm (6–9")
Wt:	50–100 g (1·8–3·5 oz)

Demidoff's Dwarf Galago is a very small, mouse-sized galago with a light brown to dark brown back and limbs, and light brown underparts. The tail has short hairs and is the same colour as the body. The advertising call of the Demidoff's Dwarf Galago is a crescendo that increases in speed and pitch, ending with a very rapid, high-pitched series of notes, which is delivered once or twice per bout.

Where to look

The only opportunity to see this species in Tanzania is by spotlighting in Minziro FR.

Similar species
The only other dwarf galago in Minziro FR is the Thomas's Dwarf Galago. This species has a paler body and a less defined contrast between the upperparts and underparts. Thomas's Dwarf Galago is usually found in the upper forest strata (12–20 m | 40–70 ft), while Demidoff's Dwarf Galago typically occurs in the lower forest strata (less than 5 m | 15 ft). Thomas's Dwarf Galago tends to jump and run along branches, whereas Demidoff's Dwarf Galago has a scurrying gait.

Ecology and social behaviour
In Tanzania it is found only in seasonally-flooded swamp forest. This animal lives in dispersed groups of up to 12 individuals, although it usually forages alone. The diet consists of invertebrates, tree gum and fruit. It typically nests in self-made vegetation nests lower than 5 m (16 ft) off the ground.

Distribution in Tanzania
Known only from the Minziro FR in Tanzania. During a survey of this Forest Reserve, Demidoff's Dwarf Galago was only recorded in the forest interior, in the vicinity of pit saw and tree-fall sites.

Population size and conservation status
Demidoff's Dwarf Galago is uncommon in Minziro FR. Since Minziro FR is only 290 km^2 (112 mi^2), the total population of this species is likely to be small.

Demidoff's Dwarf Galago
(Democratic Republic of Congo)

E Zanzibar Dwarf Galago

Galagoides zanzibaricus

SWAHILI: Komba

A very small galago that is yellowish-grey to grey-brown or cinnamon above and creamy-white, white or pale yellow below. The tail is grey-brown above and light beneath, with the lower third being dark. This galago makes a series of 'single-unit' rolling calls, the calls becoming louder and increasing in frequency until a crescendo is reached that then trails off.

Subspecies
G. z. zanzibaricus: Zanzibar.

G. z. udzungwensis: mainland Tanzania.

Similar species
The Zanzibar Dwarf Galago is separated from the Grant's Dwarf Galago (*page 82*) by range. Its range may overlap with the Diani Dwarf Galago (*page 83*) and Mountain Dwarf Galago (*page 80*) on the lower northern slopes of the East Usambara Mountains, although it is restricted to forest areas with higher rainfall. The Zanzibar and Mountain Dwarf Galagos also overlap in range in the Uluguru Mountains, but the latter is smaller, darker, and usually found at higher altitudes (above 1,000 m | 3,280 ft). The ranges of Zanzibar Dwarf Galago and Rondo Dwarf Galago (*page 81*) overlap in the coastal forests north of the Rufiji River but the latter is much smaller and has a 'bottle-brush' tail tip.

Ecology and social behaviour
Zanzibar Dwarf Galagos are found in primary and secondary lowland forest, bushland and thicket between sea level and 1,000 m (3,280 ft). They live in small groups of 2–4 individuals that use high-pitched calls for communication and nest in tree holes and tangles of vegetation. They feed on invertebrates and fruit, and typically forage alone below 10 m (33 ft).

Distribution in Tanzania
The Zanzibar Dwarf Galago is endemic to Tanzania and occurs in the coastal forests north of the Rufiji River and most of the Eastern Arc Mountains, except for the North Pare and Mahenge Mountains. It is found

Least Concern	
HB:	12–15 cm (5–6")
Tail:	20–24 cm (8–10")
Wt:	100–170 g (3–5 oz)

Where to look
Frequently seen in and around Jozani Chwaka Bay NP on Zanzibar at dusk and early evening, and is occasionally seen in Sadaani NP and the areas surrounding the Park, including around Kisampa Lodge.

in Udzungwa, Sadaani, Mikumi and Jozani Chwaka Bay NPs, and on the islands of Zanzibar and Mafia, but not on Pemba.

Population size and conservation status
The population density is estimated to be 500 animals per km² (1,300 animals per mi²) in the Matundu Forest in Udzungwa NP, and the species is generally common in the lowland Udzungwa Mountains but uncommon in the lowland Uluguru Mountains. It is common on Zanzibar, with estimated populations of up to 200 animals per km² (520 per mi²) in places.

E Rungwe Dwarf Galago

Galagoides sp. nov.

SWAHILI: Komba

A small galago with a dark brown pelage, light tan hands and feet and a very bushy, dark brown tail with a black tip. The advertisement call has double or triple notes that rise then fall in pitch, and is usually repeated 6–8 times.

Similar species
The Rungwe Dwarf Galago is not known to overlap in range with any other dwarf galago species.

Ecology and social behaviour
The Rungwe Dwarf Galago occurs in montane forest including the bamboo *Oldeania alpina*. In parts of its range it is found in forested areas with stands of wild bananas, although on northern Mount Rungwe it occurs in *Hagenia*-dominated forest, where wild bananas are scarce. It has been observed feeding on nectar from banana flowers, as well as on a variety of invertebrates. Little is known about its social behaviour.

Distribution in Tanzania
The Rungwe Dwarf Galago is endemic to Tanzania and, to date, has been recorded from Mount Rungwe, Mporoto Ridge FR, Livingstone FR in Kitulo NP, Madehani Forest Reserve, and other smaller Forest Reserves in the Southern Highlands.

Population size and conservation status
Rungwe Dwarf Galagos are locally common on Mount Rungwe and parts of the Mporoto Ridge and Livingstone FRs. The total area of remaining forest in these areas is probably less than 300 km² (116 mi²) and these forests are all affected by logging and charcoal production. Specimens of this species were first collected in the Livingstone Mountains in the 1930s although were incorrectly identified as a different species. A formal description of those and more recent specimens is presently being made.

FACING PAGE: **Zanzibar Dwarf Galago:** ssp. *zanzibaricus*, Jozani Chwaka Bay NP; RIGHT: **Rungwe Dwarf Galago:** Mount Rungwe

Not Assessed	
HB:	14–15 cm (5·5–6")
Tail:	16·5–19·0 cm (6–7")
Wt:	not known

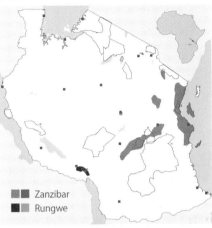

Zanzibar
Rungwe

Where to look
This species can be observed by spotlighting in the Livingstone forest around Kitulo NP and in parts of the Mount Rungwe Nature Reserve.

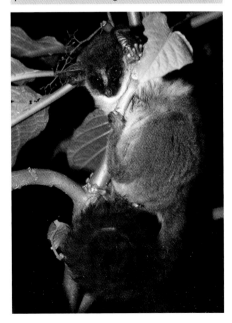

E Mountain Dwarf Galago

Galagoides orinus

SWAHILI: Komba

A tiny galago that is dark brown above, creamy-white below and has yellowish-brown on the lower part of the limbs. The tail is slightly bushy, brown or reddish-brown at the base and dark at the tip. In the Udzungwa Mountains it has a single-note repetitive call, while in other parts of its range it has a double-note call.

Similar species
The Mountain Dwarf Galago overlaps in range with the Zanzibar Dwarf Galago (*page 78*) in the Uluguru Mountains although the latter is a lighter colour and typically found at lower altitudes (below 1,000m | 3,300ft).

Ecology and social behaviour
Mountain Dwarf Galagos are restricted to moist submontane and montane forest within an altitudinal range of 600–2,600 m (2,000–8,500 ft). They live in dispersed groups of up to nine individuals although typically forage alone. They feed on invertebrates, tree gum, and fruit, and spend most of their time in the canopy.

Near Threatened	
HB:	13 cm (5")
Tail:	18 cm (7")
Wt:	75–100 g (3–4 oz)

Where to look
This is not an easy species to see. A good place to look is the Amani Nature Reserve, on the trail from the guest house to Mbomole hill, at dusk, before they disperse into the forest. Also try the forest above Tchenzema village in the Uluguru Mountains, or forests around Mufindi.

Distribution in Tanzania
The Mountain Dwarf Galago is endemic to the Eastern Arc Mountains. It is known from the South Pare, Usambara, Nguu, Nguru, Ukaguru, Rubeho, Uluguru and Udzungwa Mountains, including Udzungwa NP.

Population size and conservation status
During nocturnal surveys, this species was most frequently encountered in disturbed forest in the Uluguru and Usambara Mountains. It is found at low densities in the Udzungwa Mountains and probably throughout most of its range. Habitat loss through deforestation is the primary threat.

E Rondo Dwarf Galago

Galagoides rondoensis

SWAHILI: Komba

A tiny galago with a brown back, flanks and limbs. It is creamy-white below and can show yellow on the chest. The reddish-brown tail is 'bottle-brush'-shaped and has short hair at the base and longer hair at the tip. Its call is a rolling double-note.

Similar species
The Rondo Dwarf Galago overlaps in range with the Zanzibar Dwarf Galago (*page 78*) and Grant's Dwarf Galago *page 82*), although these species are twice the size and do not have a 'bottle-brush' tail-tip.

Ecology and social behaviour
Rondo Dwarf Galagos are found in patches of dense forest along the coast, typically utilizing the lower strata of the forest. They feed mostly on invertebrates, and sometimes fruits, flowers and tree gum. They are usually solitary, but occasionally seen in pairs or small groups.

Distribution in Tanzania
The Rondo Dwarf Galago is endemic to Tanzania, recorded from just nine locations. In the south, it is found in the Rondo, Litipo, Ziwani, Ruawa and Chioa FRs. There are three populations close to Dar es Salaam in the Pugu–Kazimzumbwi and Ruvu South FRs and the Pande GR, and a further population in the Zoraninge Forest in Sadaani NP.

Population size and conservation status
The Rondo Dwarf Galago is one of the rarest primates in the world, with a total known range of approximately 100 km^2 (40 mi^2). It is locally common in Pugu and Rondo FRs, within a very localized area. Many of the sites where it occurs have little or no effective protection, and are being rapidly degraded due to charcoal production, logging and agricultural expansion. The most secure populations are in the Zoraninge Forest in Sadaani NP and in the Chitoa FR, which is surrounded by plantation woodland.

FACING PAGE:
Mountain Dwarf Galago: Udzungwa NP;
RIGHT: **Rondo Dwarf Galago:** Rondo FR

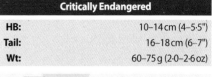

Critically Endangered	
HB:	10–14 cm (4–5·5")
Tail:	16–18 cm (6–7")
Wt:	60–75 g (2·0–2·6 oz)

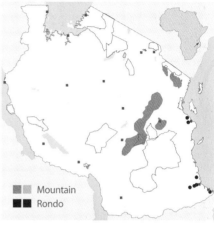

Mountain
Rondo

Where to look
Spotlighting in the Rondo FR for one or two nights should be sufficient to see this species.

Grant's Dwarf Galago

Galagoides granti

Mozambique Dwarf Galago

SWAHILI: Komba

A small galago that is light brown above and has creamy-yellow underparts. The inner side of each limb is also creamy-yellow, the outer side pale brown. The forehead is grey and the ears mostly black. This species has an incremental advertising call, which rises and then falls in volume; the number of notes within each phase gradually increases during the call.

Similar species

Grant's Dwarf Galago overlaps in range with Rondo Dwarf Galago (*page 81*) in the coastal forests south of the Rufiji River but the latter species is half the size and has a 'bottle-brush'-tipped tail. Its range may also overlap with the Southern Lesser Galago (*page 74*), although this is mainly a dry woodland specialist and has a grey, rather than brown, back.

Ecology and social behaviour

Grant's Dwarf Galagos are found in evergreen forest, although they also occur in coastal forest and scrub, and agriculture and forest–woodland mosaics up to an altitude of 1,800 m (5,900 ft). Up to six animals may share sleeping nests in tree holes and tangles of dense vegetation. Typically, one male associates with one or two females, using high-pitched calls

Least Concern	
HB:	15–18 cm (6–7")
Tail:	20–22 cm (8–9")
Wt:	110–160 g (3–5 oz)

Where to look
Frequently seen at night in the Rondo FR.

for communication, although individuals usually forage alone for invertebrates, fruits and tree gum.

Distribution in Tanzania

The Grant's Dwarf Galago is found between the Ruvu and Rufiji Rivers, with most records coming from coastal forest in the southeast, including the Rondo Plateau. It is also known from the Mahenge Mountains, Lulanda Forest in the Udzungwa Mountains, Milo FR in the Livingstone Mountains, the Sitebe Mountains and Mahale NP.

Population size and conservation status

The highest hourly encounter rates for Grant's Dwarf Galagos during nocturnal counts were in the Namatimbili, Mtopwa and Noto Forests and the Rondo FR in the southeast of the country. The species is uncommon in the Lulanda FR in the Udzungwa Mountains, but it is believed to be widespread and not threatened across much of its range.

RIGHT:
Grant's Dwarf Galago: northern Livingstone Mountains (Tanzania);
FACING PAGE:
Diani Dwarf Galago: (Kenya)

Diani Dwarf Galago

Galagoides cocos

Kenya Coast Dwarf Galago

SWAHILI: Komba

Buffy-brown above and grey-white below. Has prominent black marks on the muzzle on either side of the white facial stripe. It has an incremental advertising call. The call usually starts with a rapid chirrup and then high frequency units arranged in phases, with an incremental increase in the number of units in each phase until the call ends.

Similar species
Likely to overlap with Mountain Dwarf Galago (*page 80*) and Zanzibar Dwarf Galago (*page 78*). Most reliably differentiated by their calls.

Ecology and social behaviour
Dry mixed woodland, primary and secondary coastal forest, and areas of mixed cultivation with large trees. Occurs in dispersed groups with one adult male associating with one or two adult females and their offspring, maintaining contact through high-pitched calls. Typically forages alone for insects, fruit, and tree gum.

Distribution in Tanzania
Restricted to the very northeast corner of Tanzania, although may occur in other mixed woodlands along the coastal area. Known only from Bombo East I and II FRs

Least Concern	
HB:	14–18 cm (5–7")
Tail:	18–23 cm (7–9")
Wt:	110–170 g (3–5 oz)

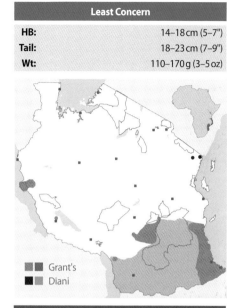

■ ■ Grant's
■ ■ Diani

Where to look

Try spotlighting at night in Mgambo FR or Bombo East FR in the Usambara Mountains.

and the Mgambo FR on the northern slopes of the East Usambara Mountains.

Population size and conservation status
Nothing is known about its status in Tanzania.

East African Springhare

Pedetes surdaster

SWAHILI: Kamendegere

This species resembles a small kangaroo, with long, powerful back legs, very short front legs, and a long tail. The body is yellowish or reddish-brown and the underparts are pale or white. The tail, which is used for balance, is the same colour as the body but has a long, bushy black tip. The ears are long and erect. There are four toes on the hind legs and five on the front legs. It moves by hopping on its hind legs, leaping as much as 2 metres (6 feet) with each bound.

Subspecies
Previously described as a subspecies of South African Springhare *Pedetes capensis*, the East African Springhare was recently reclassified and is now treated as a full species.

Similar species
Unlikely to be mistaken for any other mammal. At night it is easily identified by the bobbing movement of its reflected eyeshine.

Ecology and social behaviour
East African Springhares are restricted to open grasslands with relatively sandy or well-drained soils. They dig an extensive burrow system with up to ten entrances, which they use for shelter during the day. Burrows are occupied by only one animal or a mother with offspring, although several different burrow systems may be concentrated in one area. Springhares feed on grasses and roots, and sometimes seeds and fruits, and are water-independent. They are strictly nocturnal and often feed in small groups.

Distribution in Tanzania
The East African Springhare has a patchy distribution in Tanzania, largely dictated by its preference for dry, sandy soils. It is mostly associated with the *Acacia–Commiphora* bushland in the north and central areas of the country, although its distribution extends into the dry miombo woodland in western Tanzania. In the north it ranges from West Kilimanjaro to the western Serengeti, the Yaeda Valley and much of the Maasai Steppe.

Least Concern	
HB:	30–45 cm (12–18")
Tail:	35–45 cm (14–18")
Wt:	2·5–4·0 kg (5·5–9 lb)

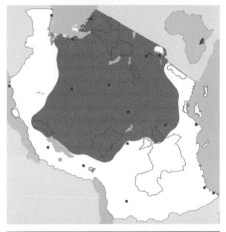

Where to look
East African Springhares are regularly seen on night drives in Manyara Ranch, Ndarakwai Ranch and northern Tarangire NP.

There are records from Shinyanga and Tabora regions, Swagaswaga GR, the Ruaha–Rungwa ecosystem, the Katavi–Rukwa ecosystem and Ugalla GR. There are historical records from around Kilosa, west of Morogoro, and from Laela southeast of Sumbawanga, but the current status of the latter population is not known.

Population size and conservation status
Population sizes are not known for this species. Its restricted habitat can result in it being very common in one part of a reserve but absent from an adjacent area. It is common in parts of northern Tanzania, including the Ndutu–Serengeti short-grass plains, Manyara Ranch, the Simanjiro plains and West Kilimanjaro, including Ngaserai and Enduimet WMA. It is fairly common in the Yaeda Valley. In the west, it is common in parts of the Katavi–Rukwa ecosystem,

including Rukwa–Lukwati GRs and Mlele hunting block. It is fairly common in Muhesi–Kizigo GRs, although uncommon in Ruaha NP. Habitat loss to agriculture presents a threat to this species in its range in the centre of the country, and populations are also vulnerable to subsistence hunting. Numbers inside protected areas are probably stable.

East African Springhare
TOP: (Kenya); BOTTOM: Loliondo (Tanzania)

Crested Porcupine
Hystrix cristata

Cape Porcupine
Hystrix africaeaustralis
South African Porcupine

SWAHILI: Nungunungu

Both Crested and Cape Porcupines are large rodents with long, very sharp, black-and-white quills on the lower back. A crest of long, thick, black hair with white tips runs from the top of the forehead to the centre of the back. The legs and underparts are covered with short, coarse black hairs, and there is often a white chin patch. The short tail is covered with short quills. The two species are very difficult to identify in the field. The most reliable feature is the colour of the short quills covering the lower rump: those of the **Crested Porcupine** are black, those of the **Cape Porcupine** are white.

Similar species
A third species, the **African Brush-tailed Porcupine** *Atherurus africanus* (*opposite, bottom*), also occurs in western Tanzania in the dense forests of Mahale NP. It is much smaller (HB: 36–60 cm | 14–24"; Wt 2·5–4·0 kg | 6–9 lbs), has no spines on its head, shorter spines on its back, and a long, naked tail tipped with yellow-white bristles.

Ecology and social behaviour
Both **Crested** and **Cape Porcupines** are found in a wide variety of habitats, including savanna grasslands, bushland, *Acacia* woodland, miombo woodland, and both lowland and montane forests. They feed on fruits, roots and bark. Porcupines are nocturnal, resting during the day in burrows. When threatened or alarmed, porcupines raise their quills and may back rapidly towards the predator, stabbing it with their quills that detach easily from the loose skin. Porcupines are monogamous and live in small family groups with their offspring. Home range sizes may be up to 2 km² (0·8 mi²).

Distribution in Tanzania
Porcupines are distributed throughout Tanzania, including all mainland National Parks, except Rubondo NP.

Least Concern	
HB:	65–86 cm (26–34")
Tail:	10–13 cm (4–5")
Wt:	10–20 kg (22–44 lb)

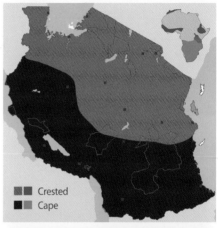

Crested

Cape

Where to look
Porcupines are regularly seen on the grounds of the Vuma Hills Lodge in Mikumi NP. They are also occasionally seen at night in Loliondo and on the slopes of West Kilimanjaro, including Simba Farm and Ndarakwai Ranch.

However, the two species are difficult to distinguish in the field, and the ranges shown on the distribution map are speculative. Further research may show that both species overlap widely in Tanzania. All verified records of **Crested Porcupines** come from north of Mbeya, and their occurrence in the south and southwest of the country is uncertain. There are possible records from Zanzibar. Confirmed records of **Cape Porcupine** come from southern Tanzania and a few locations in central and western Tanzania, including Tabora and northern Moyowosi GR, and there is also a record from near Mount Kilimanjaro, in the north of the country.

Population size and conservation status

Porcupines are common across much of Tanzania, with camera trap surveys suggesting that they are very common in Maswa and Uvinza GRs, in the forests of Ngorongoro CA and in Ufiome FR. They are also common around Lake Natron and in Mahale NP, the Selous–Niassa corridor and Sadaani NP. No information on population trends is available for these two species and more research is needed to determine their range and status.

Crested Porcupine:
TOP: (Kenya); CENTRE LEFT: (Italy)
– note the dark rump;
Cape Porcupine: CENTRE RIGHT: (South Africa)
– note the white rump and long tail quills;
African Brush-tailed Porcupine:
BOTTOM: captive individual

African Savanna Hare
Lepus victoriae
Scrub Hare
Cape Hare
Lepus capensis

SWAHILI: Sungura

Both the African Savanna Hare and the Cape Hare have long ears, well-developed hind legs, small tails and flecked brown-grey backs with white underparts. Although they are extremely difficult to tell apart in the field, a range of morphological and ecological characteristics can help to identify them in East Africa.

The **African Savanna Hare** is relatively dark, has a distinct rufous nape and ears that are longer than its head. It also commonly has a white spot on its forehead. The shape of the head is gently convex from the forehead to the tip of the nose, and it has a long muzzle. This species favours grassy areas with bushes and woodland for cover.

The **Cape Hare** is paler than the African Savanna Hare and has a grey-buff, often indistinct, nape. The ears are roughly the same length as its head, and have rounded tips that are fringed with short black hairs. The forehead is angular, bending sharply downwards above the eye. It has a shorter muzzle than African Savanna Hare, and rarely has a white spot on the forehead. It is usually found in open grassland.

Another useful field identification feature is their behaviour: the **African Savanna Hare** runs for cover when disturbed, whereas the **Cape Hare** frequently runs into the open.

Specimens can be positively identified by their incisor tooth structure: **Cape Hare** has a light groove with no cement; **African Savanna Hare** has a deep groove filled with cement.

Similar species
The Smith's Red Rock Hare (*page 90*) has much smaller ears and a rufous body and tail.

Ecology and social behaviour
While there is some overlap in habitat preference, **African Savanna Hares** are typically found in woodland and wooded grassland, and generally prefer grassland with more scrub cover; **Cape Hares** are restricted

Least Concern	
HB:	40–60 cm (8–10")
Tail:	1–1·5 cm (0·5")
Wt:	1·3–3·0 kg (3–7 lb)

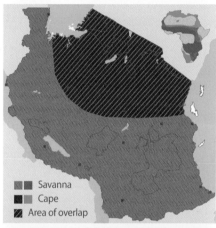

■■ Savanna
■■ Cape
▨▨ Area of overlap

Where to look
The African Savanna Hare can be commonly seen on night drives in most areas in Tanzania. The Cape Hare can be observed on the open plains of the Serengeti NP and Ngorongoro CA, where it is often flushed by vehicles during the day, and around the Lake Natron area.

to more open grasslands. Both species feed on grasses, but African Savanna Hares have a higher proportion of herbs in their diet. Both species are solitary and mostly nocturnal, although they may be active during the late afternoon on cloudy days.

Distribution in Tanzania
The **African Savanna Hare** is very widely distributed in Tanzania, occurring in all lowland habitat types except forests, and is found in every Game Reserve and mainland National Park, except Rubondo NP.

The **Cape Hare** is restricted to the drier areas of northern and central Tanzania, and is probably absent from the miombo woodland in the south and west of the country. However, its precise distribution in Tanzania is not known and requires more research. The Cape Hare is known from the Serengeti NP and Ngorongoro CA, and it probably also occurs in Tarangire, Manyara, Arusha and Mkomazi NPs. There is one record from near Lindi in the southeast of Tanzania from 1951, although its validity is unclear.

Population size and conservation status

Hares are abundant across much of Tanzania. They are often common around human habitation, and their nocturnal habits and high birth rates make them less susceptible to hunting pressure than larger species of mammal.

Cape Hare: MAIN PHOTO: Serengeti NP (Tanzania)
African Savanna Hare: INSET: (Kenya)

Smith's Red Rock Hare

Pronolagus rupestris

SWAHILI: Sungura Mwekundu, Kitengule

A medium-sized hare with dense, soft fur. The back is a grizzled rufous-brown or grey colour and the underside is a light tawny-white. The front legs are only slightly shorter than the hind legs and have bright red fur. The tail is bushy and rufous with a black tip. There is a rufous patch behind the neck. The ears are relatively short and not longer than the head.

Similar species
The African Savanna Hare and Cape Hare (*page 88*) are larger with much longer ears and are not typically found in rocky and hilly habitat.

Ecology and social behaviour
Smith's Red Rock Hares occupy rocky hillsides and ravines with boulders and rock crevices that offer suitable cover. Although they are mostly nocturnal, they sometimes emerge during the late afternoon and early morning, in areas where they are not hunted, and may occasionally be seen sitting on boulders. During the day they hide in rock crevices or in thick grass tussocks. They are generally solitary, although several individuals may live in close proximity in areas of suitable habitat. Their diet is exclusively grasses and herbs, and they seldom graze far from cover. Their latrine sites, often on flat rocks, are large with heaps of droppings of varying age. They often lie still when approached, only bolting at the last moment, and sometimes making loud screams as they run.

Distribution in Tanzania
There are few records for this species in Tanzania, probably because it is a shy, nocturnal animal. However, it is likely to be more widespread than current sightings suggest and probably occurs in suitable habitat throughout northern, central and western Tanzania. It has been recorded in Loliondo, eastern Serengeti NP, the Sangaiwe Hills in Tarangire NP, Swagaswaga, Rungwa and Piti GRs, the Ufipa Plateau, the Sitebe–Syampemba Highlands, Mpanga–Kipengere

Least Concern	
HB:	32–50 cm (13–17")
Tail:	6–11 cm (2–4")
Wt:	1·5–2·5 kg (3–6 lb)

Where to look
Good places to look are rocky areas on the Ufipa Plateau and Mpanga–Kipengere GR. They usually hide in tussock-grass between rock outcrops and can be readily flushed by walking through areas with fresh middens. Another option is to locate a midden and spotlight the area at night.

GR and Idobogo Hill east of Iringa. It is also likely to occur on the Isunkaviola Plateau in Ruaha NP. There are records from 1951 for this species east of Tabora and from the Iramba Hills north of Singida.

Population size and conservation status
There are no population estimates for the Smith's Red Rock Hare, although it is very common on parts of the Ufipa Plateau and in the Sitebe–Syampemba Highlands, locally common in the Sangaiwe Hills in Tarangire NP and generally uncommon in the Serengeti ecosystem. This species is heavily hunted using dogs and fire to flush them out, and is probably declining anywhere near human settlements. It is also susceptible to predation by many species.

Smith's Red Rock Hare
TOP and BOTTOM: (South Africa)

White-bellied Hedgehog   *Atelerix albiventris*

SWAHILI: Kalunguyeye

A small animal with numerous short spines (1·5–2·5 cm | 0·6–1" long) covering the upperparts of the body. The underparts and front and sides of the face are white, while the nose and ears are black. The spines are white at the base, black or brown at the centre, and tipped with white. There are five toes on the front feet and four on the hind feet.

Least Concern	
HB:	15–24 cm (6–9")
Tail:	1·5 cm (0·5")
Wt:	270–700 g (10–25 oz)

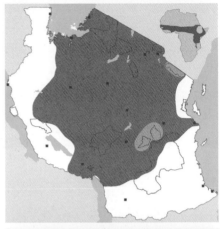

Similar species
Unlikely to be mistaken for any other mammal.

Ecology and social behaviour
White-bellied Hedgehogs are found in a wide variety of habitats including open grassland, wooded savanna, open forests, urban gardens, and agricultural land. They are associated with dry soils, avoiding swampy vegetation. Their diet consists mostly of small invertebrates including beetles, snails, slugs, centipedes and earthworms, although they will also consume small rodents, small reptiles, eggs, roots and fruits. Hedgehogs are nocturnal and mostly solitary, although they occasionally travel in mother–infant pairs. During the day they shelter under vegetation or in holes. In East Africa, the White-bellied Hedgehog frequently aestivates during the dry season (July–September), possibly linked to a decline in food availability. When disturbed, they will roll into a tight ball, shielding their face and underparts, using their spines as a defence mechanism. They often react to strong smells by licking or chewing the object, including poisonous toads, and will then produce a toxic saliva mixture that they use to anoint their spines. Pricking a finger on the spines can be painful and lead to infection.

Distribution in Tanzania
White-bellied Hedgehogs are well distributed in north and central Tanzania; there are very few records from the west and east of the country and no confirmed records south of the Rufiji River. They are widespread in the towns of Arusha, Moshi, Babati, Singida, Kondoa, Mwanza, Dodoma and Morogoro, and are known from parts of Dar es Salaam,

Where to look
White-bellied Hedgehogs are found in many urban gardens of hotels, restaurants, and private residences in major towns and cities. In Arusha they can be easily found in the gardens of the Blue Heron cafe and Outpost Lodge, among others. A good tactic is to ask the night watchmen of the hotel to keep a lookout for them and call you when they find one.

the Serengeti, Manyara, Tarangire and Arusha NPs, the lower slopes of Mount Kilimanjaro, the Pare Mountains, Lushoto town, and likely into Mkomazi NP. There are a few records from Iringa and Mbeya regions, Ruaha NP and the Selous GR, and old records (1950s) from southern Tabora Region.

Population size and conservation status
The population size is unknown. White-bellied Hedgehogs are most common in the north of Tanzania, and are particularly abundant around Arusha, Moshi, Babati and parts of Kondoa District. They are also common in gardens in Morogoro. They are uncommon in Dar es Salaam, and rare in Ruaha NP, the Selous GR and around Mbeya. Hedgehogs are

most abundant in areas of human habitation where there are relatively few predators; they are uncommon or rare in most National Parks. Despite having spines as a defence mechanism, White-bellied Hedgehogs are frequently predated by Verreaux's Eagle Owls *Bubo lacteus*, which may significantly depress local populations. One pair of owls on the outskirts of Arusha fed on hedgehogs almost nightly, sometimes consuming more than one in a night. Hedgehogs are also commonly seen dead on roads.

White-bellied Hedgehog
TOP: Arusha; BOTTOM: an individual adopting a defensive posture, Arusha

Ground Pangolin

Smutsia temminckii

SWAHILI: Kakakuona

Ground Pangolins are covered in large, broad, brown scales made of fused hair. There are 11–13 rows of scales between the back of the head and the base of the tail. The head is small and the nose is short and pointed. The tail is very muscular and broad at the base, with 11–13 rows of scales along its length and a rounded tip. All feet are covered in scales. The front feet are short with five strong claws, the central claw reaching up to 6 cm (2") long. The soles of the hind feet are rounded. Ground Pangolins frequently walk by balancing on their hind feet, with their front feet and tail held off the ground. When walking on all four feet, the front claws curl inwards and the animal walks on the outside of its front wrists. Males are typically 50% heavier than females.

Similar species
The Giant Pangolin (*page 98*) is a forest species, is larger, has a longer muzzle, longer front legs, and has more rows of scales on its body and tail.

Ecology and social behaviour
Ground Pangolins live in savanna and woodland with annual rainfall between 250–1,400 mm (10–55") and are absent from forests, swamps and deserts. They feed exclusively on ants and termites, which they ingest by licking them off the ground or out of underground nests with their enormous tongue (25–40 cm | 10–16" long). Pangolins occupy a well-defined home range of 0·2–11 km² (up to 4 mi²), with the home ranges of the two sexes showing little overlap. Within a home range they use a large number of burrows, which are usually abandoned Aardvark (*page 26*) or Warthog (*page 174*) holes, or sometimes crevices among rocks. When alarmed, they roll up into a tight ball with their scaly tail protecting their head and belly. They are solitary and predominantly nocturnal with activity peaks between 7:00 p.m. and 1:30 a.m., although subadults are more active during the day.

Least Concern	
HB:	30–67 cm (12–26")
Tail:	22–50 cm (9–20")
Wt:	5–18 kg (11–40 lb)

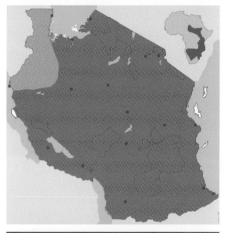

Where to look
Most experienced guides have only seen this animal once or twice, if ever, so count yourself very lucky if you do see one. A combination of their rarity, shyness, and nocturnal habits makes them very difficult to find. The only place where Ground Pangolins have been recorded relatively frequently is on the 'Triangle' of short-grass plains linking the entrance to the Serengeti NP, Naabi Hill, and the start of the Ndutu woodlands.

Distribution in Tanzania
Widespread in Tanzania, with records from across much of the country. This species has been reported from the Serengeti NP, Ngorongoro CA, Katavi, Tarangire, Mkomazi, Mikumi, Ruaha, Saadani, and Udzungwa NPs, and Selous GR. Records for Mahale NP may be the result of confusion with the Giant Pangolin, although it is likely to occur in the miombo woodland in the east of the National Park. Its status in the far northwest of Tanzania is unclear as there are no confirmed records from that area.

Population size and conservation status
Despite being widespread, Ground Pangolins are rare across most of Tanzania. There may be pockets of high densities within protected areas where food sources are abundant, although their reclusive habits means they are seldom recorded. In Tanzania, pangolins are widely collected for use by witch doctors and their scales are worn as good luck amulets. The collection of pangolin parts for the Asian medicine trade is now a major threat. Pangolins are sometimes killed when they wrap themselves around the live wires of an electric fence.

Ground Pangolin
TOP: captive individual; BOTTOM: Maswa GR

Tree Pangolin

Phataginus tricuspis

White-bellied Pangolin

SWAHILI: Kakakuona

A small pangolin with a very long tail and small, delicate scales with three cusps on their outer edge. There are no scales on the snout, chin, belly, or the inside of the legs. The underparts and throat are white or whitish. There are five claws on all feet, and the forelegs are slightly shorter than the hind legs. The prehensile tail has 30+ rows of scales along its length and a sensitive pad at the tip.

Similar species
Both the Giant Pangolin (*page 98*) and Ground Pangolin (*page 94*) are significantly larger and have proportionally shorter tails.

Ecology and social behaviour
Tree Pangolins are found in woodland and forests, including secondary forest growth and cultivation. They are nocturnal, solitary, semi-arboreal, and shelter mainly in tree hollows, which they change every few days, although they will also dig shallow burrows in the ground. Male and female home ranges overlap, with males occupying much larger home ranges (30 ha | 75 acres) than females (3–4 ha | 7–10 acres). Their main food source is termites and, less commonly, ants, which they lick up with their long (30 cm | 12") tongue. Most foraging activity takes place on the ground, although they will also break open ants' nests up in trees.

Distribution in Tanzania
Known only from two locations in Tanzania: Minziro FR, on the northwest border with Uganda, where it was camera trapped in 2006, and near Katoke village, just south of Bukoba. It may also occur in other forests in northwest Tanzania, including Burigi GR, but has not been reported from other Guinea–Congo lowland forest further south, such as Gombe and Mahale NPs.

Population size and conservation status
The population size is unknown but numbers are likely to be low given that Tanzania is at

Near Threatened	
HB:	25–35 cm (10–14")
Ht:	35–60 cm (14–24")
Wt:	1·6–3·5 kg (3·5 7·7 lb)

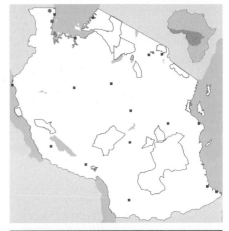

Where to look
Minziro FR is probably the only place in Tanzania where you may see this species, although since it is both nocturnal and arboreal, the chances of observing one are very low.

the very edge of this species' range. Two Tree Pangolins were photographed in 1,500 camera trap nights in Minziro FR, suggesting that the species is rare there. Dry season densities in Benin (West Africa) were estimated at 0·84 individuals per km^2 (2 individuals per mi^2). Based on these density figures, the population in Minziro FR (an area of 250 km^2 | 100 mi^2) is unlikely to exceed 250 individuals. Tree Pangolins are threatened by hunting for meat and their scales, which are used by local witch doctors, and also exported to Asian markets. Hunting levels in Minziro FR are reportedly high, and researchers visiting the area were shown a Tree Pangolin skeleton that had been kept for sale. The Minziro FR is protected against logging, but habitat loss is a threat to other nearby forests that may harbour Tree Pangolin populations.

Tree Pangolin
TOP: (location unknown); BOTTOM: captive individual

Giant Pangolin

Smutsia gigantea

SWAHILI: Kakakuona

A large, heavy-set pangolin with very large, rounded scales. There are 15–17 rows of scales from the back of the head to the base of the tail. The face is naked with a long muzzle. There are three large claws and two vestigial claws on the front legs. When walking the outside of the wrists are used with the claws turned inwards. Giant Pangolins have relatively long front legs and adopt a more quadrupedal stance than other pangolins. The tail is shorter than the body, has thick scales on the dorsal surface with 15–19 scales along each side, and a pointed tip.

Similar species

Large male Ground Pangolins (*page 94*) overlap in size with small or young Giant Pangolins. The Ground Pangolin has a shorter snout and tail, and smaller front legs, giving it a distinctive hunched appearance when it walks – as opposed to the more upright stance of the Giant Pangolin. Ground Pangolins more commonly walk on their hind legs.

Ecology and social behaviour

Giant Pangolins are found in areas of Guinea–Congo lowland forest and savanna-forest mosaic. They are solitary and completely water-dependent. This species is predominantly nocturnal, with activity peaks between 11:00 p.m. and 4:00 a.m. During the day they rest in thick vegetation or deep burrows, which they dig themselves or use those of other species. Giant Pangolins feed mainly on termites and ants, ripping open the termite mounds with the large front claws; they will also consume other invertebrates and larvae. They are believed to aestivate for long periods during times of poor food supply. When disturbed, they will curl up into a tight ball for protection, and will sometimes swing their heavy tail at an intruder.

Distribution in Tanzania

There are only two known populations of Giant Pangolin in Tanzania: Mahale NP on the edge of Lake Tanganyika and Minziro FR on the border with Uganda. In Mahale NP,

Near Threatened	
HB:	75–100 cm (30–39")
Tail:	55–70 cm (22–28")
Wt:	30–35 kg (66–77 lb)

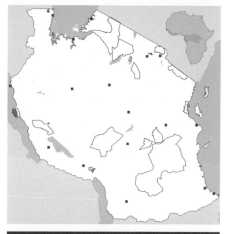

Where to look

Giant Pangolins are very difficult to see in Tanzania. Although common in Mahale NP, their nocturnal habits mean they are unlikely to be seen as night spotlighting is prohibited in the National Park. Spotlighting in Minziro FR might yield results, although beware of being trampled by buffalo.

this species was recorded in the Kasoge and Kabezi areas of the National Park during camera trap surveys. Kasoge, which is close to the National Park headquarters, is characterized by secondary lowland forest. In Kabezi, Giant Pangolins were found in areas of solid stands of dense bamboo, *Oxytenanthera abyssinica*, surrounded by miombo woodland. It is likely that populations also exist in other areas of Guinea–Congo lowland forest in Tanzania, including Gombe NP, where records of Ground Pangolins may have been confused with this species.

Population size and conservation status

In Mahale NP, seven Giant Pangolins were camera trapped in 653 camera trap nights, suggesting that the species is relatively common in the area. This population is well protected and likely to be either stable or expanding. In Minziro FR, only two individuals were camera trapped in 1,500 camera trap nights, indicating a much smaller population. Wildlife densities in Minziro FR are generally very low, suggesting heavy human pressure, and this population is probably declining steadily. Pangolins are heavily hunted both for their meat and, increasingly, for their scales, which are widely used in Asia in traditional medicine and as fashion accessories. Habitat destruction of remaining Guinea–Congo lowland forest in Tanzania is also a threat.

Giant Pangolin
TOP and BOTTOM: camera trap photos from Mahale NP.
These are the first images of this species from Tanzania.

Side-striped Jackal

Canis adustus

SWAHILI: Bweha Miraba

The Side-striped Jackal is the largest jackal in Tanzania. The body is a dull grey colour, with a white or buff-coloured side stripe, of variable prominence, running from the shoulder to the hip with a black margin below. The legs are a light grey-brown, and the underside and throat are cream-coloured. It has a dog-like face with relatively small ears that are grey on the back. The tail is mostly black with a distinctive white tip, although the white tip is sometimes absent. Side-striped Jackals in southern Tanzania can be quite dark.

Similar species

Can usually be easily distinguished from the Black-backed Jackal (*page 104*) and the Golden Jackal (*page 102*) by its white-tipped tail. Its vocalizations are a series of yaps, rather than the drawn-out howls of Golden or Black-backed Jackals. In areas where the three species overlap, the Side-striped Jackal occupies denser vegetation, whereas the other species tend to favour more open habitats. The face of the Side-striped Jackal is more dog-like compared to the other two species, which have more fox-like faces. From a distance, the Side-striped Jackal may also be confused with a domestic dog.

Ecology and social behaviour

Found in a wide variety of habitats from bushland, wooded grassland, woodland, mountains and farmland. They have a varied diet, consisting primarily of fruits, seeds, small rodents, hares, gazelle fawns, invertebrates, and carrion. They are typically more nocturnal than other jackals, although diurnal sightings are not infrequent. The basic social unit is a monogamous, territorial pair, although individuals often forage alone. Family groups with up to seven individuals, comprising a breeding pair and their young, can occasionally be seen. Home range sizes of between 12–20 km² (5–8 mi²) have been recorded.

Least Concern	
HB:	72–77 cm (28–30")
Ht:	45–50 cm (18–20")
Tail:	30–40 cm (12–15")
Wt:	M 7–12 kg (15–26 lb) | F 7–10 kg (15–22 lb)

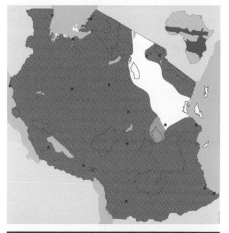

Where to look

In the Serengeti NP it can occasionally be seen near Mukoma Hill, along the road from Seronera to Serengeti Sopa Lodge, around the Seronera airstrip, and in the vicinity of Kusini Camp. Another place to try is Simba Farm on West Kilimanjaro at night. It is also quite frequently encountered in Kitulo NP.

Distribution in Tanzania

The most widely distributed jackal in Tanzania and the only jackal species found in the miombo woodland in the south and much of the west of the country. It is found in most National Parks, except Tarangire, Manyara, Sadaani, and Rubondo. It has not yet been recorded in Arusha and Mikumi NPs, although its presence in nearby areas, such as the coffee farms around Arusha and in the Selous GR photographic area, adjacent to Mikumi NP, suggests it is likely to occur in both National Parks. It is absent from most of the Maasai Steppe and Lake Natron.

Population size and conservation status

The only density estimate in Tanzania is from the Serengeti NP (0·5 animals per km² | 1·3 animals per mi²), where it is fairly common across northern, central, and western areas, and in Maswa GR. It is uncommon on Mount Kilimanjaro, in the Ruaha–Rungwa ecosystem, and across most of central Tanzania. It is fairly common in the Southern Highlands, including Kitulo NP, Mount Rungwe and other montane forests up to an altitude of 2,800 m (9,185ft). It is also common in parts of western Tanzania including Ugalla, Moyowosi and Lukwati GRs. The species is rare in the Selous GR and uncommon in southern Tanzania.

Threats to the Side-striped Jackal include canid diseases, such as rabies and canine distemper virus, collisions with vehicles, and sometimes retribution killings by poultry farmers. Densities in southern Serengeti are low, but stable or possibly increasing. Nothing is known about population trends in the rest of the country, although the species is not threatened in Tanzania.

Side-striped Jackal
TOP and BOTTOM: Serengeti NP

Golden Jackal

Canis aureus

SWAHILI: Bweha Dhahabu

A scruffy-looking jackal with a sandy or yellow-brown body and a relatively long muzzle. The back often has black, white, and brown streaks of hair and may even have a dark 'saddle'. The legs are reddish and the lower half of the tail is black. The throat is white and the belly is a pale cream colour. Males are slightly larger than females.

Least Concern	
HB:	65–85 cm (26–33")
Ht:	40–45 cm (16–18")
Tail:	20–25 cm (8–10")
Wt:	6–10 kg (13–22 lb)

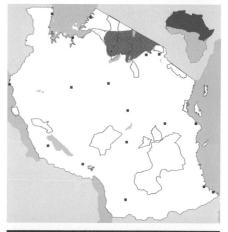

Similar species

The Side-striped Jackal (*page 100*) usually has a white tip to its tail. The Black-backed Jackal (*page 104*) has a distinct black line separating the back from the flanks. The black 'saddle' occasionally found on Golden Jackals in the Serengeti NP has more diffuse colour separation between the back and flanks, and the patterning is also more patchy than that observed in the Black-backed Jackal (*see bottom photo opposite*).

Ecology and social behaviour

In Tanzania, Golden Jackals are restricted to arid, open grasslands and open bushland, although in Asia this species occupies a wide range of habitat types including forest and woodland. They are highly adaptable to a human landscape and frequently found around villages.

Golden Jackals are omnivorous, feeding on invertebrates, fruits, reptiles, rodents, birds and small ungulates up to the size of juvenile Thomson's Gazelles (*page 212*). Carrion and human refuse is also consumed. In the Ngorongoro Crater highlands they also feed on mole rats (*Tachyoryctes* spp.), stalking and then digging them out of their holes. Adult jackals form monogamous pairs that defend permanent territories of 2–4 km² (0·8–1·5 mi²). One or two pups from a previous litter may accompany the breeding pair to assist in raising the current litter of pups. Average group size in the Serengeti is 2·5 individuals. They may be active at all hours of the day, although are mainly nocturnal in areas of human habitation.

Where to look

The most reliable areas to search for Golden Jackals are the short-grass plains between Ndutu and the main Serengeti–Ngorongoro road, around Naabi Hill, and on the Serengeti–Ngorongoro boundary road leading to Loliondo. They are also commonly seen on the floor of the Ngorongoro Crater. Although they can be active at all times of the day, particularly during cloudy weather, they are more likely to be encountered during the early morning and late afternoon.

Distribution in Tanzania

The Golden Jackal is restricted to a small section of northern Tanzania between the central Serengeti and the western slopes of Mount Kilimanjaro. In the Serengeti ecosystem it is concentrated around the short-grass plains, the floor of Ngorongoro Crater, and on the plains between Olmoti and Empakai Crater. It is sparsely distributed in Serengeti, Loliondo, and Maswa GR. It is found across the Lake Natron area and West Kilimanjaro, as far east as the Kitenden corridor on the northern slopes of Mount

Kilimanjaro, and is occasionally recorded in the north of Arusha NP. The most southerly record for this species is from Manyara Ranch.

Population size and conservation status
Golden Jackal density ranges between 0·5–1·5 animals per km^2 (1·3–4·0 animals per mi^2) on the short-grass plains in the Serengeti NP and Ngorongoro CA, where they are regularly seen during the day. However they are uncommon or rare on the long-grass plains and in western Serengeti NP where the vegetation is thicker. They are very common in Ngorongoro Crater, and are also common on the northern slopes of Mount Meru, particularly around villages where they scavenge for food. They are uncommon around Lake Natron and rare on Manyara Ranch. The Golden Jackal population has declined by 60% on the southern plains in the Serengeti NP since the early 1970s for reasons that are unclear.

Golden Jackal
TOP: typical colour form, Serengeti NP; BOTTOM: individual with black 'saddle', Ngorongoro CA

Black-backed Jackal

Canis mesomelas

SWAHILI: Bweha Mgongo Mweusi

A jackal with a dark 'saddle' on the back, reddish-brown legs and flanks, and a bushy, mostly black, tail with a black tip. The underparts are usually white. The 'saddle' is usually black, flecked with white and, in some cases, brown fur; there is a distinct black stripe separating the 'saddle' and the flanks. The 'saddle' reaches halfway down the flank at the shoulder, narrowing towards the base of the tail. The face is a light grey with reddish tinges, and the lower lip, throat and chest are white; the ears are relatively large.

Subspecies
C. m. schmidti: only subspecies found in Tanzania.

Similar species
Side-striped Jackals (*page 100*) usually have a white tip to their tail; the grey on the back extends to the lower flanks and they have a more dog-like face, compared to the fox-like face of the Black-backed Jackal. Golden Jackals (*page 102*) are typically sandy coloured. In some cases Golden Jackals may have a black 'saddle', although they lack the sharp contrast between the 'saddle' and the flank found in the Black-backed Jackal.

Ecology and social behaviour
Found in a wide range of habitats including grassland, wooded savanna, and agricultural land, although it avoids dense vegetation. A generalist feeder, consuming birds, carrion, invertebrates, plants, and human refuse, as well as small- and medium-sized mammals. Mostly nocturnal and crepuscular, although activity periods frequently extend into the day. Adults form life-long monogamous pairs and may be seen with 1–2 offspring from previous years who assist with raising young. Each pair defends a stable territory ranging in size from 0·7–3·5 km² (0·2–1·0 mi²).

Distribution in Tanzania
Distributed across northern and central Tanzania but absent from the south and much of the coastal area. Its distribution in

Least Concern	
HB:	63–81 cm (25–32")
Ht:	45–50 cm (18–20")
Tail:	20–24 cm (8–9")
Wt:	M 6–11 kg (13–24 lb) | F 6–10 kg (13–22 lb)

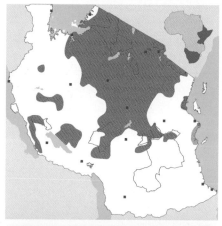

Where to look
Frequently seen in Serengeti NP, particularly in the long-grass plains and woodlands, including around Ndutu and Seronera, and at dawn or dusk in Tarangire and Manyara NPs. It can also be reliably seen along Mwagusi River in Ruaha NP.

the west of Tanzania is patchy, with a single camera trap record from Moyowosi GR, and one camera trap record and several sighting records from Ugalla GR and the adjacent Ipole WMA. There are also records from Katavi NP, Lwafi GR, Loasi FR and possibly Kalambo FR, and the hunting blocks north of Lake Rukwa. There are historical records (1950s) from Mbeya, Mufindi and Njombe districts. Formerly widespread across the Tabora Region, it probably still occurs there in areas with lower human impact. It is found in all of the northern National Parks, as well as in Ruaha and Mikumi, and possibly in the lowlands of Udzungwa NP. There are a few records from Sadaani NP and it is occasionally recorded in northern Selous GR and the Kilombero Valley.

Population size and conservation status
Common across much of the *Acacia–Commiphora* savanna bushland in Tanzania including in the Maasai Steppe, Ngorongoro Crater, Serengeti ecosystem, West Kilimanjaro, Mkomazi NP, and the Ruaha ecosystem. It is typically rare in the miombo woodlands in the west and south of the country, where it is mostly replaced by the Side-striped Jackal.

It is uncommon in Katavi and Mikumi NPs and rare in Saadani NP, the northern section of the Selous GR, and the Kilombero Valley, which forms the southern edge of its range in Tanzania. The principle threats to this species are diseases such as rabies and canine distemper virus and deliberate or accidental poisoning. It is frequently found close to human habitation, and population numbers in Tanzania are probably stable or declining slowly.

Black-backed Jackal
TOP: Serengeti NP (Tanzania); BOTTOM: (Kenya)

African Wild Dog

Lycaon pictus

Painted Hunting Dog

SWAHILI: Mbwa Mwitu

A tall, lean canid with long legs, a bushy tail, and characteristically large, round ears. The fur is distinctively blotched white, black, and tan, with each individual having a unique colour pattern. Black tends to dominate, although there is large variation between individuals. Males are slightly larger than females.

Similar species

The Bat-eared Fox (*page 108*) is substantially smaller than the African Wild Dog, with an even colouration, and its ears, although large, are pointed rather than round. Jackals (*pages 100–104*) are smaller and lack the multi-coloured patterning of African Wild Dogs.

Ecology and social behaviour

African Wild Dogs are found across a wide variety of habitats, ranging from arid grasslands to thick woodland and even some forest habitats. They have been recorded on the summit of Mount Kilimanjaro at 5,895 m (19,340 ft). Their prey consists mainly of medium-size ungulates, particularly Impalas (*page 230*), but may range in size from hares (*pages 88–90*) up to Common Elands (*page 186*). They only rarely scavenge. They occasionally take sheep and goats where wild prey populations are seriously depleted, although they will avoid livestock that is closely attended by herdsmen. African Wild Dogs are highly social and live in packs ranging from six to 13 adults, although usually only one dominant male and female will breed, and all pack members cooperate to rear the pups. Home ranges are large, averaging 400–800 km^2 (150–300 mi^2). They are predominantly diurnal.

Distribution in Tanzania

This species is widely distributed in Tanzania, with resident populations in the south, west, and north of the country. They are found in Mikumi and Udzungwa NPs, and Selous GR south to the Mozambique border.

Endangered	
HB:	100–120 cm (39–47")
Ht:	65–80 cm (25–31")
Tail:	23–35 cm (9–14")
Wt:	35–40 kg (77–88 lb)

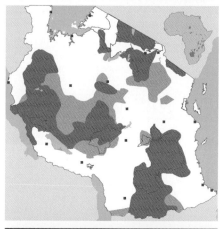

Where to look

The Selous GR and Ruaha NP offer the best opportunities to observe African Wild Dogs. In Selous GR they are most often seen around Mwanamungu, and in the area between Lake Mzizimia and Lake Manze. The best times of year are from June–August and January–March. They may be seen in Ruaha NP along the Mwagusi River, and on the Never-Ending Road early in the morning between Ruaha NP and Iringa town. There are occasionally sightings around some of the lodges and camps around Loliondo, and in southwest Ngorongoro CA, although frequency of sightings varies annually.

They also occur in Singida District, the Ruaha–Rungwa ecosystem, Katavi and Mahale NPs, and Ugalla, Moyowosi and Kigosi GRs. In northern Tanzania they are found in Tarangire NP, the Maasai Steppe, the eastern boundary of Serengeti NP to West Kilimanjaro, and in Mkomazi NP. Formerly distributed throughout the Serengeti ecosystem, they were largely absent from the Serengeti NP since the early 1990s until their recent reintroduction. They are also found in the surrounding areas, including Loliondo, Ngorongoro CA and Maswa GR. There are records of non-resident populations in Sadaani NP and Wami–Mbiki WMA.

Population size and conservation status
African Wild Dogs are dependent on large areas of contiguous habitat, and are rare everywhere but are at their highest densities in the Selous and Ruaha ecosystems. In 2007 there were an estimated 1,800 African Wild Dogs in Tanzania, comprising 20% of the global population of this species, thus making

Tanzania critical for their conservation. The Selous ecosystem alone harbours an estimated 800 African Wild Dogs, one of the world's largest single populations. Very little is known about population trends, although their range in Tanzania is contracting. Because African Wild Dogs are wide-ranging and occur at low densities, they are particularly vulnerable to habitat loss and fragmentation. They also face persecution in some areas due to retaliation by livestock herders for livestock predation, and are vulnerable to snaring and vehicle road kill. The population in the Serengeti was severely reduced in the 1990s by disease.

African Wild Dog
TOP and BOTTOM: Ngorongoro CA

Bat-eared Fox

Otocyon megalotis

SWAHILI: Bweha Masikio

A small fox with a long, bushy tail, a dense coat, and large, bat-like ears, from which it derives its name. The body is a grizzled grey, and the legs are black. The ears, which are 12–13 cm (5") long, are black or dark brown above and on the tips, and white on the inside. The forehead is white and there is a dark band around the eyes and the sides of the cheeks. The tail is a light beige at the base and black at the tip.

Least Concern	
HB:	48 67 cm (19–26")
Ht:	35–40 cm (14–16")
Tail:	25–30 cm (10–12")
Wt:	3–5 kg (7–11 lb)

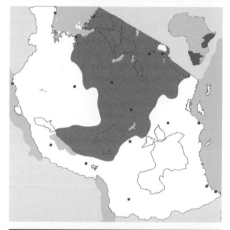

Subspecies
O. m. virgatus: only subspecies found in Tanzania.

Similar species
Unlikely to be mistaken for any other mammal; it is much smaller than all other canid species in Tanzania.

Ecology and social behaviour
Found in open grassland and woodland with little cover in drier areas of the country where rainfall is between 200–800 mm (8–31") per year. In the Serengeti NP they are common in grassland–woodland boundaries but avoid the open grass plains. A high proportion of their diet consists of termites, particularly *Hodotermes* and *Microhodotermes* harvester termites. During the wet season when termites are scarce, dung beetles and beetle larvae form the bulk of their food. They also feed on other small invertebrates and, less commonly, small rodents and fruit. Most foraging occurs at night, although they may be active throughout the day. Bat-eared Foxes live in stable family groups consisting of a male and up to three closely related females with cubs. Home range size varies between 100–300 ha (250–750 acres). Home ranges may overlap, but areas containing important harvester termite colonies are often defended.

Distribution in Tanzania
This species mainly occurs in the *Acacia–Commiphora* bushland, and occasionally in grassy areas in miombo woodland. Its distribution is similar to that of the

Where to look
Often seen on the open plains and along the woodland edge across much of Serengeti NP. They are also easily observed around Ndutu in the Ngorongoro CA, particularly early morning and late afternoon. In Ruaha NP they can often be found along the River Drive or near Mwagusi Camp.

Aardwolf (*page 148*), which also feeds principally on termites. It is found throughout the Serengeti ecosystem, Lake Natron, West Kilimanjaro, Tarangire and Mkomazi NPs, the Maasai Steppe, and the Ruaha–Rungwa ecosystem. It is also occurs in Chunya Open Area and Piti GR. It is absent from most of the south, east and west of the country.

Population size and conservation status
Published density estimates for the Serengeti vary between 0·3–1·0 animals per km² (0·8–3·0 animals per mi²). There are no population estimates for the rest of Tanzania, although it is generally common in the north of the country and increasingly uncommon in the southern parts of its range. The species is

abundant in the Gelai Game Controlled Area, and common across most of the Serengeti ecosystem, the Yaeda Valley, West Kilimanjaro, Tarangire NP, the Maasai Steppe, Mkomazi NP and eastern Ruaha NP. It is uncommon around Lake Rukwa. Habitat loss is the main threat to this species outside protected areas, and, in Tanzania, it is susceptible to significant population declines as a result of disease, including rabies and canine distemper virus. The population of Bat-eared Foxes in Tarangire NP crashed in the mid-1990s due to the outbreak of an unknown canine disease but has since recovered.

Bat-eared Fox
TOP: (Kenya); BOTTOM: Ngorongoro CA (Tanzania)

Zorilla

Ictonyx striatus

Striped Polecat

SWAHILI: Kicheche

A small weasel with long body hair and four distinctive black and white stripes running from the head to the tail. The underside and legs are black and the tail is mostly white, although sometimes the black base hairs can be seen. There is a white patch on the forehead and two white patches above the eyes on an otherwise black face. Males are approximately 50% heavier than females.

Similar species

The African Striped Weasel (*page 112*) has a white head, shorter fur, much shorter legs, and keeps its tail down when it runs (see comparative photographs, *page 263*). The Zorilla has a distinctive bouncing gait and generally runs with its tail raised.

Ecology and social behaviour

Found in a wide range of habitats, including dense forests, open savannas, dry bushland, and cultivated land. These animals are solitary and strictly nocturnal, spending the day in burrows that they either dig themselves or modify from other species, such as Springhares (*page 84*). If disturbed, they will erect the fur on the body and tail and raise the tail up in the air. If further provoked, they eject a foul-smelling liquid from their anal glands, which is difficult to remove and can last for days. This defence mechanism probably accounts for their distinctive, skunk-like, warning colouration. Most of their diet is comprised of rodents and invertebrates, although they may also feed on a range of small animals including amphibians, birds, and reptiles, including large snakes.

Distribution in Tanzania

The Zorilla probably occurs across most of mainland Tanzania, although there are no records from the northwest and few confirmed records from the southwest of the country. It has been recorded in all of the northern National Parks, except Rubondo

Least Concern	
HB:	28–38 cm (11–15")
Ht:	10–13 cm (4–5")
Tail:	24–30 cm (9–12")
Wt:	0·5–1·4 kg (1–3 lb)

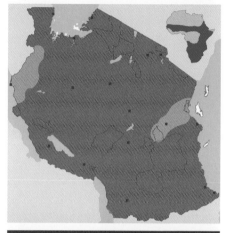

Where to look

Seeing a Zorilla requires a certain amount of luck. It can be seen at night on the farms around West Kilimanjaro, particularly in May and June when the crops are near harvest and the rodent population is high. Spotlighting in areas surrounding the Serengeti NP is another good option that is worth trying.

NP, and in the south it is known from Ruaha, Udzungwa, Kitulo and Mahale NPs, and the Selous GR. There are no records from Sadaani and Mikumi NPs, although being a small, nocturnal carnivore, the species may have been overlooked in these National Parks.

Population size and conservation status

There are no population estimates for this species in Tanzania. The Zorilla is locally common in parts of the country, including Kitulo NP and in the forests of Ngorongoro CA, where it was camera trapped regularly. Camera trap surveys found it was uncommon in both the forests and bushland around Gelai Mountain, in Arusha and Tarangire NPs, and in Lukwika–Lumesule GRs and Muhuwesi FR in southern Tanzania. It is uncommon on the lower slopes of Mount Kilimanjaro.

Habitat loss is the primary threat to this species, and it is also frequently seen as road kill in northern Tanzania.

Zorilla
TOP: captive individual; BOTTOM: location unknown

African Striped Weasel — *Poecilogale albinucha*

White-naped Weasel

SWAHILI: Chororo

A small black-and-white weasel with a very long body and short legs. The coat is black with four white stripes down the back, and the legs and underparts are black. The fur on the forehead, top of the head and the tail is completely white, and the coat is short and sleek. Males are larger than females.

Similar species

The Zorilla (*page 110*) has much longer legs, a very shaggy coat (in contrast to the short fur of the weasel), white above the eyes, and a distinctive black band across its forehead (see comparative photographs, *page 263*).

Ecology and social behaviour

Found in a variety of habitats including forest edge, grassland, and marshes, typically in areas with rainfall above 600 mm (24"). Also occasionally reported from lowland rainforest. Optimal habitat is likely to occur in areas of high rainfall with consistently high densities of rodents, including montane grasslands, agricultural land, and savanna–forest mosaics. In the Southern Highlands, scat records were distributed in bamboo forest (45%), grassland (26%) and cultivated areas (23%). The African Striped Weasel is usually seen singly although, rarely, mother–offspring groups of three or four individuals have been recorded. When travelling together, young animals typically move directly behind the mother, creating a distinctly 'snake-like' appearance. It is mainly nocturnal, although sometimes seen in the early morning or late afternoon, lying up in a burrow during the day – either an old rodent burrow or a hole that it has dug for itself. This species is a rodent specialist, its low, slender body allowing it to follow and hunt rodents in their burrows, although it will also dig them out of the ground. It is voracious, sometimes feeding on three or four rodents a night. Once killed, prey is always taken to the burrow to be eaten or stored. It will also occasionally eat birds,

Least Concern	
HB:	27–33 cm (11–13")
Ht:	7–8 cm (3")
Tail:	16–20 cm (6–8")
Wt:	M 220–350 g (8–12 oz) | F 230–260 g (8–9 oz)

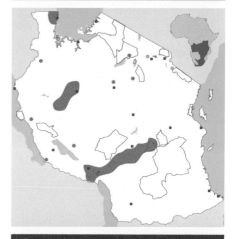

Where to look

This species is very difficult to see in Tanzania as it is nocturnal and probably spends much of its time in burrows. Spotlighting along the roads in the Minziro FR probably provides the best opportunity to observe it, and with time and luck it might be seen around the villages of Mount Rungwe and in Kitulo NP.

and has been known to raid chicken coops, although this behaviour is uncommon. If threatened, an individual may secrete a strong-smelling, thick, yellowish liquid from its anal glands.

Distribution in Tanzania

This species is sparsely distributed in Tanzania. Most records are from the west and southwest of the country, particularly around Mbeya, the Rukwa Valley, Mount Rungwe, and Kitulo and Udzungwa NPs. There are also records from near Iringa, Tabora, Ugalla GR, and from Minziro FR and Bukoba. In the north, there are two published records from Singida and the Mount Hanang area. There was also a sighting in 2012 from the grounds of Rhino Lodge in the Ngorongoro Crater, and a possible record from Monduli. It appears to be absent from east and southern Tanzania. For reasons that are unclear, there are no camera trap records of African Striped Weasels from Tanzania, despite intensive surveys in areas where there are regular scat records.

Population size and conservation status
The African Striped Weasel is probably uncommon or rare in most parts of the country, although its mainly nocturnal habits and small size mean it is easily overlooked.

A survey of scat suggested it is fairly common in Kitulo NP, and uncommon to rare on the slopes of Mount Rungwe. Most residents around Mount Rungwe reported seeing them in and around the village and farms. It is widely captured for use in traditional medicine in Tanzania and many other parts of Africa, which has probably severely depleted local populations. Skins of this species are thought to bring the owner good luck, including protection from crop thieves and curing back pain; it is also used to protect the owner from witchcraft and to pay respects to the deceased. Skins are often placed above doorways in the belief that they will keep out rodents.

African Striped Weasel
captive individual

African Clawless Otter

Aonyx capensis

SWAHILI: Fisi Maji Mkubwa

A large otter with a light brown to dark brown body and a large white patch that extends from the face onto the sides of the neck and throat. Some individuals may lack the white throat patch, and others may have white patches above the eyes. The front feet have no webbing and the hind feet are only partially webbed; they are clawless, as the name suggests.

Similar species

The Spotted-necked Otter (*page 116*) is much smaller, approximately half the weight of an African Clawless Otter, has very little white on the throat, webbed feet and claws on its toes. Both species may appear black when seen in the water and can be difficult to distinguish when swimming without a good size reference.

Ecology and social behaviour

This otter occurs both in freshwater and coastal areas. They inhabit freshwater rivers, forest streams in montane habitats, and the edges of lakes, and are frequently found in areas with large reed beds. They occasionally use semi-permanent rivers, moving to permanent water sources when these dry up. Along the coast they remain close to rivers and estuaries as they require freshwater to drink and to clean their fur. Crabs form the majority of their diet in freshwater habitats, while fish are important in coastal areas. They also eat frogs, invertebrates, and occasionally birds and small mammals. They are mainly crepuscular and move alone or occasionally in pairs, although they are sometimes observed in family groups of two adults and two to three young.

Distribution in Tanzania

The distribution of the African Clawless Otter in Tanzania is poorly known, and they are probably more widespread than records suggest. They are known from Rubondo NP, although there are no other known records from Lake Victoria. They are also present in Serengeti, Manyara, Arusha, Udzungwa,

Least Concern	
HB:	110–140 cm (43–55")
Tail:	45–57 cm (18–22")
Wt:	10–18 kg (22–40 lb)

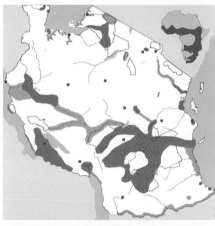

Where to look

African Clawless Otters are not easy to observe as they are shy and mainly nocturnal. They are occasionally seen in the Lumemo River in Udzungwa NP, and in small ponds and rivers at altitudes between 1,200–1,900 m (4,000–6,200 ft) within the tea estates around Sao Hill, Iringa. Also seen infrequently along the edge of Lake Tanganyika in Mahale NP very early morning and at dusk. In Tukuyu district in the Rungwe area, they can be seen in the catchment of the Kiwira, Lufirio and Mbaka rivers at altitudes between 1,000–1,500 m (3,300–4,900 ft).

Mikumi, Ruaha, Mahale, Gombe, Kitulo, and Sadaani NPs, as well as the Selous GR. They occur on the southern slopes of Mount Meru, much of the Udzungwa Mountains, including Sao Hill River, on Mount Rungwe, the Ufipa Plateau down to Lake Tanganyika and in the Loasi and Kalambo River watersheds; they are also found in higher ground on the border between Tanzania and Zambia as far south as Tunduma. They are probably widespread on the Tanzanian coast, and there are records from the Salander Bridge in Dar es Salaam. There are also records from the Wami River, the Nguru Mountains, and Ugalla and Moyowosi GRs. Although there are no data, it is likely to occur in the Ruvuma River on the border with Mozambique.

Population size and conservation status
The population size of the African Clawless Otter in Tanzania is unknown. Although it is locally common in the Moyowosi wetlands, in most parts of the country it is either uncommon or rare. In some areas it is hunted for its fur, which is used in local medicine and witchcraft. It is also persecuted for its habit of stealing fish from fish traps. This species can tolerate a relatively high level of disturbance to its riparian habitat and is still found in areas with high human activity.

African Clawless Otter
TOP: (South Africa); BOTTOM: (The Gambia)

Spotted-necked Otter

Hydrictis maculicollis

SWAHILI: Fisi Maji Mdogo / Madoa

A small, slender otter with a dark brown to reddish-brown coat, and white or creamy-white speckling on the chin. There is considerable variation in the amount of speckling and some individuals may have none at all. The body can appear almost black when wet. Its feet are fully webbed and have claws.

Subspecies
H. m. kivuana: only subspecies found in Tanzania.

Similar species
The African Clawless Otter (*page 114*) is much larger and usually has a large, distinct white patch on the throat and neck. The ranges of the two species overlap in western Tanzania, and they are able to co-exist because of their different feeding requirements: the Spotted-necked Otter feeds mainly on fish and the African Clawless Otter mainly on crabs.

Ecology and social behaviour
An aquatic animal that is mainly found in lakes and larger rivers and less commonly in swamps with large sections of open water. It also occurs in smaller montane streams. This species is completely water dependent and is seldom found more than 10 m (33 ft) from water. It is predominantly diurnal, with most activity occurring in the early morning and late afternoon, although nocturnal activity increases during a full moon. They rest and den under the roots of trees, in dense vegetation, or in holes that they excavate in soft soil. In Lake Victoria, group size typically ranges from three to five animals, although groups of up to 20 individuals have been recorded; solitary sightings are uncommon. Group size is probably determined by food availability. It is not territorial and home ranges overlap both within and between the sexes. This species feeds predominantly on fish, although crabs and frogs can make up a significant portion of its diet in some areas.

Least Concern	
HB:	60–76 cm (24–30")
Tail:	40–44 cm (16–17")
Wt:	3·8–6·5 kg (8–14 lb)

Where to look
Can be reliably seen at Rubondo NP in Lake Victoria by taking a boat trip around the Island. Other good sites include Lukuba Island, also in Lake Victoria, Lakeshore Lodge near Kipili village on Lake Tanganyika and Lake Ngwazi at Sao Hill.

Distribution in Tanzania
The Spotted-necked Otter is found in all of Tanzania's major lakes, including Victoria, Tanganyika, Nyasa and Rukwa. It was formerly widespread in Lake Victoria, occurring along the entire coastline, but is now restricted to less disturbed areas including Rubondo Island, Spekes Bay, Lukoba Island and probably the islands east of Bukoba. In Lake Tanganyika it is known from Mahale NP and Kipili village, though now extinct in Gombe NP. It is also known from Lake Ngwazi, Lake Inzivi, Lake Kyanga and Ruaha marsh in the Sao Hill area south of Iringa, and Lake Sagara near Ugalla GR. There is a scat record possibly from this species for Lake Manyara, and it may also be found in the wetlands of Moyowosi and Burigi–Biharamulo GRs, although there are no confirmed records from these areas.

Population size and conservation status
No overall population figures are available.
Otter densities are highest in protected parts
of Lake Victoria, including Rubondo NP,
where a high density of approximately 1 otter
per km (1·6 otters per mile) of shoreline was
recorded. Populations in other parts of the
lake are much lower. This species is also locally
common along the shores of Lakes Nyasa and
Tanganyika. Otters are persecuted by local
fishermen who perceive them as competitors,
and are also widely killed for their meat and
skin. Loss of riparian habitat to agriculture is
a serious threat to otters in many areas, and
agricultural run-off causes both pollution and
siltation which reduces water visibility and
affects the ability of otters to see and catch fish.

Spotted-necked Otter
TOP: (Botswana); BOTTOM: (Kenya)

Honey Badger

Mellivora capensis

Ratel

SWAHILI: Nyegere

A powerfully built, stocky carnivore with short, muscular legs and a short tail. The upperparts are white or grey surrounded by a white border, while the underparts and limbs are black. Melanistic individuals have been recorded. The front legs have very large, strong claws (up to 3.5 cm | 1·4" long), while the hind feet have only small nails. The skin skin is loose and extremely tough. The tail is black. Anal glands secrete a foul smelling liquid when under stress, possibly as a defence mechanism.

Similar species

Unlikely to be mistaken for any other mammal.

Ecology and social behaviour

Honey Badgers occur in a diverse array of habitats, from dry, open country and grassland, to agricultural land and dense montane forests. They will eat a wide variety of food including dung beetle larvae, invertebrates, small mammals, birds, vegetation, reptiles and honey, and are not averse to high quality cheese! They use their powerful front claws to dig out most of their food. Males can cover 30 km (19 miles) in one night while foraging. A symbiotic relationship between Honey Badgers and a bird, the Greater Honeyguide *Indicator indicator*, has been reported – the honeyguide directs a badger to a bees' nest using a characteristic call, the badger opens the nest to eat the honey and the bird feeds on the residue honey and grubs. Hadzabe hunter-gatherers in the Yaeda Valley (who themselves regularly follow honeyguides to locate bees' nests) claim this is a common occurrence. Honey Badgers emit a noxious smell from their anal glands that can reportedly immobilise bees and may be used to deter predators. They are generally seen alone or in pairs. Home ranges of males are significantly larger than those of females, but neither sex appears to defend a territory. The species has a well-deserved reputation for

Least Concern	
HB:	60–80 cm (30–35")
Ht:	23–28 cm (9–11")
Tail:	16–24 cm (6–9")
Wt:	M 7·5–14 kg (17–31 lb) | F 7–13 kg (15–29 lb)

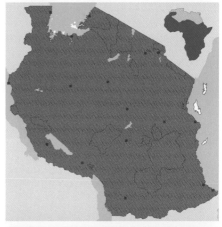

Where to look

There are frequent sightings at night in the grounds of the Vuma Hills Lodge (Mikumi NP) and at several of the lodges in Ruaha NP. Honey Badgers often visit lodge or bush camp kitchens and garbage sites in search of food, so it is always worth enquiring with lodge or camp staff if they are seeing them. They are quite often seen on the plains close to Ndutu and sometimes seen on the open grass plains in the Serengeti NP and Ngorongoro CA, around Gol Kopjes, and on the Makao road in the early morning and late afternoon. They are frequently encountered on night drives in Katavi NP, and occasionally in Tarangire NP.

being very aggressive and devoid of fear; they have been known to steal kills off adult male lions and attack and bite car tyres.

Distribution in Tanzania

The Honey Badger is extremely widespread in Tanzania, where it is known from all mainland National Parks (except for Rubondo NP) and Game Reserves.

Population size and conservation status

There are no density records for Tanzania. This species is common in Mkomazi NP and Maswa GR and fairly common on the short-grass plains of the Serengeti NP and Ngorongoro. It is also fairly common in the west of the country, around Lake Rukwa, Katavi NP, Mlele FR and Moyowosi GR, and in Mikumi NP. It is uncommon in Ruaha, Sadaani, Tarangire, and Kilimanjaro NPs and the Selous GR. This species is often trapped and killed in retaliation by beekeepers and small livestock farmers, and it is also known to suffer from canine distemper virus.

Honey Badger
TOP: (Botswana); BOTTOM: Serengeti NP (Tanzania)

African Palm Civet

Nandinia binotata

SWAHILI: Fungo

A genet-like animal with an olive-brown body, black spots on the back and sides of the body, and pale yellow or grey underparts. There is a single white or yellowish spot on each shoulder, although this may be very pale or missing entirely. The muzzle is long and pointed. The tail is long with 12–15 faint dark rings. Males are larger and heavier than females.

Subspecies
N. b. arborea: northern Tanzania; black neck stripes.

N. b. gerrardi: southern Tanzania and Zanzibar; no black neck stripes.

Similar species
When on the ground, the African Palm Civet could be confused with a Bushy-tailed Mongoose (*page 152*) or Marsh Mongoose (*page 150*), but it is paler in colour and has a proportionately longer tail, which is roughly the same length as the body. If seen in a tree at night, the civet looks dark brown with a bushy tail; genets (*pages 134–140*) have black-and-white tails, and all non-flying squirrel species are diurnal. Greater galagos (*pages 70–72*) have longer hind legs, bushier, unstriped tails and much larger ears.

Ecology and social behaviour
African Palm Civets are typically found in montane and lowland forest, although they also frequent riverine forest, dense miombo thicket, bamboo forest and cultivated areas, particularly banana plantations. They feed mainly on fruit, but will also prey on birds, small mammals and invertebrates. Highly arboreal, they can run rapidly along tree branches in the high canopy, but they will also come to the forest floor to feed. This species is nocturnal and solitary, although will occasionally be attracted in larger groups to fruiting trees. In West Africa, males have territories of approximately 100 ha (250 acres), overlapping with a number of female territories that average 45 ha (110 acres).

Least Concern	
HB:	44–60 cm (17–24")
Ht:	22 cm (9")
Tail:	46–62 cm (18–24")
Wt:	1–3 kg (2–7 lb)

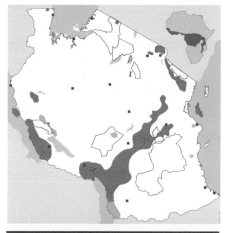

Where to look
This species is cryptic, nocturnal and uncommon in most parts of Tanzania – it is more likely to be heard at night, rather than seen. It is quite often seen in Nkuka Forest and in the adjacent Mount Rungwe Nature Reserve.

African Palm Civets have a very distinctive, haunting, loud call sounding like a long "*hoo*".

Distribution in Tanzania
This species has a scattered distribution in dense forests in north, west, central and coastal Tanzania. It is known from northern Serengeti, Manyara, Kilimanjaro, Arusha, Mikumi, Udzungwa, Kitulo, Mahale, and Gombe NPs, and is possibly in Ruaha and Katavi NPs. It is found throughout the Eastern Arc Mountains, and has been recorded in both East and West Usambaras, South Pare Mountains, Chome FR, Nguru North, Uluguru South, and West Kilombero Scarp Forest. It is also found on Mount Rungwe and other Southern Highland forests, and Mbizi FR. There are camera trap records from Minziro FR and Issa, west of Ugalla GR.

The distribution of this species in the coastal area is unclear, although there are possible records in the literature from Pugu and Tong'omba FRs. It was recently discovered in Jozani Chwaka Bay NP on Zanzibar. This species is easily overlooked and is likely to be more widespread in Tanzania than records suggest.

Population size and conservation status
There are no density data for the African Palm Civet in Tanzania, although in Bwindi Impenetrable Forest in Uganda it can reach densities of 2–3 individuals per km² (5–8 individuals per mi²). It was camera trapped regularly in Ufiome FR south of Babati, and is probably also common in the nearby Nou FR. It is fairly common on Mount Rungwe. This species is rare in Mikumi NP, where it has been recorded close to Vuma Hills Lodge and on Malundwe Mountain. Densities in other areas are not known, although three individuals were caught in Chome FR during a period of a few weeks, suggesting it is relatively common there.

African Palm Civet
TOP: ssp. *arborea* (Rwanda); BOTTOM: camera trap photo ssp. *gerrardi*, Udzungwa NP (Tanzania)

Cheetah

Acinonyx jubatus

SWAHILI: Duma

A tall, slender cat with a long tail and small head. The fur is a yellowish-beige with distinct black spots across most of the body. The face is marked by black 'tear lines' falling from each eye, around the muzzle, to the upper lip. The tail is long with spots merging to a series of black and white stripes at the end, and the tip is usually white. Cheetahs have semi-retractable claws that are not protected by a sheath as in other cats, and so their claws are blunt. Males are slightly larger than females.

Similar species

The Leopard (*page 132*) looks similar to the Cheetah, but has blotched rosettes rather than the clearly defined spots of a Cheetah, and its face lacks 'tear lines'. The Serval (*page 126*) is much smaller, with a shorter tail, and has spots that merge into stripes towards its back.

Ecology and social behaviour

Cheetahs are found in a wide variety of habitats, ranging from desert to thick woodland. They feed on a wide range of prey, from hares (*pages 88–90*) up to adult Common Wildebeests (*page 238*), although they prefer prey the size of gazelles (*pages 212–214*) or Impalas (*page 230*). They occasionally take sheep and goats. Cheetahs have a unique social system whereby males hold small territories (approx. 50 km² | 20 mi²), while females and non-territorial males roam across large areas, averaging 800 km² (300 mi²) in the Serengeti, and up to 3,000 km² (1,150 mi²) elsewhere. Females are solitary or accompanied by dependent cubs, while males can live in 'coalitions' of 2–3 individuals, who are usually brothers. They are predominantly diurnal, being most active in the early morning and evening.

Distribution in Tanzania

Cheetahs are found throughout the Serengeti ecosystem. They range from Lake Natron to West Kilimanjaro, across the Maasai Steppe, and into Manyara, Mkomazi and Tarangire NPs; there are also records from the Yaeda Valley and Wembere Wetland. They occur in

Vulnerable	
HB:	110–140 cm (43–55")
Ht:	65–80 cm (26–31")
Tail:	60–74 cm (24–29")
Wt:	35–50 kg (77–110 lb)

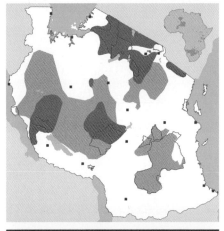

Where to look

The plains of the Serengeti NP and Ngorongoro CA are one of the best places in the world to observe Cheetahs. They can be seen throughout the Serengeti at any time of year, with the best dry season viewing in the woodland at the edge of the plains around Seronera, Ndutu, Kusini and Serengeti Sopa; wet season sightings are best on the plains around Ndutu, Naabi Hill, Lemuta and Gol kopjes. Cheetahs tend to be shy in other areas in Tanzania, although they are occasionally seen in Tarangire NP and Ruaha NP, particularly along the River Drive and Mwagusi Sand River.

Ruaha NP and Rungwa, Rukwa, and Ugalla GRs and surrounding areas. They formerly occurred in Mikumi NP and the Selous GR, although the last known sighting in the Selous GR was in the late 1990s.

Population size and conservation status

The Cheetah is rare in much of Tanzania outside the Serengeti ecosystem, seldom reaching densities above 1 animal per 100 km² (3 animals per 100 mi²). Estimates from the

Serengeti ecosystem suggest a population of 210–280 individuals, and an estimated total of 1,180 Cheetah in the country, representing just over 10% of the global population. In the Serengeti ecosystem, the population has been roughly stable over the last 40 years, although there has been a recent decline on the short grass plains. Very little is known about population status elsewhere, although the Cheetah is now restricted to just 14% of its historical range in Tanzania. Because Cheetahs are wide-ranging and occur at low densities, they are particularly vulnerable to habitat loss and fragmentation. In some areas they are persecuted in retaliation for livestock loss, and they also face an increasing threat of capture for the captive animal trade.

Cheetah
TOP: Ngorongoro CA; BOTTOM: female with cubs, Serengeti NP

Caracal

Caracal caracal

SWAHILI: Simbamangu

A medium-sized, stocky cat with a tawny-brown or red body. The underparts are white and may be lightly spotted. The face is very distinctive, with white on the chin and throat and a black line from the eye to the nose. The tail is relatively short. The ears are black on the back and distinctly tufted with long black hairs approximately 4·5 cm (2") in length.

Similar species
The Wild Cat (*page 128*) is occasionally the same colour as the Caracal, but typically has stripes on the legs and tail, is significantly smaller and has a proportionately longer tail. The Golden Cat *Profelis aurata* is similar in size and colour but has a longer tail and lacks the distinctive black ear tufts.

Note: There are persistent reports of Golden Cats occurring in northern Tanzania, including on Monduli Mountain and the Nou FR, although as yet there are no verified records. The species may occur in Tanzania given the proximity to known populations in southern Kenya, Uganda, and Rwanda.

Ecology and social behaviour
A dry country species, inhabiting savanna, woodland and scrub. Caracals feed principally on small- to medium-sized mammals such as rodents, hares (*pages 88–90*), Kirk's Dik-diks (*page 208*) and Bush Duikers (*page 196*). They also eat birds, including storks, and, rarely, carrion. They are predominantly nocturnal but can be observed during the day in protected areas. Caracals are solitary, although occasionally mother–offspring units are seen together. Home range size varies considerably by habitat type, with male ranges typically being three times larger than those of females. Male home ranges encompass several female home ranges with reported overlap of approximately 50% with other males. Female home ranges have very slight overlap.

Distribution in Tanzania
Most of the records for this species are from northern and central Tanzania. It is found in

Least Concern	
HB:	60–100 cm (24–39")
Ht:	40–50 cm (16–20")
Tail:	20–34 cm (8–13")
Wt:	M 8–19 kg (18–42 lb) | F 8–16 kg (18–35 lb)

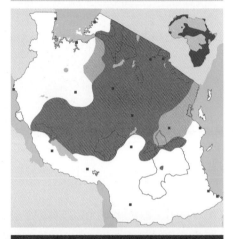

Where to look
The Caracal is not easily seen in Tanzania. The best place is in the Serengeti ecosystem, on the open grassland around Ndutu, Naabi Hill, Seronera, Five Hills track, and Semetu. It is also occasionally seen in Mkomazi NP.

Mkomazi, Tarangire, Kilimanjaro, Serengeti, Ruaha, Mikumi, and Udzungwa NPs, and probably Katavi NP, although there are no confirmed records. It is also found in the Maasai Steppe, West Kilimanjaro to Lake Natron, Ngorongoro CA, Rungwa GR, the Rukwa Valley and Ugalla GR. There are few records of this species from southern Tanzania, although it is known from the photographic area of Selous GR and there is one record from a hunting block in the south. It is similarly scarce in coastal areas, with a single record from Sadaani NP. It is believed to be absent from the far west and northwest of Tanzania.

Population size and conservation status
There are no density estimates for this species in Tanzania. It was frequently camera trapped

in Mkomazi NP, which is the only part of the country where it appears to be relatively common. It is otherwise uncommon in Serengeti NP, Maswa GR, the grasslands of Ngorongoro CA, Lake Natron, West Kilimanjaro, the Yaeda Valley and Swagaswaga GR. It is rare in Tarangire NP, the Maasai Steppe, Rukwa and Ugalla GRs. Population trends are unknown. Habitat loss is likely to be the principal threat to this species.

Caracal
TOP: (Namibia); BOTTOM: Serengeti NP (Tanzania)

Serval

Leptailurus serval

SWAHILI: Mondo

Least Concern	
HB:	60–92 cm (24–36")
Ht:	54–62 cm (21–24")
Tail:	24–35 cm (9–14")
Wt:	M 8–13 kg (18–29 lb) | F 6–10 kg (13–22 lb)

A slender, spotted cat with long legs, a small head, and a short tail. The coat is a yellowish-tan colour, with bold, elongated black spots that tend to merge into longitudinal stripes on the upper neck, shoulders, and insides of the legs. The underparts are white or off-white. The tail is the same colour as the body with black rings towards the tip. On the back of the large ears are two black stripes and one prominent white lateral stripe. In montane areas, individuals have much denser fur and are commonly melanistic.

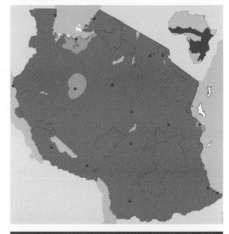

Similar species
Cheetahs (*page 122*) and Leopards (*page 132*) also have spotted coats, although the Serval is smaller, has proportionately much longer legs, and a significantly shorter tail. The Caracal (*page 124*) is similar in size and shape but lacks spots.

Ecology and social behaviour
Servals are primarily found in savanna habitat, but are also common in reed beds, marshes, subalpine habitat, agricultural land and along the margins of forests, but seldom in dense forest. Hares and rodents form a major part of their diet, and they also feed on birds, reptiles, invertebrates, fruits and vegetation. Servals are solitary and territorial. The home range (12 km² | 5 mi²) of one male in the Ngorongoro Crater overlapped with the ranges of at least two females. Females also have discrete, non-overlapping ranges, estimated at 9·5 km² (4 mi²) for one female. Camera trap records from Tanzania show that they are active at all hours of the day, with the majority of activity occurring at night.

Where to look
Frequently seen on night drives on the lower slopes of Mount Kilimanjaro at Simba Farm and Ndarakwai Ranch, and occasionally seen on the road up to the Shira Plateau. In the Serengeti it can be found in the triangle area of Ndutu and around the Seronera River, while in Tarangire NP it is sometimes seen along the edge of Silale Swamp in the early morning or late afternoon.

Distribution in Tanzania
Extremely widespread in Tanzania, with records from much of the country and all habitat types. There are no records from central Tabora and Shinyanga regions. It has been reported from every Game Reserve and mainland National Park with the exception of Rubondo NP. An adaptable species, it is also found on the outskirts of big cities, including Arusha. Melanistic Servals have been recorded in Serengeti, Mkomazi and Kitulo NPs, and on Mount Kilimanjaro; three out of nine Servals camera trapped on the Shira Plateau on Mount Kilimanjaro were melanistic individuals, suggesting that this is a common trait in this area.

Population size and conservation status
Most common in the north and in highland areas, and less common in the west, south and coastal areas. In Tarangire NP, density was estimated at 11 individuals per 100 km² (29 individuals per 100 mi²). It is very common on Mount Kilimanjaro and it is

also common in Maswa GR, much of the Serengeti NP, the Ngorongoro CA, and in the Southern Highlands including Mount Rungwe and Kitulo NP. It is less common but still frequently encountered in Lake Natron, West Kilimanjaro, the Maasai Steppe, Mkomazi NP, Burigi–Biharamulo GR and the Ruaha–Rungwa ecosystem. It is uncommon around Katavi NP, Ugalla GR, Moyowosi GR and rare across most of the Selous ecosystem and Selous–Niassa corridor. Population trends are not known. Little is known about threats and causes of mortality, although individuals are occasionally killed by domestic dogs.

Serval
TOP: (Kenya); BOTTOM: camera trap photo, melanistic individual, Kilimanjaro NP (Tanzania)

Wild Cat

Felis silvestris

SWAHILI: Paka Mwitu / Pori, Kimburu

The Wild Cat is very similar in size and appearance to the domestic cat, to which it is closely related, but is larger, has longer legs, and reddish or rusty-brown backs to its ears. There is a wide variation in coat colour – most individuals in Tanzania have a light grey or tawny coat, with grey-black or brown spots or stripes on the back and flanks and bold stripes on the legs, but sandy-yellow individuals with no spots or stripes have been recorded from the Serengeti. The chin is white and the underparts are white or buff. The tail has several dark bands and a black tip.

Similar species
The Wild Cat can be difficult to distinguish from a domestic cat, and the two often interbreed. Pure Wild Cats can be identified by the russet colour on the backs of the ears. Caracals (*page 124*) are larger, have long tufts on their ears, and are more uniform in colour with proportionately shorter tails.

Ecology and social behaviour
Wild Cats occur in a wide range of habitats, including open grassland, bushland, woodland, agricultural land and around human settlements. They avoid areas of thick forest. Rodents are the main prey species, although hares, birds, reptiles, amphibians and a variety of invertebrates are also eaten. They are mainly nocturnal, but can also be active in the early morning and late afternoon. Camera trap records from northern Tanzania showed activity peaks between 9:00–11:00 p.m. and 3:00–6:00 a.m. Little is known about their social behaviour although they are solitary and probably territorial, with the range of one male overlapping with that of several females.

Distribution in Tanzania
Most Wild Cat records in Tanzania are concentrated in the north and central parts of the country. The species has been recorded in all of the northern National Parks, as well as Ruaha, Katavi and Kitulo. There is also a record from Mahale NP. There are possible sighting records from the Kilombero Valley,

Least Concern	
HB:	47–66 cm (19–26")
Ht:	30–36 cm (12–14")
Tail:	24–38 cm (9–15")
Wt:	M 3·5–6·5 kg (7–14 lb) | F 2·4–5·5 kg (5–11 lb)

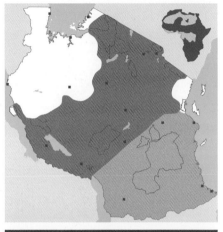

Where to look
Wild Cats are occasionally seen in the early morning and late afternoon on the short-grass plains around Ndutu in the Ngorongoro CA and Seronera in the Serengeti NP, as well as on night drives in areas surrounding the Serengeti NP. They are also frequently encountered on night drives in the West Kilimanjaro area, and less commonly in Tarangire NP and Manyara Ranch.

the Udzungwa Mountains and parts of northern Selous GR, although these need to be confirmed. Records from Mikumi NP are believed to be of domestic cats. There are very few confirmed records from south and west Tanzania, suggesting that the species may be absent from large areas of miombo woodland. Wild Cats may be more widely distributed in Tanzania than current records suggest, but confusion with domestic cats makes it difficult to determine their exact range.

Population size and conservation status
Wild Cats are widespread and common in northern Tanzania. They are common in

the Serengeti NP, where densities have been estimated at 0·1–1·0 animals per km^2 (less than 0·5 animals per mi^2). Camera trap surveys have shown that this species is particularly abundant in the Lake Natron and West Kilimanjaro ecosystems and in Mkomazi NP. There are also high densities on the outskirts of Arusha, although many of these individuals are probably Wild Cat × domestic cat hybrids.

Wild Cats are uncommon in Manyara and Tarangire NPs, the Maasai Steppe and in the Ruaha–Rungwa and Katavi–Rukwa ecosystems, and rare or absent from the Selous GR and most of southern and northwestern Tanzania. Hybridization with domestic cats poses a major threat to Wild Cats and pure populations are now probably confined to remote areas far from human habitation.

Wild Cat
TOP: Individual with tawny pelage, Ngorongoro CA (Tanzania); BOTTOM: (South Africa)

Lion

Panthera leo

SWAHILI: Simba

A very large cat with a tan-brown coat and white underparts. Adult males have large manes extending around the neck, from the forehead to the shoulder blades, and between the front legs. Mane colour ranges from light to dark brown, or black in some older males. Male Lions without manes have been recorded in the Tarangire and Ruaha ecosystems. Cubs have light spotting, and adults may also have faint spots on the underparts and the inner sides of the legs. The tail is long with a distinct black tuft at the tip. The nose colour of adult male Lions changes from pink to black when they are approximately five years old.

Subspecies
P. l. nubicus: only subspecies found in Tanzania.

Similar species
Both the Leopard (*page 132*) and the Cheetah (*page 122*) have distinctly spotted coats.

Ecology and social behaviour
Lions are found in a wide range of habitats including savanna grassland, bushland, woodland and forest. They take a broad range of prey, from duikers (*pages 194–202*) and gazelles (*pages 212–214*) up to buffalos (*page 180*) and occasionally Giraffes (*page 178*) and young Elephants (*page 38*). They also frequently scavenge from other predators, and may kill livestock, including cattle. Although hunting can take place at any time of day, most activity is at night. Females do much of the hunting, although males will frequently cooperate when catching larger prey. Lions live in prides of closely related females, usually with 3–10 adult females a nd 1–3 adult males, although prides of up to 39 animals led by 'coalitions' of 7–9 males have been reported. Male 'coalitions' can comprise both related and unrelated animals. Pride members frequently split into smaller groups or move alone within the home range. Males taking over a new pride will usually kill all of the cubs, thereby ensuring paternity of the new offspring. Pride home ranges are

Vulnerable	
HB:	M 190–250 cm (75–98")
	F 160–190 cm (63–75")
Ht:	90–120 cm (35–47")
Tail:	70–95 cm (27–37")
Wt:	M 150–270 kg (330–600 lb)
	F 90–190 kg (200–420 lb)

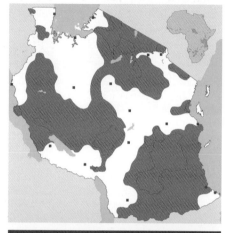

Where to look
The best place to see Lions is in the Ngorongoro Crater and on the Serengeti plains, where the short grass and good visibility make them relatively easy to find. They can also be seen regularly in several other National Parks including Ruaha, Mikumi and Tarangire.

25–225 km² (10–85 mi²), depending on prey density.

Distribution in Tanzania
Lions are still widely distributed across Tanzania. They are found in all mainland National Parks with the exception of Gombe NP, where they are extinct, and Arusha and Kitulo NPs, where vagrant animals are occasionally recorded. There are also populations on village land across much of the Maasai Steppe, Lake Natron, Singida Region, southern Tanzania, and parts of coastal Tanzania. Lion sightings are still reported from areas of high human habitation, including close to major cities; in November

2012 a Lion killed a goat at Ras Dege, just south of Dar es Salaam. Lions in these areas are not resident, and are typically transient young males dispersing from protected areas, in the latter case the Selous GR.

Population size and conservation status

There are estimated to be approximately 15,000 Lions in Tanzania. While still is the largest population in Africa, this figure is significantly less than it was just two decades ago. The highest numbers are in the Selous ecosystem followed by Serengeti NP, which has around 3,000 animals. Other important populations include the Ruaha–Rungwa ecosystem with 1,450, and the Tarangire ecosystem with 400–600 individuals.

The majority (80%) of Lions occur within National Parks and Game Reserves, with the remainder on community land.

Its reputation for livestock depredation (real or perceived), leads to many Lions being killed in retaliation. Other threats to Lion populations include loss of habitat, declines in prey populations, disease, and the use of their bones in Chinese medicine.

Lion
Male and female, Ngorongoro CA

Leopard

Panthera pardus

SWAHILI: Chui

A large cat with a distinctly spotted coat. The background pelage is yellow or golden-yellow, and the underparts are white. The spots on the back, sides, and top of the legs are rosette-shaped, with broken circles of black spots on the outside and brown on the inside. There are solid black spots on the lower half of the legs, head, neck and belly. The tail is long, with black rosettes or spots above and white below. Melanistic individuals have been recorded.

Subspecies
P. p. pardus: Tanzania mainland.
P. p. adersi: Zanzibar (probably extinct).

Similar species
The Cheetah (*page 122*) has a more upright stance, solid black spots across the body, and a smaller head with black 'tear lines' running from the eyes to the cheek. Servals (*page 126*) are much smaller and have a short tail.

Ecology and social behaviour
Leopards occupy a very diverse range of habitats, including forests, woodland, swamps, mountain ranges, and urban areas. They eat a wide variety of food including beetles, rodents, hares, primates, birds, carrion, and medium-sized to large ungulates. Prey is often stashed in trees to feed on at a later time. Leopards are solitary, although mating pairs or females with one or two cubs are sometimes seen together. Home range sizes of 16–18 km² (6–7 mi²) were recorded in the Serengeti NP and 25–135 km² (10–50 mi²) in Piti GR in western Tanzania, but are often much smaller in isolated forest patches. Several female ranges may overlap with the range of one male. Leopards are mostly nocturnal, although in areas of low human disturbance they are frequently active throughout the day.

Distribution in Tanzania
Leopards are widely distributed across Tanzania and have the broadest range of any of the large cat species. They occur in all mainland National Parks except Gombe NP,

Near Threatened	
HB:	90–140 cm (35–55")
Ht:	70 cm (27")
Tail:	50–80 cm (20–31")
Wt:	M 34–70 kg (75–155 lb) | F 20–42 kg (45–90 lb)

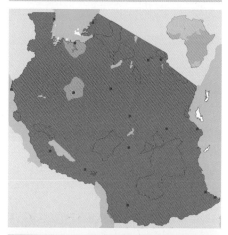

Where to look
Leopards are frequently sighted around the Seronera area in the central Serengeti NP. Drive along the riverine areas and scan the *Acacia* and *Kigelia* trees bordering the rivers, particularly at dawn or dusk. Leopards are also regularly, although less reliably, seen along the main river in Ruaha NP and around Silale Swamp in Tarangire NP, particularly during the dry season. Although Leopards are common in many parts of Tanzania, their cryptic habits means they are seldom seen outside protected areas.

where they are now extinct, and Rubondo NP. They are also found in all Game Reserves and Nature Reserves, and many of the larger Forest Reserves around the country. Their secretive nature allows them to live in close proximity to humans, including in and around large cities such as Dar es Salaam and Arusha, where they occasionally prey on domestic dogs.

Population size and conservation status
Leopards in Tanzania are common or abundant in many protected areas and on

community lands with low human density. Particularly high densities have been recorded in submontane or montane forest areas, with camera trap surveys showing that they are abundant in the forests of Gelai Mountain, the Ngorongoro CA, and Mahale NP. They are also common in Tarangire NP, where densities of 8 animals per 100 km² (21 animals per 100 mi²) were recorded.

The species is uncommon, but widespread, in much of the coastal area. It is now extinct on Zanzibar, where the last confirmed sighting was in the 1980s, although there is some evidence of its continued existence until the mid-1990s. Threats to Leopards include persecution (poisoning or trapping) for killing livestock, and accidental capture in snares set for other animals. Their skins are sometimes used for charms or in traditional medicine.

Leopard
TOP: (Botswana); BOTTOM: Tarangire NP (Tanzania)

Common Genet

Genetta genetta

Small-spotted Genet

SWAHILI: Kanu

The Common Genet has a small head, long ears, and a relatively long tail. The background coat colour is whitish-grey and the spots are small, rusty-coloured or black. There is a large strip of black hairs on its back that can be raised into a crest when alarmed. The rear of its legs are black and the tip of the tail is white.

Subspecies
G. g. dongola: only subspecies found in Tanzania.

Similar species
The Common Genet overlaps with the Large-spotted Genet (*page 138*) across much of its range, although the Large-spotted Genet is absent from very dry areas, notably Ndutu and the area between Lake Natron, West Kilimanjaro and Mkomazi NP. The Large-spotted Genet has larger, bi-coloured spots, a black tip to its tail and little or no black on the hind legs. The Common Genet may overlap with the Miombo Genet (*page 140*) at the western and southern edges of its range; the latter can be distinguished by the black inner thighs on its hind legs. The Miombo Genet usually has a black tip to its tail (see comparative photographs, *page 262*).

Ecology and social behaviour
The Common Genet is found in open woodlands, semi-arid bushland and rocky outcrops, in areas with annual rainfall of less than 680 mm (27"). It avoids areas with dense vegetation, such as forests and moist miombo woodland. This species frequents areas of human habitation and may be commonly found in settlements and towns where there is some vegetation cover. It is nocturnal and mainly solitary, although occasionally seen in pairs. Its diet consists mainly of small mammals, but also reptiles, amphibians, birds, invertebrates and fruit.

Distribution in Tanzania
In Tanzania, this species' distribution is closely associated with the *Acacia–Commiphora*

Least Concern	
HB:	46–51 cm (18–20")
Ht:	15–20 cm (6–8")
Tail:	40–52 cm (16–20")
Wt:	1·4–2·6 kg (3–6 lb)

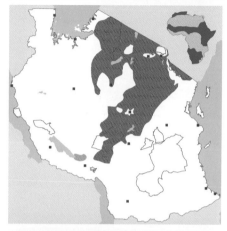

Where to look
Ndutu Safari Lodge in the Ngorongoro CA offers excellent opportunities to see this species – many individuals can be seen on the beams of the dining room in the early evening. It is also frequently seen on night drives in Tarangire and Manyara NPs, and on Manyara Ranch and Ndarakwai Ranch.

bushland. In northern Tanzania, it is found in the Serengeti NP and Maswa GR, Ngorongoro CA (but not in the Ngorongoro Crater itself), Tarangire, Manyara, and Mkomazi NPs, and the low-lying areas of Arusha NP. In the south of its range it is found in the Ruaha ecosystem, and there are historical records from the southern end of Lake Rukwa; it is absent from most of western and southern Tanzania.

Population size and conservation status
The total population size is unknown. The only density estimate for this species comes from the southern Serengeti where there were an estimated 1·5 individuals per km² (4 individuals per mi²). This species

is abundant in Tarangire NP and common in the drier areas of northern Tanzania including much of the Maasai Steppe, Lake Natron, West Kilimanjaro and Mkomazi NP. It is also common in the eastern section of Ruaha NP and the surrounding WMAs. Domestic dogs and vehicle traffic occasionally kill Common Genets and it is also hunted in some areas; however, the population is large and probably stable.

Common Genet
Ngorongoro CA

Servaline Genet

Genetta servalina

SWAHILI: Kanu

The Servaline Genet has short fur and numerous spots aligned tightly together over a light grey or yellow background, giving it a dark appearance. The spots are generally black, although occasionally the top two rows on the upper back are black with pale brown centres. The tail has 8–12 white and black rings, the black rings being double the width of the white rings, and the tip of the tail is pale. It has a narrow face, relatively long legs, and no dorsal crest.

Subspecies
G. s. lowei: mainland Tanzania.

G. s. archeri: Zanzibar.

Similar species
Easily distinguished from the Large-spotted Genet (*page 138*) and Miombo Genet (*page 140*) by its very tight spot pattern and the wide black rings on its tail (see comparative photographs, *page 262*). It is the only genet found on Zanzibar, and is also the only genet recorded in the upper levels of the forest in the Uluguru Mountains during camera trap surveys.

Ecology and social behaviour
Found in dense forest in areas of high rainfall, usually in excess of 1,800 mm (71") per year. On Zanzibar, it inhabits dense lowland forest and coral rag, while on the mainland it is generally restricted to montane forest above an altitude of 1,000 m (3,300 ft). This species is strictly nocturnal and is usually solitary, feeding mainly on rodents. Little is known about its behaviour.

Distribution in Tanzania
On the Tanzanian mainland, the Servaline Genet is known only from the Eastern Arc Mountains, where it was rediscovered in 2002 having not been recorded for 70 years. In the Udzungwa Mountains it has been recorded from Udzungwa NP and the West Kilombero Scarp FR, and there is an old specimen record from the Dabaga area. In the nearby Mufindi forest complex it is found in the Kigogo,

Least Concern	
HB:	45–50 cm (18–20")
Ht:	18–20 cm (7–8")
Tail:	35–48 cm (14–19")
Wt:	1–2·4 kg (2–5 lb)

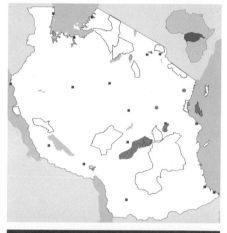

Where to look
There are no easy sites to see this species in Tanzania. Spotlighting in the forests close to the Mufindi Highland Lodge, such as the Calderara and Lulanda forests, probably offers the best option. Both forests are accessible by vehicle and on foot. Night walks on the outskirts of the Jozani Chwaka Bay NP on Zanzibar may also offer opportunities to see this species.

Lulanda, Calderara and Mufindi Scarp West forests. It is also known from the Uluguru and Nguru South Mountains, and from Amani Nature Reserve in the Usambara Mountains. On Zanzibar, the species probably occurs in most intact forests, including the Jozani Chwaka Bay NP, where it is found both in the groundwater forest and coral rag forest. It is absent from the islands of Pemba and Mafia.

Population size and conservation status
Camera trap surveys suggest the species is very common in the forests of Udzungwa NP, but uncommon in Jozani Chwaka Bay NP on Zanzibar and the Uluguru Mountains.

Its status in the forests of Mufindi is unclear, although it is probably uncommon. It is rare in the Usambara Mountains. Deforestation is the principle threat to this species, although most of the forests in its range have some level of protection. On Zanzibar, the species is hunted for its meat and pelt and numbers are likely to be dwindling rapidly. In other countries, the species has been recorded in degraded forest habitat, but its narrow ecological niche in Tanzania suggests it may be out-competed in such areas by the Large-spotted Genet.

Servaline Genet
TOP: camera trap photo, ssp. *lowei*, Uluguru Mountains; BOTTOM: camera trap photo, ssp. *lowei*, Udzungwa Mountains. This species has rarely been photographed in the wild.

Large-spotted Genet

Genetta maculata
(Genetta tigrina)

Blotched Genet, Rusty-spotted Genet

SWAHILI: Kanu

Least Concern	
HB:	42–52 cm (17–20")
Ht:	16–18 cm (6–7")
Tail:	40–53 cm (16–21")
Wt:	1·3–3·0 kg (3–7 lb)

The Large-spotted Genet has short, soft fur and little or no dorsal crest, which, if present, rises only from the lower part of the back. The background coat colour is whitish-grey or pale yellow. The top two dorsal rows of spots are generally round or square rosettes with a black exterior and brown or ochre centre. The rest of the spots are either solid black or brown. It has a continuous black dorsal stripe running the length of its back. The tip of the tail is black. Melanistic individuals are fairly common in the montane forests of northern Tanzania, the Udzungwa Mountains and occasionally the Southern Highlands.

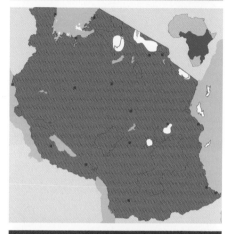

Similar species
Often confused with the Common Genet (*page 134*), which has small, uniformly coloured spots and a long tail with a white tip. The Servaline Genet (*page 136*) has many small dark spots across its body, making it appear dark, and often has a light tip to the tail. The Miombo Genet (*page 140*) has black 'socks' on its hind legs and a bushier tail (see comparative photographs, *page 262*). Large-spotted Genets that are partially melanistic, and which also have black hind legs, have been recorded in the Minziro FR, although the species does not overlap with the Miombo Genet in that part of its range.

Ecology and social behaviour
The Large-spotted Genet is found in a wide range of habitat types, including moist bushland, woodland mosaics, riverine vegetation and forest, although it avoids open grassland and arid scrubland. It is frequently found in close proximity to human habitation and may become quite tame. This species is strictly nocturnal and generally solitary, although is sometimes seen in pairs or mother–offspring groups. It feeds on a wide variety of foods including invertebrates, birds, rodents, reptiles and fruits. Foraging usually occurs on the ground although it is an excellent climber.

Where to look
Common at many lodges in the Selous GR at Lake Manze, and in forest lodges and campsites in the Udzungwa Mountains. Also seen at many lodges in Ruaha NP. Night drives in Manyara NP and on Simba Farm in West Kilimanjaro also provide good viewing opportunities. Regularly seen in the grounds of several of the lodges on the edge of the Ngorongoro Crater at night, including Gibbs Farm.

Distribution in Tanzania
Very widely distributed across Tanzania. The Large-spotted Genet is found in all of the mainland National Parks and is the only species that overlaps in range with all three other genet species. Its range overlaps with the Common Genet in Ngorongoro CA, Serengeti, Tarangire, Arusha, Mkomazi and Ruaha NPs, although the two species are generally separated by habitat: the Large-spotted Genet is found in areas of riverine forest or dense habitat, whereas the Common Genet occurs in grassland or wooded grassland. Its range overlaps

with the Servaline Genet in the lowland and submontane forest in the Udzungwa Mountains, Amani Nature Reserve and in the Nguru Mountains. The Large-spotted Genet occurs throughout the known range of the Miombo Genet. It is absent from parts of the upper montane forest in the Udzungwa and Uluguru Mountains, and from areas of dry, open savanna, including Lake Natron, West Kilimanjaro, most of Mkomazi NP and the open plains of the Serengeti. It is also absent from the islands of Zanzibar, Pemba and Mafia.

Population size and conservation status
This is the most common and widespread genet in Tanzania, and is abundant in many parts of its range. It has been recorded at high densities in many northern National Parks, as well as in Mahale NP and in the southern Selous GR. This species is very adaptable and is commonly found close to human habitation, including in big cities such as Dar es Salaam and Arusha. Large-spotted Genets are killed as retribution for attacking poultry and for use in local medicine in central and southern Tanzania.

Large-spotted Genet
TOP: camera trap photo, Ukaguru FR (Tanzania); BOTTOM: (Zambia)

Miombo Genet

Genetta angolensis

SWAHILI: Kanu

The pelage of the Miombo Genet has a light brown background colour. The throat and chest are light grey or grey-black. The mid-dorsal line is black, with three (in some cases four) distinct rows of small square, round, or irregularly shaped brown or black spots along the flanks. The last three or four spots on the rump are often fused. The tail has 7–9 dark rings and the tip is typically black, but can be white in some individuals. The guard hairs on the tail are long, sometimes giving it a bushy appearance. It has distinctive black 'socks' on the hind legs and the forelegs may also be blackish or black. Semi-melanistic individuals with all-black tails have been recorded in Tanzania.

Similar species

The Large-spotted Genet (*page 138*) lacks black on the inside of its hind legs and has shorter tail hairs. Partially melanistic Large-spotted Genets, with black hind legs, have been recorded in the Minziro FR where their range does not overlap with the Miombo Genet. The Common Genet (*page 134*) is not know to overlap in range with the Miombo Genet, although the two species may co-exist in parts of eastern Singida district. The Common Genet has a longer tail with a white tip and a paler body colour (see comparative photographs, *page 262*).

Ecology and social behaviour

The Miombo Genet is found in miombo woodland and wooded grassland, and in coastal bushland. This species is solitary and nocturnal, feeding on a wide variety of small mammals and birds, reptiles, invertebrates and probably fruits. Little is known about its behaviour, which is presumably similar to that of the Large-spotted Genet.

Distribution in Tanzania

Until recently there were very few confirmed records for this species in Tanzania. However, camera trapping surveys have greatly expanded its known range, and there are now records throughout the miombo

Least Concern	
HB:	44–48 cm (17–19")
Ht:	18–20 cm (7–8")
Tail:	38–42 cm (15–17")
Wt:	1–2 kg (2–4 lb)

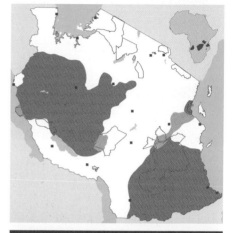

Where to look

May be observed on the outskirts of Sadaani NP, including the area around Kisampa Lodge, to the south of the Park.

woodland as far north as the Moyowosi GR. It is found in Katavi NP, and Ugalla, Swagaswaga, Lukwika, Muhuwesi GRs, Mbangala FR, and in the Selous GR, where there is one sighting record from the northern photographic area. It has been camera trapped in Rungwa GR, and is likely to be present in the west of Ruaha NP although has yet to be recorded there. It is also found in the coastal bushland around Sadaani NP and in the Rungo FR, northwest of Lindi; it probably occurs in areas of dense bushland and open woodland throughout much of the coastal zone. This species is replaced by the Large-spotted Genet in forested areas.

Population size and conservation status

The Miombo Genet occurs at low densities throughout its range, although it is widely distributed and not threatened. Camera trap surveys recorded it most frequently in the

Muhuwesi GR, the Mbarangandu WMA in the Selous ecosystem, and in Ugalla GR. Camera trap surveys have also shown the Large-spotted Genet to be, on average, three times as common as Miombo Genet where the ranges of the two species overlap. The Miombo Genet probably suffers from being killed in retribution for attacking poultry.

Miombo Genet
TOP: camera trap photo, Luganzo Open Area; BOTTOM: camera trap photo, Mlele FR.
Most known images of this species are from camera trap surveys.

African Civet
Civettictis civetta

SWAHILI: Ngawa, Paka wa Zabidi

A medium-sized carnivore with a long, shaggy coat and a stocky build. Females are usually slightly larger than males. The base coat is white or grey-white, with irregular black stripes, spots, and rings on the back and flanks. There are distinctive black and white stripes on the neck, the throat is black, and the face has a black mask. There is a dorsal crest of black hairs running from the neck to the tail. The basal half of the tail has black and white rings, and the distal half is all black. The legs are black.

Least Concern	
HB:	67–84 cm (26–33")
Ht:	35–40 cm (14–16")
Tail:	34–50 cm (13–20")
Wt:	9–13 kg (20–29 lb)

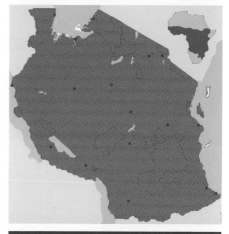

Similar species
The Small Indian Civet *Viverricula indica* (*inset opposite*), was introduced onto the islands of Zanzibar, Pemba and Mafia, and its range overlaps with that of the African Civet on Zanzibar. It has a greyish-brown coat, small black or brown spots in rows across its body, and black and white or cream stripes on the neck. It is much smaller than the African Civet, weighing 2·5–3·5 kg (5·5–8 lb), has smaller spots, and no dorsal crest. It also has black and white rings running the length of the tail, whereas the lower half of the tail of the African Civet is all black (see comparative photographs, *page 262*).

Ecology and social behaviour
African Civets are found in a large variety of habitats that offer suitable cover, including wooded grassland, montane grassland, bushland, riverine areas, cultivated land, human settlements, marshland, and both open and dense forests, up to 2,800 m (9,184 ft). Omnivorous, they feed on fruit, grass, invertebrates, reptiles, small mammals and birds, and will readily take carrion, household waste and crops. They are nocturnal and rarely seen during the day. African Civets are solitary, and their social system in the wild is poorly known. They use defecation sites called latrines or civetries, which might be associated with territorial boundary marking, although it is unclear whether

Where to look
African Civets often walk on roads, paths, and trails, resulting in frequent sightings when spotlighting. Good places to try are Simba Farm and Ndarakwai Ranch on West Kilimanjaro and night game drives in Manyara NP and on the outskirts of Serengeti NP. They are also frequently seen on Madete Beach in Saadani NP.

both or either sex is territorial. Civetries are very obvious and typically attended by butterflies (*Charaxes* spp.).

Distribution in Tanzania
This species is very widely distributed in Tanzania. It is known to occur in every National Park except Rubondo NP and is also present in most Game Reserves and Forest Reserves around the country. It is also found on Zanzibar but not on the islands of Pemba or Mafia. Zanzibar formerly had a flourishing trade in civet musk, which was used in the perfume industry, so it is possible this species was introduced to the Island.

Population size and conservation status
This species is very common in the coastal and southern parts of the country, including Pangani, Sadaani NP, the southern Selous GR and the Selous–Niassa corridor. It is also common in Ugalla GR, the Southern Highlands, Udzungwa Mountains, Maswa GR, the lower slopes of Mount Kilimanjaro, and on Zanzibar. Density records for the Serengeti NP have been estimated at 1 animal per 10 km² (3 animals per 10 mi²). The population of African Civets in Tanzania is likely to be stable, although it is hunted in some areas, including the Southern Highlands. This species benefits from its highly varied diet and its adaptability to a human environment, where it may also profit from lower competition by other predators.

African Civet
TOP: (Sierra Leone); BOTTOM: (South Africa); INSET AT TOP: **Small Indian Civet** (India)

Spotted Hyaena

Crocuta crocuta

SWAHILI: Fisi

A large, muscular hyaena, with sandy-brown upperparts that are covered in black or dark brown spots, and paler underparts. The muzzle is black and hairless. Females are generally 10% larger than males and have an elongated clitoris, similar to the male penis, making it difficult to distinguish the sexes. The tail is short with a black tassel at the tip. Juvenile Spotted Hyaenas often have black legs.

Similar species
The Striped Hyaena (*page 146*) has distinct stripes on the body and pointed, rather than rounded, ears.

Ecology and social behaviour
Found in a wide variety of habitats including grassland, woodland, lowland, and montane forest. A social species, this hyaena lives in multi-male and multi-female clans, with females socially dominant to males. Clan size varies with food availability, ranging from four up to 80 individuals in areas with abundant food. Clan territory size in East Africa is typically 20–60 km² (8–23 mi²). Clan members frequently split into subgroups or travel alone, although they all raise their cubs in communal dens. Spotted Hyaenas have highly varied diets, feeding predominantly on medium- and large-sized ungulates, including Common Wildebeest (*page 238*), Plains Zebra (*page 170*), hartebeest (*pages 234* and *236*) and Thomson's Gazelle (*page 212*), although they will also eat fruits, small mammals, carrion and human refuse. They have massive, powerful jaws that allow them to chew bones. Spotted Hyaena dung is green when fresh and turns white when dry from the calcium of digested bones. They are mostly nocturnal or active at dawn and dusk. Spotted Hyaenas have a distinctive whooping call that is individually recognizable by other clan members. This call serves to bring clan members together or as a form of display, particularly by high-ranking individuals.

Least Concern	
HB:	125–180 cm (49–71")
Ht:	80–87 cm (31–34")
Tail:	22–30 cm (9–12")
Wt:	45–80 kg (100–175 lb)

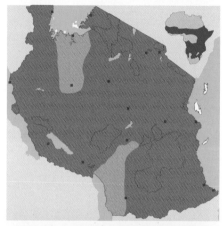

Where to look
Spotted Hyaenas can be reliably seen in the Ngorongoro Crater and on the short-grass plains between the Serengeti and Ngorongoro. They are also commonly seen in the savanna grassland and riverine areas in Ruaha NP, on the edges of the floodplains in Katavi NP, and in open areas in Mikumi NP.

Distribution in Tanzania
The Spotted Hyaena is extremely widespread in Tanzania. It is found in all mainland National Parks with the exception of Gombe and Kitulo, where it is now extinct, and Rubondo NP. It also occurs in all of the Game Reserves. It is one of the few species of large predator that survives in close proximity to human settlement, including on the outskirts of Arusha and Dar es Salaam.

Population size and conservation status
This species is very common in Tanzania. There are believed to be 7,200–7,700 animals in the Serengeti ecosystem, where densities up to 2 individuals per km² (5 individuals per mi²)

have been recorded in the Ngorongoro Crater. The Spotted Hyaena is also abundant in the Selous GR and the northern Selous–Niassa corridor. Density estimates for the tourism area in the north of the Game Reserve were estimated at 0·3 animals per km^2 (1 per mi^2) in 1996, and there are probably over 10,000 individuals in the entire Game Reserve. Camera trapping has shown that the Spotted Hyaena is also abundant in Arusha NP, Gelai Mountain, and Tarangire NP, and is very common in Ugalla, Swagaswaga, Moyowosi and Burigi–Biharamulo GRs. The species is also common in Katavi, Ruaha, and Mikumi NPs. Populations in most of the protected areas are probably stable. Threats include poisoning and snaring, with snares set for ungulates causing high hyaena mortality in the Serengeti NP.

Spotted Hyaena
Serengeti NP

Striped Hyaena

Hyaena hyaena

SWAHILI: Fisi Milia, Fisi Miraba

A hyaena with long, shaggy hair, a large head and a back that slopes down to the hindquarters. The fur is white or grey-white, with vertical black stripes on the body and horizontal stripes on the legs. There is a black patch on the throat and a long crest that runs from the top of the neck to the tail. The muzzle is hairless. The ears are long and pointed at the tip and the tail is bushy and usually white at the tip. Males are slightly larger than females.

Similar species
The Aardwolf (*page 148*) looks like a small Striped Hyaena, although the body is light brown, it lacks a black throat patch, and the lower half of the tail is black rather than white. The Striped Hyaena's head and jaw are much heavier (see comparative photographs, *page 264*).

Ecology and social behaviour
Striped Hyaenas occur in dry, open habitat or *Acacia* bushland up to an altitude of 3,300 m (10,800 ft). Although mainly a carrion scavenger, they also feed on small vertebrates, invertebrates and fruits, as well as human refuse and vegetable matter. Their powerful jaws also allow them to crush bones. There are reports of them taking sheep and goats in Tanzania, although this behaviour is rare. They are solitary when foraging, although they often rest in pairs or in small groups usually consisting of one female and one to three males. During conflicts with other individuals, Striped Hyaenas will often erect their long mane hairs, which can make their body size appear over 30% larger than usual. Striped Hyaenas are non-territorial. Home range sizes for a female and male in the Serengeti were 44 km² (17 mi²) and 72 km² (28 mi²), respectively. They are active throughout the night, with activity peaks between 10:00 p.m. and midnight, although they may be encountered in the early morning or late afternoon. Striped Hyaenas are generally silent, and are not known make the 'whooping' calls typical of the Spotted Hyaena (*page 144*).

Near Threatened	
HB:	100–120 cm (39–47")
Ht:	65–80 cm (25–31")
Tail:	23–35 cm (9–14")
Wt:	25–35 kg (55–77 lb)

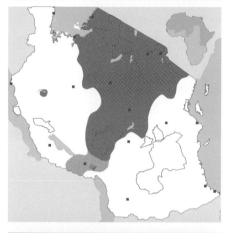

Where to look
Frequently encountered at Kisima Ngeda Lodge and campsite near Lake Eyasi, usually in the early morning or late afternoon. They can be seen daily when denning, which generally occurs between December and March. Three days at the Lodge is usually sufficient to see this species. Other good areas to look are the short-grass plains around Ndutu, Naabi Hill, Kusini Camp and Olduvai Gorge in the Serengeti ecosystem, and on night drives on Manyara Ranch.

Distribution in Tanzania
Restricted to the north and central parts of the country, where it is closely associated with the *Acacia–Commiphora* bushland. It is found throughout the Serengeti ecosystem, with most records from southern Serengeti NP and western Ngorongoro CA, and is widespread across Lake Natron, West Kilimanjaro, Tarangire NP, the Maasai Steppe and Mkomazi NP. It also occurs around Arusha city and the Kilimanjaro International Airport. There are records from Dodoma, and it is

found in Ruaha NP, Rungwa GR and the surrounding WMAs. There are local names for this species from the Ufipa Plateau and Lake Rukwa, suggesting its historical presence in these areas. There is an historical record from the Songwe Valley, east of Mbeya, and villagers living around the Kitulo NP and Mount Rungwe have reported seeing Striped Hyaena, although these sightings have not yet been confirmed. There is a camera trap record of the species from Luganzo in western Tanzania. Records of Striped Hyaenas wandering through the streets of Dar es Salaam are almost certainly of escapees from captive populations.

Population size and conservation status
This species occurs at low densities throughout its range. Estimates from the Serengeti

ecosystem suggest a population of 100–1,000 individuals. A camera trap survey found that it is very common around Gelai Mountain. It is also common in the dry bushland in the Yaeda Valley, Lake Natron, West Kilimanjaro and Manyara Ranch. It is uncommon in Tarangire NP, the Maasai Steppe, and is rare in the Ruaha ecosystem and Mkomazi NP. Nothing is known about population trends, but it is probably stable in its strongholds in the Lake Natron and Serengeti ecosystems. Being mainly carrion eaters, Striped Hyaenas are not actively persecuted by humans, although their scavenging habits make them very vulnerable to incidental poisoning, even if they are not the intended target. They are also vulnerable to snaring, probably because they are attracted to the cries of animals caught in nearby snares.

Striped Hyaena
Serengeti NP

Aardwolf

Proteles cristata

SWAHILI: Fisi ya Nkole, Fisi Mdogo

A small, jackal-sized hyaena. The body is yellowish or tan with vertical black stripes on the back and sides and horizontal stripes across the legs. The feet are black. There is a prominent mane running from the neck to the base of the tail. The hairs on the mane are tan at the base, tipped with black, and 15–20 cm (6–8") long. The tail is bushy, with the basal half the same colour as the body and the remainder black.

Subspecies
P. c. septentrionalis: only subspecies found in Tanzania.

Similar species
The Striped Hyaena (*page 146*) is nearly twice as large, has a comparatively larger and heavier head and a distinct black throat patch. It has a white tail (tipped black in some cases) that reaches halfway down its hind legs. The tail of the Aardwolf is proportionally longer, reaching two-thirds of the way down the hind legs, and the lower half is black (see comparative photographs, *page 264*).

Ecology and social behaviour
The Aardwolf is found in open grassland and bushland in arid areas. In East Africa, it relies on one species of harvester termite (*Trinervitermes bettonianus*) as its main prey, and its distribution is closely tied to the availability of this food source. In the wet season, when *Trinervitermes* are less active, other termites, particularly from the genera *Odontotermes* and *Macrotermes*, supplement their diet. The Aardwolf feeds by licking the termites off the soil surface and may consume as many as 300,000 termites in one night. It is mostly solitary and nocturnal, which is when its prey is active. This species is monogamous and forms stable adult pairs that share a territory with their most recent offspring. Average territory size in East Africa is 1·5 km² (0·6 mi²).

Least Concern	
HB:	65–80 cm (26–31")
Ht:	45–50 cm (18–20")
Tail:	19–28 cm (7–11")
Wt:	8–14 kg (18–31 lb)

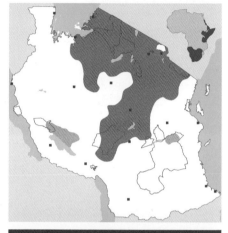

Where to look
Probably the best opportunity to see this species is on night drives on Manyara Ranch, where they are seen on average once every two nights. They are also occasionally seen in Ruaha NP in the mornings and in Serengeti NP around Gol and Simba Kopjes, Seronera and Soit Lemoytoni, although sightings here are uncommon.

Distribution in Tanzania
The Aardwolf occurs predominantly in *Acacia–Commiphora* bushland, and is most widespread in areas with less than 700 mm (28") of annual rainfall. It is found in the Ngorongoro CA and the Serengeti, Tarangire, Manyara, Mkomazi and Ruaha NPs, and there is a road kill record from Udzungwa NP. There are single sighting records from Katavi NP, Chunya Open Area and Beho Beho in the Selous GR. It is also found in Lake Natron, West Kilimanjaro, the Yaeda Valley and the Maasai Steppe, although its southern range in the Steppe is unclear.

Population size and conservation status
The only density estimate in Tanzania is from central Tarangire NP where 0·9 animals per km² (2 animals per mi²) were recorded. It is most common in the drier parts of the country. Camera trap surveys have shown it to be abundant around Gelai Mountain, common in Mkomazi NP, fairly common around Maswa GR, Ruaha NP and the adjacent Lunda WMA, and uncommon in the Maasai Steppe. The main threat to Aardwolves is poisoning, particularly from agricultural pesticides, including large-scale spraying for locust and African Armyworm *Spodoptera exempta*. Population trends are unknown, although studies suggest that grazing by livestock at medium intensity might increase termite densities and benefit Aardwolves.

Aardwolf
TOP: (Kenya); BOTTOM LEFT: (Botswana); BOTTOM RIGHT: camera trap photo of startled individual showing erect mane, Tarangire NP (Tanzania).

Marsh Mongoose
Atilax paludinosus

Water Mongoose

SWAHILI: Nguchiro Maji

A large, heavy-bodied mongoose with a long, shaggy, dark brown coat, sprinkled with black guard hairs. The head is usually paler than the back, with a distinctive pale lower lip. The tail is bushy at the base and strongly tapered at the tip, and is usually carried low to the ground. The toes are long with no webbing, allowing them to spread in soft mud. There are five toes on each foot, although the first digit is very small and often absent in tracks. It walks with its head down giving it a characteristic hunched appearance.

Similar species

The Bushy-tailed Mongoose (*page 152*) is a similar colour but is smaller, has shorter fur, and a distinctive bushy tail that does not taper at the tip. Meller's Mongoose (*page 162*) has longer legs and has long, black guard hairs along the length of its tail (see comparative photographs, *page 263*). Long spreading toes are characteristic of Marsh Mongoose tracks.

Ecology and social behaviour

Marsh Mongooses are found in a variety of habitats but seldom far from water sources, usually bordered by dense vegetation. Favourite haunts are marshes, riverbeds and estuaries, and they are also common in montane forest with high rainfall. They are excellent swimmers and divers. Marsh Mongooses are solitary and predominantly nocturnal. They feed on a wide range of prey including crabs, snails, rodents, frogs, and birds, and will also consume carrion.

Distribution in Tanzania

This species is very widely distributed in Tanzania and probably occurs wherever there is permanent water or suitable habitat with high rainfall. It is known from every mainland National Park except Mahale NP, where it has probably been overlooked. It is also found throughout the Selous ecosystem and occurs in many of the Eastern Arc Mountain forests,

Least Concern	
HB:	48–64 cm (19–25")
Ht:	18–20 cm (7–8")
Tail:	31–41 cm (12–16")
Wt:	2–5 kg (4–11 lb)

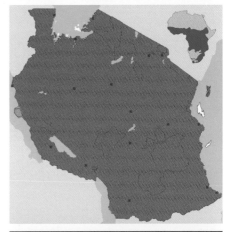

Where to look

Despite being widespread, this species is seldom seen because of its mainly nocturnal habits. A good site is Kisima Ngeda Lodge and the adjacent campsite at Lake Eyasi. Several individuals have become habituated there, and they are frequently seen behind the Lodge kitchen in the late afternoon and in the reed beds by the permanent springs in the early morning or after dark.

including the Usambara, Uluguru, Ukaguru, Udzungwa and Mahenge Mountains, and around the Mufindi highlands, Mount Rungwe, and the Livingstone Mountains. It is also found on Pemba Island but not the islands of Zanzibar or Mafia.

Population size and conservation status

No population figures are available for Marsh Mongoose. It is common in the marshland ecosystems of Tanzania including the Moyowosi and Malagarasi. It was camera trapped frequently in the river system in Majegeja in the Selous–Niassa corridor and is probably common across the Selous ecosystem. It is reported as being common on Pemba Island. The main threat to this species is loss of habitat, particularly the draining of marshes and wetlands, and pollution of water sources.

Marsh Mongoose
TOP and BOTTOM: Lake Eyasi

Bushy-tailed Mongoose

Bdeogale crassicauda

SWAHILI: Nguchiro Kijivu, Chonjwe

A medium-sized mongoose with a very bushy tail and four toes on the front and hind feet. Coat colour is usually black or dark brown, less commonly light brown or orange. Both dark and light colour forms can occur in the same area (in Burigi GR they have been photographed at the same camera trap). The legs and guard hairs on the tail are always black, and the tail is usually bushy along its entire length.

Subspecies

B. c. puisa: mainland Tanzania.

B. c. tenuis: Zanzibar.

B. c. omnivora: Sokoke Bushy-tailed Mongoose. Possibly northeast Tanzania; slightly smaller than *B. c. puisa*. Some references list this as a full species, but it is treated in this text as a subspecies due to a high level of individual variation in coat pattern.

Similar species

The Marsh Mongoose (*page 150*) has a tapered rather than a bushy tail and has a light-coloured lower lip. The Meller's Mongoose (*page 162*) is similar in colour to the light form of the Bushy-tailed Mongoose, but is significantly larger and has longer hind legs (see comparative photographs, *page 263*).

Ecology and social behaviour

Bushy-tailed Mongooses are found in areas of dense vegetation, including lowland and montane forests, groundwater forest, thick bushland, coral rag thicket, and dense miombo woodland. They are mostly insectivorous, but also eat small rodents, amphibians and reptiles. They are solitary and almost strictly nocturnal.

Distribution in Tanzania

Until recently this species was originally known only from a few records on the Tanzanian mainland, mostly in the south and coastal areas and from a few forests

Least Concern	
HB:	39–42 cm (16–17")
Ht:	18–20 cm (7–8")
Tail:	22–26 cm (9–10")
Wt:	1·3–2·0 kg (3–4 lb)

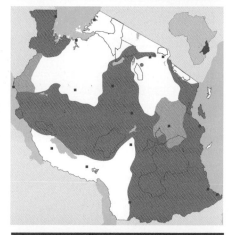

Where to look

Bushy-tailed Mongooses are seen fairly regularly on night drives in Manyara NP, particularly in the bushland areas. On Zanzibar they may be encountered at night at the rubbish tip near the National Park headquarters at Jozani Chwaka Bay NP. Individuals are also occasionally seen in the evening around campsites in the Udzungwa NP.

in the Eastern Arc Mountains. However, camera trapping surveys have shown that in fact it is widely distributed across the country and occurs in most areas of thick bushland, woodland or forest. In the Eastern Arc Mountains it is known from the Pare, Usambara, Ukaguru, Uluguru north, Nguru and Udzungwa Mountains, where it was recorded up to an atitude of 1,850 m (6,650 ft). It has also been recorded in the forests of Arusha, Manyara, and Mahale NPs, Ngorongoro CA, and the mountains around Babati. There are recent records from the Burka Forest in Arusha and from riverine forest due east of Tarangire NP. It is widespread in areas of dense miombo woodland including the southern Selous, Swagaswaga, and Ugalla GRs. It has also been camera trapped along riverine forest in Burigi–Biharamulo GRs. It is found throughout Pemba and Zanzibar, including in farmland around Stone Town. It has not been recorded on Mount Kilimanjaro or Mount Rungwe, although both mountains have similar habitat to other areas where the species is common.

Population size and conservation status
This mongoose is widespread and can be locally common or abundant. It occurs at highest densities in montane forest, and was the most frequently photographed species of carnivore during camera trapping surveys in Arusha and Mahale NPs and the Udzungwa Mountains. It is also common in Ufiome Forest near Babati and in the coastal forests around Pangani and Zanzibar. Densities in miombo woodland are considerably lower. There are no known threats to this species.

Bushy-tailed Mongoose
TOP: camera trap photo, ssp. *puisa*, Ufiome FR; BOTTOM: camera trap photo, ssp. *puisa*, light colour form, Burigi GR. Prior to the widespread use of camera traps in surveys, this species had seldom been photographed in the wild.

Jackson's Mongoose   *Bdeogale jacksoni*

SWAHILI: Nguchiro

A large mongoose with a grizzled grey-white or grey-brown body, black legs, a white bushy tail, and vibrant yellow on the side of the neck and throat. It has round, broad ears and a blunt muzzle.

Near Threatened	
HB:	50–57 cm (20–22")
Ht:	18–20 cm (7–8")
Tail:	27–34 cm (11–13")
Wt:	2–3 kg (4–7 lb)

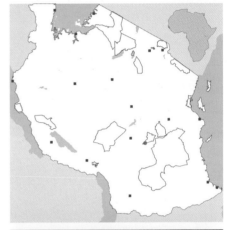

Similar species
Range overlaps with the Bushy-tailed Mongoose (*page 152*) and Marsh Mongoose (*page 150*), both of which are dark and have a black or brown rather than a white tail. The White-tailed Mongoose (*page 160*) is much larger and is not found in dense montane forest.

Ecology and social behaviour
In Kenya, Jackson's Mongoose is known from montane forest and bamboo up to an altitude of 1,700 m (5,600 ft). In Tanzania, it is only known from lowland *Anthocleista*-dominated swamp forest and groundwater forest with mixed evergreen and deciduous trees at an altitude of 300–400 m (985–1,310 ft). It feeds primarily on invertebrates, especially ants, but also eats rodents, birds, amphibians and reptiles. Analysis of stomach contents found they contained a high proportion of rodents that inhabit thick grassland and swamps, suggesting these are the preferred hunting habitats for this species. This species is solitary and strictly nocturnal, with most activity occurring between 7:00 p.m. and midnight.

Distribution in Tanzania
This species was discovered in Tanzania in 2002 during a camera trap survey of the Udzungwa Mountains. It was previously only known from forests in southeast Uganda and central and southern Kenya. It is currently only known from a small area of approximately 30 km² (11·5 mi²) within the Matundu Forest, a lowland semi-deciduous forest in the Udzungwa NP and adjacent Matundu FR and West Kilombero Nature Reserve. Jackson's Mongoose was recorded at only five of a total of 76 camera trap sites surveyed in the Udzungwa Mountains over

Where to look
This species is very difficult to observe. Currently, the best chance of seeing it in Tanzania is by spotlighting outside Udzungwa NP in the Matundu FR or West Kilombero Nature Reserve in the Udzungwa Mountains.

a period of three years, all within the Matundu Forest, suggesting that its presence in the Udzungwa Mountains is extremely localized. During the same survey, villagers also reported the presence of a mongoose corresponding to the description of Jackson's Mongoose at the edge of bamboo forest at 1,700 m (5,600 ft) in Kihulula, Mwanihana Forest in the east of the National Park, although this record has not yet been verified. It is likely that more populations will be discovered with further camera trapping surveys in appropriate habitat types within the Eastern Arc Mountains.

Population size and conservation status
A total of 25 camera trap pictures were taken of Jackson's Mongooses at the five sites where it was recorded, suggesting that it is locally

common within its very narrow range. However, such a small population will be vulnerable to stochastic environmental events, such as a disease outbreak or a large fire.

At least part of the Matundu Forest lies within the Udzungwa NP, which has a high level of protection.

Jackson's Mongoose
TOP and BOTTOM: camera trap photos, Udzungwa Mountains.
This species has rarely been photographed in the wild.

Egyptian Mongoose
Herpestes ichneumon

Large Grey Mongoose, Ichneumon Mongoose
SWAHILI: Nguchiro Mkubwa, Karasa

Least Concern	
HB:	50–60 cm (20–24")
Ht:	19–20 cm (7")
Tail:	43–60 cm (17–24")
Wt:	2·4–4·0 kg (5–9 lb)

A large, grizzled grey mongoose with a relatively long head and body and short legs. The face and legs are black, and the tail is long and tapered with a conspicuous black tuft at the tip. The fur on the hindquarters and hind legs is long. When running it has a distinctive smooth, gliding gait and keeps very low to the ground, often concealing its legs. It usually keeps its tail down when it moves. This is the largest diurnal mongoose.

Similar species
The Slender Mongoose (*page 158*) has a similar body shape but is much smaller and has no black on the legs and shorter fur. The Marsh Mongoose (*page 150*) is dark brown, smaller and has a much shorter tail. Other similar-sized mongooses such as the White-tailed Mongoose (*page 160*) and Meller's Mongoose (*page 162*) are nocturnal (see comparative photographs, *page 263*).

Ecology and social behaviour
Widely distributed in savanna habitats, although closely associated with riparian habitat, including the edge of rivers, swamps, lakes, and reed beds. It has been recorded in lowland forest at an altitude of 2,000 m (6,600 ft) on Mount Kilimanjaro, although it is not usually a forest species. Strictly diurnal, in Tanzania it is usually solitary or occasionally seen in pairs. This species is most active in the late morning and early afternoon, feeding on a variety of foods including birds, frogs, reptiles, crabs, rodents and invertebrates. It is capable of killing large snakes and has been found to be little affected by the venom of some snake species.

Distribution in Tanzania
It is widely distributed in the north, central, southwest and coastal areas of the country. There are few records from miombo woodland in the west of the country, although it is known from Katavi NP, Lukwati GR and

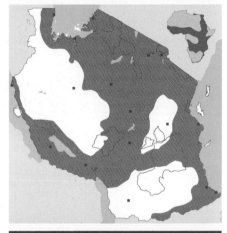

Where to look
The Egyptian Mongoose can occasionally be seen in the Serengeti NP, particularly around Simba and Moru Kopjes in the south. It can also be found around Silale Swamp in Tarangire NP during the early morning and late afternoon. Most views of this species are brief glimpses as it crosses between areas of dense vegetation.

Lake Rukwa. There is also a record from just north of Mahale NP. It is found in the Ngorongoro CA, Serengeti, Tarangire, Kilimanjaro, Mkomazi, Gombe and Ruaha NPs, and the Selous GR and Kilombero Valley. It is also known from Mount Rungwe, and although there are no records for Kitulo NP, it is likely to occur there.

Population size and conservation status
There are no population figures for Tanzania, although it is uncommon in most areas. This species was rarely recorded during camera trap surveys across the country, probably a result of naturally low densities

156

and infrequent use of wildlife paths. It is fairly common in the cultivated land along the lower slopes of Mount Kilimanjaro, and in southern Serengeti NP. It is uncommon in the highlands of Mbeya and rare in the Selous GR and southern Tanzania.

Egyptian Mongoose
TOP: Serengeti NP (Tanzania); BOTTOM: (Kenya)

157

Slender Mongoose

Herpestes sanguineus

SWAHILI: Nguchiro Mwembamba, Kicheche

Least Concern	
HB:	27–34 cm (11–13")
Ht:	10–12 cm (4–5")
Tail:	20–30 cm (8–12")
Wt:	280–680 g (10–24 oz)

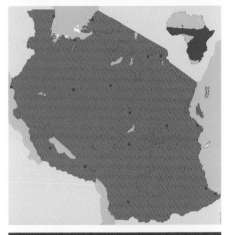

A small mongoose with a long, slender body, short legs, and a long tail with a distinctive black tuft at the tip. Males are larger and heavier than females. The short coat hair is usually reddish-brown in colour but can range from black to light yellow-brown. Melanistic individuals are common in montane forests of northern Tanzania and are sometimes also seen in savanna areas. There are faint transverse bands across the neck and back that are usually only visible at close range.

Similar species

The Egyptian Mongoose (*page 156*) is a similar shape and also has a black tip on the tail, but is much larger, has black legs, and denser fur (see comparative photographs, *page 263*). All other diurnal mongooses are social. The Small Indian Mongoose *Herpestes auropunctatus* (*pictured opposite*) is a similar-sized mongoose on Mafia Island that was introduced some time before 1958, probably to control rodents. It has a grizzled reddish to yellow-brown coat and lacks a black tip to the tail. The Slender Mongoose does not occur on Mafia Island.

Ecology and social behaviour

This species inhabits a wide range of habitats including open savanna, swamps and dense forest, and is often seen in farmland and areas of human habitation. Home ranges are approximately 50–100 ha (125–250 acres), with male territories usually overlapping with those of several females. It is one of the few mongoose species that can climb trees, which it does either chasing prey or to escape when threatened. When foraging, it trots rapidly, occasionally standing up on its hind legs to scan the surroundings. It is solitary and strictly diurnal, and is often seen moving along the edges of animal paths or roads. While walking or running, it carries its tail low with the tip of the tail erect. It feeds mostly on invertebrates but also takes small vertebrates, amphibians and reptiles.

Where to look

Slender Mongooses are seen fairly frequently around Seronera in Serengeti NP. Although common in many other protected areas, there are few places where they can be reliably seen and most sightings are brief glimpses of them crossing a road. They frequent lodge and camp rubbish pits so these can be good places to look.

Distribution in Tanzania

This is the most widely distributed mongoose in Tanzania, occurring in all parts of the country including in heavily cultivated areas and gardens in all the major towns and cities. It is known from all of the National Parks except Rubondo NP and occurs in all Game Reserves. It occurs on the islands of Zanzibar and possibly Pemba, but not Mafia.

Population size and conservation status

This species is relatively common in most parts of the country. Camera trap surveys showed high densities in Ngorongoro CA and on Gelai Mountain, and it was also common in Tarangire NP, Ufiome FR and fairly common in the Serengeti NP. Observation records suggest it is also common in much of western Tanzania. The Slender Mongoose is often killed in retaliation for preying on chickens, although its ability to adapt to areas with high human density means the population is probably stable in Tanzania.

Slender Mongoose
TOP: Arusha (Tanzania); BOTTOM: Ruaha NP (Tanzania);
INSET CENTRE: **Small Indian Mongoose** (Croatia)

White-tailed Mongoose

Ichneumia albicauda

SWAHILI: Nguchiro Mkia Mweupe

Least Concern	
HB:	47–70 cm (19–28")
Ht:	22–25 cm (9–10")
Tail:	36–48 cm (14–19")
Wt:	3–5 kg (7–11 lb)

A large mongoose with a pointed head, long hind legs and a hunched appearance. The coat is coarse, the body is a grizzled grey or grey-brown colour and the legs are black. The tail is bushy and grizzled grey at the base, tapering to white at the tip. There is one record of an individual with a black, rather than white, tail from Lake Eyasi in northern Tanzania – a colour form that is common in West Africa and parts of Uganda.

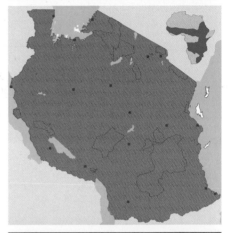

Subspecies
I. a. ibeana: only subspecies found in Tanzania.

Similar species
Jackson's Mongoose (*page 154*), which was recently discovered in the Udzungwa Mountains, is a similar colour, although it is smaller, has shorter hind legs, a bushy tail, and yellow on the neck and throat. In the Udzungwa Mountains the two species can also be separated by habitat: Jackson's Mongoose is found in deciduous lowland forest and White-tailed Mongoose in woodland and grassland. Meller's Mongoose (*page 162*) has a similar body shape but has a brown body and black tail with long guard hairs.

Ecology and social behaviour
The White-tailed Mongoose is found in a wide range of habitat types including open savanna, savanna woodland and farmland, and frequently around areas of human habitation. It avoids dense forest, but has been recorded in open forest in Mahale NP and the lower slopes of Mount Kilimanjaro. It is strictly nocturnal and mostly solitary, but occasionally seen in mother–offspring groups. Home range size in the Serengeti NP is approximately 1 km² (less than 0·5 mi²). Both males and females are territorial, although there may be considerable overlap in territories, particularly among females. It feeds predominantly on invertebrates, including termites, ants, and dung beetles, but will also prey opportunistically on small vertebrates and reptiles. It walks or trots in a distinctive zigzag pattern while foraging.

Where to look
Frequently seen on night drives on Manyara Ranch, in Tarangire NP and in West Kilimanjaro. May also be seen while spotlighting around camps on the western boundary of the Serengeti NP, and in Loliondo.

Distribution in Tanzania
Very widely distributed throughout the country, except for areas of montane woodland and grassland, and dense lowland forest. It has been reported from all mainland National Parks except Kitulo and Rubondo.

Population size and conservation status
This species is very common in the *Acacia–Commiphora* bushland in northern Tanzania. In Serengeti NP it can reach densities as high as four animals per km² (11 animals per mi²). It is abundant in Tarangire NP and common in Mkomazi and Ruaha NPs, Lake Natron, and West Kilimanjaro. It is fairly common in the west of the country, including Ugalla GR and the Rukwa Valley, and occurs at much lower densities in coastal areas, the Selous GR,

and in most of southern Tanzania. Domestic dogs around areas of human habitation often kill this species, which can cause local population extinctions. Nothing is known about population trends.

White-tailed Mongoose
TOP: Subadult (South Africa); BOTTOM: (South Africa)

Meller's Mongoose   *Rhynchogale melleri*

SWAHILI: Nguchiro

Least Concern	
HB:	44–50 cm (17–20")
Ht:	15–18 cm (6–7")
Tail:	28–40 cm (11–16")
Wt:	1·8–3·0 kg (4–7 lb)

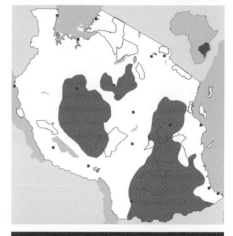

A large mongoose with a reddish-brown coat, dark brown or black feet, and a light grey-brown face. The tail is shaggy with dense black guard hairs and a light undercoat. The animal's rear haunches are raised above the shoulders and the tail is carried high at the base and then droops downwards, giving it a similar appearance to that of the White-tailed Mongoose (*page 160*). The hairs on the side of its throat grow in a reverse direction, although this is not easily visible in the field. The tail is often flared at the base when running.

Subspecies
R. m. melleri: only subspecies found in Tanzania.

Similar species
Both the Marsh Mongoose (*page 150*) and the Bushy-tailed Mongoose (*page 152*) are smaller, darker, and have shorter rear legs; neither species has white in the tail (see comparative photographs, *page 263*). The White-tailed Mongoose has a grizzled grey rather than brown body, black legs, a white tail tip, and a shorter, blunter muzzle.

Ecology and social behaviour
A solitary species found predominantly in areas of miombo woodland, particularly in open grassland within miombo. Termites form an important part of its diet, particularly *Macrotermes* and *Hodotermes* species, and its distribution may be closely associated with termitaria of these species. Little is known about its social behaviour. The Meller's Mongoose is strictly nocturnal, with camera trap records suggesting peak activity between 1:00–3:00 a.m.

Distribution in Tanzania
There are few records for this species in Tanzania, although recent camera trap surveys suggest that it is probably widespread across miombo woodland. The species has been recorded in Swagaswaga GR, in woodland west of the Itigi thicket, and in Mbarang'andu

Where to look
This mongoose is not easily seen in Tanzania. Most of the sites where it is known to occur are either hunting blocks with limited access or are isolated and difficult to reach, such as the Itigi thicket. Its strictly nocturnal behaviour adds to the challenge. Driving at night on the road between Tunduru and Masasi in southern Tanzania probably offers the best opportunity to see this species.

WMA, Lukwika GR, and Mbangala FR in the Selous–Niassa Corridor. It has also been reported from Udzungwa and Ruaha NPs. There are historical records from the 1950s from Morogoro and Mkalama, north of Singida.

Population size and conservation status
Meller's Mongoose was the most frequently recorded mongoose during a camera trap survey in the Lukwika GR, suggesting that it may be locally common in appropriate habitat, particularly in the south of the

country. It was uncommon in all other survey sites where it was recorded. There are no known threats to the species, although habitat loss in miombo woodland areas could lead to a long-term range reduction. Nothing is known about population trends.

Meller's Mongoose
TOP: Mbangala FR; BOTTOM: Lukwika FR.
These camera trap photos are two of the very few images known of this species in the wild.

Banded Mongoose

Mungos mungo

SWAHILI: Nguchiro Miraba / Milia

A medium-sized mongoose with a pointed face, a relatively short tail and long legs. The coat is shaggy, grizzled grey or grey-brown. There are 10–15 alternating dark and light (in some cases white) bands running transversely from its shoulders to the base of the tail. The feet and tip of the tail are black. Males and females are the same size.

Similar species
The only other diurnal and social mongoose in Tanzania, the Dwarf Mongoose (*page 166*), is much smaller, redder, and lacks the transverse bands.

Ecology and social behaviour
Banded Mongooses occur in a wide variety of habitats, only absent from swamps and the interior of dense forest. They are strictly diurnal and are social, living in stable groups averaging 10–20 (up to 45) individuals. There is no reproductive suppression in this species (as in Dwarf Mongoose), with all adults breeding and cooperating in rearing the young. They feed predominantly on invertebrates, but will also eat reptiles, amphibians, small mammals and fruit. They also frequent rubbish dumps around lodges or human habitation. Banded Mongooses are highly vocal, and individuals communicate constantly through a twittering call with other members of their group when foraging. When threatened, they will gather together in a tightly compact group and challenge the attacker, hissing loudly. Home range size ranges from 100–400 ha (250–1,000 acres), sometimes larger, depending on the availability of food.

Distribution in Tanzania
This species is very widespread in Tanzania. It is found in all of the mainland National Parks, with the exception of Rubondo and Kilimanjaro (although it has been recorded on the lower slopes of Mount Kilimanjaro and across West Kilimanjaro), and it also occurs in most Game Reserves. The Banded Mongoose is found in Jozani Chwaka Bay

Least Concern	
HB:	33–41 cm (13–16")
Ht:	18–20 cm (7–8")
Tail:	17–28 cm (7–11")
Wt:	1·0–1·9 kg (2–4 lb)

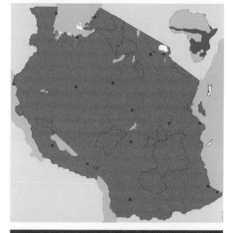

Where to look
Banded Mongooses are easily seen in many National Parks, aided by their propensity to become habituated and habit of feeding in lodge grounds. The lodges around Seronera are a particularly good place to look.

NP on Zanzibar. Its status on Pemba Island is unknown and it is absent from Mafia Island.

Population size and conservation status
The Banded Mongoose is common in most National Parks and other protected areas in Tanzania. It occurs at significantly lower densities outside protected areas, particularly in places with intensive agriculture, although it is highly adaptive and can survive in close proximity to human settlement including on the campus of the University of Dar es Salaam. In protected areas, birds of prey are probably their major predators, and Marabou Storks *Leptoptilos crumeniferus* have also been recorded killing young mongooses. The main threat to this species is habitat loss, although the population is probably stable in protected areas.

Banded Mongoose
TOP and BOTTOM: Tarangire NP

Dwarf Mongoose

Helogale parvula

SWAHILI: Kitafe

The smallest carnivore in Africa. The fur is smooth and ranges in colour from light reddish to yellowish-grey and (infrequently) dark brown. The face and ears are usually a light reddish underneath. The tail is the same colour as the body and is usually one-third to two-thirds of body length with relatively short fur that tapers evenly.

Similar species
Due to its small size and social habits, this species is unlikely to be mistaken for any of the larger mongooses. There is one unconfirmed record listed in the literature of the Somali Dwarf Mongoose *Helogale hirtula* from Mkomazi NP. This species looks very similar to the Dwarf Mongoose, but has a longer, shaggier coat with less red, and dark toes. The Somali Dwarf Mongoose has not been recorded in subsequent surveys of the National Park, and its presence in Tanzania has yet to be determined conclusively.

Ecology and social behaviour
Dwarf Mongooses are found in a wide variety of savanna and woodland habitats, although are absent from forests and montane areas. They are strictly diurnal, social animals that live in cohesive groups. In the Serengeti NP, group sizes vary from 2–21 (nine on average) adults. Groups comprise one dominant breeding pair, their offspring, and sometimes unrelated immigrants. The breeding pair suppress reproduction in other group members, and all group members help feed and care for the young. Individuals regularly make a 'peep' call to stay in contact with other pack members while foraging. Their diet is mostly invertebrates, although they occasionally feed on small vertebrates.

Distribution in Tanzania
Very widespread in Tanzania, occurring in all habitats except for montane and dense coastal forest. It is absent from Kilimanjaro, Gombe, Rubondo, Udzungwa and Kitulo NPs. There are few records for this species in southern Tanzania and no records from the

Least Concern	
HB:	16–23 cm (6–9")
Ht:	7–8 cm (3")
Tail:	14–18 cm (5–7")
Wt:	220–415 g (8–15 oz)

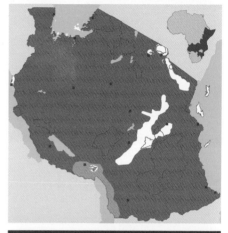

Where to look
Frequently seen in the grounds of lodges and around administration buildings in many National Parks. They are easy to see in the Serengeti around the Seronera Visitor Centre and at Seronera Wildlife Lodge, in various camps around Ruaha, such as Mwagusi and Jongomero, and in the Selous GR.

Mbeya area and the Livingstone Mountains, although there is a sighting record from the Makambako Gap.

Population size and conservation status
In appropriate habitat, such as on the Serengeti plains, Dwarf Mongoose densities can be up to 31 animals per km² (81 animals per mi²). There are no density estimates for other parts of Tanzania, but this species is common in many areas where there are large numbers of termite mounds for shelter, including Mkomazi, Tarangire, Manyara and Katavi NPs, and much of the Maasai Steppe. There are no known anthropogenic threats, beyond loss of habitat. Population trends are unknown.

Dwarf Mongoose
TOP: (Kenya); BOTTOM: Serengeti NP (Tanzania)

167

Black Rhinoceros

Diceros bicornis

SWAHILI: Kifaru

A very large, dark grey animal, with two horns on the face between the eyes and the nose. The front horn, near the nose, is generally longer (20–66 cm | 8–26" in Tanzania) than the rear horn. The skin is mostly hairless, and typically assumes the colour of the local soil as Black Rhinoceros frequently wallow in mud. The tail has a small fringe of black hair on the tip, and the edges of the ears are also lined with short, black hairs. The upper lip is pointed and used for grasping vegetation.

Subspecies

D. b. michaeli: northern Tanzania; the horn is long and curved. Often has large folds of skin on the side of the body.

D. b. minor: Selous GR; the smallest of the subspecies.

Similar species

Unlikely to be mistaken for any other mammal.

Ecology and social behaviour

Occurs in a wide variety of bushland, thicket, wooded grassland and woodland habitats. Predominantly browsers, Black Rhinoceros feed on shrubs, fruits, shoots, and leaves that they break off using their long and prehensile upper lip. They favour areas with permanent water and although generally solitary, or found in mother–offspring pairs, ten or more individuals may congregate briefly around wallows or waterholes. Like many diurnal animals, they may become increasingly nocturnal in areas of heavy poaching. Home ranges vary from 0·5–130 km² (0·2–50 mi²), depending on the quality of the habitat, with the highest densities found in areas of dense thicket. Home ranges of both sexes may overlap significantly.

Distribution in Tanzania

In the early 1960s, Black Rhinoceros were widely distributed across northern, central, and southern Tanzania, although they were absent from most of the west of the country. By the mid-1990s, uncontrolled poaching

Critically Endangered	
HB:	3–3·8 m (9–12 ft)
Ht:	1·4–1·7 m (4·6–5·58 ft)
Tail:	60 cm (24")
Wt:	850–1,400 kg (1,900–3,000 lb)

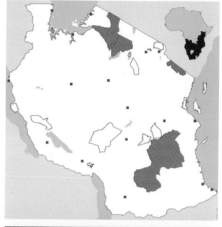

Where to look

Black Rhinoceros are most easily seen in the Ngorongoro Crater, where they are often found in the area around the Lerai Forest on the Crater floor. They are also regularly seen around Moru kopjes in the central Serengeti NP.

for their horns had decimated this species in Tanzania to such an extent that they only existed in two small populations: in the Selous GR and the Ngorongoro Crater. Since then there have been a number of re-introductions into parts of Serengeti NP and Mkomazi NP, where they are heavily protected, in some cases in fenced compounds.

Population size and conservation status

The population of Black Rhinoceros dropped precipitously in Tanzania from approximately 10,000 animals in 1970 to only 32 in 1995. It has since gradually increased to approximately 115 animals in 2010 as a result of natural births and the translocation of animals from other countries. There is little information on the status of the population in the Selous

GR, although numbers are believed to be very low, while numbers in the Ngorongoro Crater have been stable. With individual populations remaining critically low, they are vulnerable both to poaching and to stochastic events such as disease, predation and deaths resulting from fights between rivals. The demand for rhinoceros horn is so high that the survival of Black Rhinoceros in Tanzania is contingent upon 24-hour individual protection by the Tanzanian wildlife authorities. Rhinoceros horn is used in Yemen to create ornately-carved handles for ceremonial daggers, and in Asia in traditional medicine, although its reputed medicinal value has never been substantiated scientifically.

Black Rhinoceros
TOP: (Kenya); BOTTOM: female with calf (Kenya)

Plains Zebra

Equus quagga

Burchell's Zebra, Common Zebra

SWAHILI: Punda Milia

A very distinctive horse-like animal with black and white stripes across its body. The stripes on the neck and to the centre of the back are vertical, while those on the rump and legs are horizontal. It has short legs, a rounded body, relatively small ears and an erect mane. The tail is long, striped at the base, with thick black hairs at the tip.

Subspecies

E. q. boehmi: north and western Tanzania; very broad and well-defined body stripes.

E. q. chawshaii: Selous ecosystem; narrow body stripes.

Similar species

Unmistakable.

Ecology and social behaviour

Most frequently found in open and lightly wooded savanna and open scrubland with permanent water. Plains Zebras are social animals that live in small, stable harems of one male and 1–8 adult females and their offspring. The males are non-territorial and move with the family group. Large herds consist of many family groups that often move together in loose aggregations of several hundred to several thousand individuals. Home range sizes vary widely from 50 to over 600 km² (20–230 mi²). Non-harem males live in loosely aggregated bachelor herds of up to 35 animals. Zebras commonly associate with other species, particularly Common Wildebeests (*page 238*), hartebeests (*pages 234–236*) and Common Elands (*page 186*). They are almost exclusively grazers and their hindgut fermentation system allows them to feed on tougher, less nutritious grasses than other ungulates.

Distribution in Tanzania

Plains Zebras formerly occurred throughout Tanzania with the exception of the Eastern Arc and Livingstone Mountain ranges, although they are now restricted primarily to protected areas. They are found in all of the mainland

Least Concern	
HB:	220–245 cm (87–96")
Ht:	112–130 cm (44–51")
Tail:	42–50 cm (17–20")
Wt:	M 220–320 kg (480–700 lb)
	F 175–250 kg (385–550 lb)

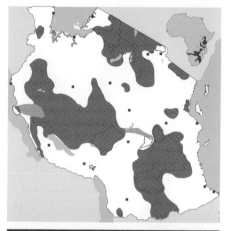

Where to look

Plains Zebras are among the most common mammals in many of Tanzania's National Parks. Sightings are guaranteed in the Serengeti NP and Ngorongoro Crater, and are very likely in Ruaha, Mikumi and Arusha NPs. In Tarangire NP they are generally absent during the wet season but very common in the dry season.

National Parks except Gombe, Udzungwa, Rubondo and Kitulo, and are also widely distributed in most of the Game Reserves, though extinct in the Ibanda–Rumanyika GRs. There are also populations in the Wami–Mbiki WMA, the Yaeda Valley, Wembere Wetland, much of the Maasai Steppe, and throughout Lake Natron and West Kilimanjaro.

Population size and conservation status

Latest counts suggest a population of nearly 250,000 Plains Zebras in Tanzania. The Serengeti ecosystem has the largest population in Africa with 160,000–200,000 individuals, equivalent to almost 30% of the global population. There are a further 10,000 zebras in the Rungwa–Ruaha ecosystem, 15,000 in the Tarangire ecosystem and 2,700 in the Katavi–Rukwa ecosystem. In 2010, 3,200 zebras were counted during an aerial total count in the Lake Natron area and a further 570 in West Kilimanjaro. In the Selous ecosystem, including the Selous GR and Mikumi NP, there are approximately 20,000 individuals of subspecies *E. q. crawshaii*. There are also small populations of 500–1,000 individuals in each of Moyowosi–Kisigo GRs, Sadaani and Mkomazi NPs.

Poaching for meat and skins poses a threat, particularly in the Tarangire and Katavi–Rukwa ecosystems where there have been significant population declines in the past ten years. Plains Zebra skins from East Africa are particularly prized as they lack the shadow stripe that is prevalent in the subspecies occurring south of the Zambezi River. Loss of migration corridors as a result of agricultural encroachment has had a negative impact on populations in the Tarangire and West Kilimanjaro ecosystems.

Plains Zebra
TOP: ssp. *boehmi*, Ngorongoro CA;
BOTTOM: ssp. *crawshaii*, Selous GR

Bushpig

Potamochoerus larvatus

SWAHILI: Nguruwe Pori / Mwitu

Least Concern	
HB:	110–154 cm (43–61")
Ht:	55–86 cm (22–34")
Tail:	30–43 cm (12–17")
Wt:	M 55–105 kg (120–230 lb)
	F 55–85 kg (120–190 lb)

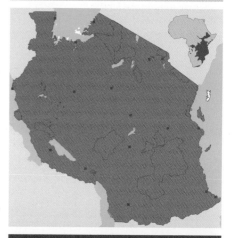

A medium-sized pig with a long muzzle. Coat colour is highly variable, ranging from light red to almost entirely black. Females and young typically have more red on the body, while older males are darker. There is a prominent dorsal crest running from the nape to the rump that is usually black-tipped with white hairs. The hairs on the body are long and coarse. The forehead is white with long white hairs on the side of the face, which are occasionally all-black in males. The lower tusks are long (up to 23 cm | 9"), although they do not protrude from the sides of the face as in Common Warthogs (*page 174*). The upper tusks are much shorter and very sharp from rubbing against the lower ones.

Subspecies

P. l. hassama: north, east and central Tanzania; has a white face.

P. l. koiropotamus: southern Tanzania; lacks contrasting black-and-white face pattern.

Similar species

Common Warthogs have grey bodies with little body hair and large, protruding warts and tusks on their faces. There are many erroneous references in the literature of Giant Forest Hog *Hylochoerus meinertzhageni* occurring in the Ngorongoro Highlands, which are based on a document that misidentified a large, dark male Bushpig. There are two reported sightings of the Giant Forest Hog from riverine forest in northwestern Serengeti in the 1970s. However, records for Tanzania have yet to be substantiated with photographs or a specimen. Feral pigs *Sus scrofa* were introduced to Pemba Island by the Portuguese in the 15th century; their current status is unknown.

Ecology and social behaviour

Bushpigs occur wherever there is dense cover and a regular water supply, including bushland, forests, reed beds, agricultural land and riparian habitat. They are omnivorous, feeding on a wide range of foods including carrion, small birds and mammals, invertebrates, fruits, grass rhizomes, tubers and crops. They use their long snouts to root through soil leaving distinctive patches of upturned vegetation. Bushpigs are mainly nocturnal, although sometimes active during the day in overcast weather. Highly gregarious, they live in groups of 4–16 individuals, led by a dominant male and female. Home ranges vary from 0·2–10 km² (0·08–4·0 mi²).

Distribution in Tanzania

Bushpigs are very widely distributed in Tanzania, occurring across the mainland. They occur in all of the National Parks, with the exception of Rubondo NP, and in all Game Reserves. They are widely reported

Where to look

Bushpigs are easily seen in the Ngorongoro CA at the staff village behind the Park headquarters at dawn or dusk. Simba campsite on the rim of Ngorongoro Crater is another good place to see them at night. Groups of Bushpigs can sometimes be seen in the Lake Mzizimia area in the Selous GR during the afternoon and at dusk, and at Mdonya Camp in Ruaha NP at night.

from agricultural areas where other mammal species have disappeared. In the south and coastal areas of the country the presence of Bushpigs has been linked with incidences of man-eating Lions (*page 130*). Bushpigs often form an important food source for Lions in areas where other large prey have been eliminated. Consequently, Lions sometimes follow them into farms and villages where they may come across (and sometimes kill) humans, who are sleeping in the fields to protect their crops from Bushpigs.

Bushpigs are present on the islands of Zanzibar and Mafia but absent from Pemba.

Population size and conservation status
There are no population estimates for Bushpigs in Tanzania, although they are common in many areas of the country and likely to number in the hundreds of thousands. They are abundant in the forests of the Ngorongoro CA and Mahale NP. Despite being widely hunted both for food and as an agricultural pest, the population is probably either stable or declining slowly.

Bushpig
TOP: male ssp. *koiropotamus* (South Africa);
BOTTOM LEFT: camera trap photo, large boar ssp. *hassama*, Swagaswaga (Tanzania);
BOTTOM RIGHT: camera trap photo, female ssp. *hassama*, Ugalla GR (Tanzania)

Common Warthog

Phacochoerus africanus

A medium-sized pig with a grey body that is sparsely covered with long bristle hairs. There is a long mane of erectile hairs running from the top of the forehead to the base of the tail. The tail is mostly naked with a small black tuft at the tip. The muzzle is long and flattened with prominent 'warts' made of thickened skin. Males have two pairs of warts: a very large pair (up to 15 cm | 6" long) below the eyes and a smaller pair on the side of the cheeks; females have only one pair of warts, below the eyes. The canine teeth develop into large, upward-curving tusks, with the upper tusk reaching 36 cm (14") long in males.

Least Concern	
HB:	110–130 cm (43–51")
Ht:	65–84 cm (26–33")
Tail:	35–50 cm (14–20")
Wt:	M 60–100 kg (230–240 lb)
	F 45–70 kg (100–150 lb)

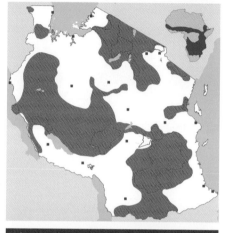

Where to look
Warthogs are easily seen in most National Parks in the north and the south of the country, and may frequently be encountered in lodge grounds.

Subspecies
P. a. massaicus: only subspecies found in Tanzania.

Similar species
The Bushpig (*page 172*) is larger, mainly nocturnal, and has a dense coat. Warthogs run with their tail held up in the air, while Bushpigs run with their tail down.

Ecology and social behaviour
Warthogs are found in open savanna grasslands, floodplains, bushland and open woodland, avoiding areas of forest and dense bush. They are principally grazers, feeding on grasses, grass rhizomes and roots, often adopting a characteristic bent-knee position when digging for food. They will also feed on fruits and tree bark, and less commonly on carrion. Females live in small groups composed of one or more related adult females and their young. Males are either solitary or associate in small bachelor groups of 2–4 males. Yearling animals also form small, transitory groups. Both males and females tend to remain in their natal home ranges, which average 165 ha (410 acres). Group home ranges overlap widely, although family groups will usually avoid each other. Strictly diurnal, Common Warthogs spend the night in burrows (often abandoned Aardvark holes) for protection. Burrows are frequently interchanged and a group may make use of up to ten on a regular basis. Warthogs are regularly preyed upon by many large carnivores, including Lions (*page 130*), Spotted Hyaenas (*page 144*) and Leopards (*page 132*). When pursued, they retreat to burrows, which they enter backwards, thereby presenting their tusks to the attacker.

Distribution in Tanzania
The Common Warthog is widely distributed in Tanzania and is recorded in all of the mainland National Parks except for Rubondo, Gombe and Kitulo; it is also present in most Game Reserves. It is now absent from most of Tabora and Mwanza Regions where much of the land has been converted to agriculture.

Population size and conservation status

There are no population estimates for this species in Tanzania. It is common in most of the National Parks and Game Reserves, and is abundant in some areas, including Tarangire and Arusha NPs. Hunting outside protected areas and habitat loss are the main threats, although the species is resilient and numbers are stable across most protected areas.

Common Warthog
TOP: male (Kenya); BOTTOM: female with young (Kenya)

Common Hippopotamus
Hippopotamus amphibius

Hippo

SWAHILI: Kiboko

A large, rotund animal with a huge head, short legs and a short tail. The hairless skin is dark grey above and pink or pinkish-grey below, with pink around the eyes and ears. There are four toes on each foot. The mouth has a very wide gape and massive incisors and lower canines. When at the surface of the water, only the nostrils, eyes and ears are visible.

Subspecies
H. a. amphibius: only subspecies found in Tanzania.

Similar species
Unlikely to be mistaken for any other mammal.

Ecology and social behaviour
The Common Hippopotamus (hereafter Common Hippo) is found in rivers, lakes and permanently flooded wetlands, where individuals may remain submerged for up to six minutes. Dispersing animals can travel long distances and in the wet season may be found far from permanent water. They feed mostly at night, spending the day wallowing or resting in water or sometimes basking on land. They are exclusively grazers, preferring short grass. Common Hippos live in herds of up to 50 individuals (known as pods), dominated by a single male that defends a narrow stretch of water of 50–500 m (160–1,650 ft) long. Non-territorial males usually form bachelor herds. Common Hippos make a very distinctive call, starting with a high-pitched note, tailing off with a long series of lower pitched grunts.

Distribution in Tanzania
Common Hippos are still widely distributed across Tanzania. There are populations in all mainland National Parks with the exception of Kilimanjaro, Mkomazi and Kitulo. For many years they were absent from Tarangire NP, until a small population re-established itself in 2007, probably from Lake Babati. Common Hippos are also found in a number of major rivers, including the Pangani, Wami, Rufiji, Ruvu and Ruvuma, and in the deltas where

Vulnerable	
HB:	2·6–4·0 m (10·2–13 ft)
Ht:	1·4–1·7 m (4·6–5·6 ft)
Tail:	40 cm (16")
Wt:	M 1,000–2,000 kg (2,200–4,400 lb)
	F 1,000–1,850 kg (2,200–4,100 lb)

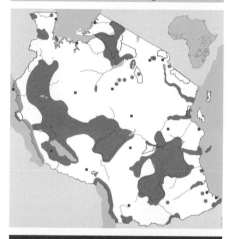

Where to look
This species is easily seen in many of the National Parks in both the north and south of the country. Many National Parks have a 'hippo pool' where permanent pods of Common Hippos can be found.

these rivers meet the coast, including at Kilwa. They are widespread in the rivers and wetlands in the west and also occur at Lake Nyasa, Lake Tanganyika, in the Mtera and Nyumbu ya Mungu dams, and Lakes Babati, Chaya and Jipe, and possibly still Lake Balangida. In the northeast they can be found in the Burigi–Biharamulo and Ibanda–Rumanyika Game Reserves and in the Kagera River.

Population size and conservation status
Common Hippos are difficult to count and there are no accurate figures for the whole country. The highest numbers are in the Selous ecosystem, where there are probably over 30,000 animals. There are also approximately 2,000 individuals in both the Katavi–Rukwa and the Ruaha–Rungwa ecosystems, and 1,300

to 2,000 in the Serengeti NP. Common Hippos are common in Moyowosi and Ugalla GRs, and Mikumi and Manyara NPs. They occur at lower densities, although are still easily seen, in Arusha NP, Ngorongoro CA, Sadaani NP and Mahale NP. They are uncommon or rare in most rivers and lakes outside protected areas, where numbers are declining due to hunting, habitat loss, drought and disease, any of which can eliminate small populations.

Common Hippopotamus
TOP: Serengeti NP; BOTTOM: Hippo pod, Serengeti NP

Giraffe

Giraffa camelopardalis

SWAHILI: Twiga

The Giraffe is the tallest land mammal, with large males reaching almost 6m (20 ft) in height. The neck and legs are each over 1·5m (5ft) long. Both sexes have short, ossified bones resembling horns on the top of the head. The body has a blotched, brown pattern, separated by lighter coloured patches. There is a great deal of variation in patterning and colouration, with the patches tending to darken with age. Both white and black forms have also been recorded.

Least Concern	
HB:	3·5–5·9m (11–19ft)
Ht:	2·8–4·0m (9–13ft)
Tail:	75–150cm (29–59")
Wt:	M 970–1,400kg (2,130–3,000lb)
	F 700–1,000kg (1,540–2,200lb)

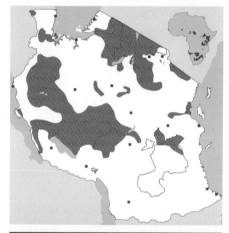

Subspecies
G. c. tippelskirchi: only subspecies found in Tanzania.

Similar species
Unlikely to be mistaken for any other mammal.

Ecology and social behaviour
Giraffes occur in open *Acacia* and miombo woodland, bushland, and grassland. They are gregarious and non-territorial, forming temporary groups of 2–32 individuals with constantly changing configurations. Only females and their young form stable units, and males frequently move alone. Giraffe infants congregate in groups, usually accompanied by one or more mothers. Males and females occupy home ranges that vary in size from 22–280 km² (8–110 mi²) depending on the density and abundance of food. Males have a complex dominance system with bulls establishing superiority with a 'necking' fight, where they stand next to each other and swing their heads at their opponents. Many of these fights are ritualized, although deaths have been recorded. Giraffes are browsers, feeding mainly on *Acacia*, *Commiphora* and *Terminalia* trees.

Distribution in Tanzania
Giraffes are widely distributed in northern, central and western Tanzania, with the Rufiji River in the Selous demarcating the limit to the species' distribution in the south of the country. They are found in all National Parks except for Udzungwa, Kitulo and Gombe.

Where to look

This species is easily seen in many National Parks including Arusha, Tarangire, Serengeti, Ruaha and Mikumi.

A population is also established on Rubondo Island in Lake Victoria, having been introduced in the 1960s. Giraffes also occur in Lake Natron, West Kilimanjaro, much of the Masaai Steppe, Wembere Wetland, southwestern Singida, Wami–Mbiki WMA and throughout the miombo woodland between the Ruaha–Rungwa ecosystem and the Moyowosi ecosystem. In addition, there are populations in the northwest of the country in Burigi–Biharamulo and Ibanda–Rumanyika GRs. Giraffes are absent from the floor of the Ngorongoro Crater, although widely distributed across the rest of the Ngorongoro CA.

Population size and conservation status
The population of Giraffes in Tanzania numbers approximately 25,000 animals,

which is roughly 25% of the global population. The largest population is in the Serengeti ecosystem with approximately 12,000 animals, while other significant populations are found in the Ruaha ecosystem with 5,000–7,000 individuals, northern Selous GR and Mikumi NP with 1,000–2,500 animals, and a further 1,000 individuals in Katavi NP. The Giraffe population in the Tarangire ecosystem declined from 4,000 animals in 1994 to 1,200 in 2011. There are approximately 500 Giraffes in Sadaani NP and 400 in Mkomazi NP.

The population in Burigi–Biharamulo GRs is very low, with less than 20 individuals recorded in 2000. The Giraffe population in Tanzania is mostly stable in protected areas, although is declining on community lands. As Tanzania's national animal, Giraffes are protected throughout the country, yet poaching for meat remains a problem. They are also susceptible to various diseases including Rinderpest, which reduced the Kenyan population by 40% in the 1960s.

Giraffe
MAIN PHOTO: female (Kenya); INSET TOP LEFT: male, Ngorongoro CA (Tanzania). Note that the male has a larger bump on the forehead and less prominent hair tufts on the 'horns' than the female.

African Buffalo

Syncerus caffer

Cape Buffalo

SWAHILI: Mbogo, Nyati

A very large, muscular animal resembling a stocky cow. Coat colour ranges from reddish-brown to black, with older males usually being totally black. Both sexes have horns that grow sideways from the skull and curve upwards at the tip. The boss on the horns of males is much heavier than those of females and the maximum recorded horn size is 162 cm (64") long. The tail is long with a black tassel at the tip.

Subspecies

S. c. caffer: only subspecies found in Tanzania.

Similar species

Unlikely to be mistaken for any other mammal.

Ecology and social behaviour

Found in a wide range of habitats, including forest, savanna, thicket, swamp, wetland and montane grassland up to an altitude of 4,700 m (15,400 ft). They are strictly grazers and need regular access to water to drink. African Buffalo form discrete population units that share a home range. Herds within these units regularly separate and regroup into smaller or larger groups, although they seldom disperse to other units. In savanna habitats, herd size can vary from 20–2,500 animals, while males can be solitary or form small bachelor groups. Home ranges vary from 100–1,000 km² (40–400 mi²). African Buffalo are most active during the morning and evening, preferring to rest in the shade during the heat of the day.

Distribution in Tanzania

The African Buffalo is widespread across Tanzania. It is found in every National Park except for Rubondo NP, and it is now extinct in Kitulo and Gombe NPs. The species also occurs in nearly every Game Reserve in the country, as well as in many lowland and montane Forest Reserves. In some parts of Tanzania, including the Masaai Steppe and south of Selous GR, it is still widespread on village land outside protected areas.

Least Concern	
HB:	230–340 cm (91–134")
Ht:	135–153 cm (53–60")
Tail:	67–90 cm (26–35")
Wt:	M 660–850 kg (1,450–1,870 lb)
	F 390–470 kg (860–1,030 lb)

Where to look

African Buffalo are easy to see in many protected areas in Tanzania. Herds of over 2,000 can sometimes be observed on the ridge roads in Tarangire NP, while large herds are also common on the open plains in Katavi NP and Mikumi NP. In Manyara NP they are often seen on the open plains close to the Hippo Pool, and in Arusha NP there is always a small group present in the grassland before the waterfall by Momella gate. Another good location is the Ngorongoro Crater, where several herds occupy the Crater floor. Large bulls often graze in the grounds of the lodges on the Crater rim, and among the buildings at the Headquarters.

Population size and conservation status

The largest population of African Buffalo in Tanzania is in the Selous GR, with an estimated population over 100,000 individuals. There are also large populations in the Serengeti ecosystem with 32,000 counted in 2009, and in the Ruaha–Rungwa ecosystem with some 20,000 animals. The Katavi Rukwa ecosystem had approximately 10,000 individuals in 2009, although numbers declined markedly in the preceeding decade. Other notable populations include the Moyowosi GR with approximately 7,000 animals in 2001, where it is the dominant large ungulate both in terms of numbers and biomass, and Tarangire NP, where numbers have remained steady at 5,000–6,000 over the past decade. African Buffalo are also very common in the forests of Ngorongoro CA, Arusha NP and Kilimanjaro NP. Hadzabe hunters report that African Buffalo are still found in the Yaeda Valley but they are now uncommon, probably only descending occasionally from the Ngorongoro Highlands. Numbers are declining in some areas including the Kilombero Valley and Katavi NP, although most of the large populations appear stable. The main threats are poaching for bushmeat and habitat loss.

African Buffalo
TOP: male (Kenya);
BOTTOM: female with calf, Serengeti NP (Tanzania)

Lesser Kudu   *Tragelaphus imberbis*

SWAHILI: Tandala Mdogo

A large antelope. Males are slate-grey, becoming darker with age, and females are grey-brown. Both sexes have 11–13 white stripes running from the back down to the belly, two white patches under the neck and an incomplete chevron on the forehead. The tail is the same colour as the body on the upper side, white on the underside, and tipped black. Only the males have horns, which are long (61–92 cm | 24–36" long) and corkscrewed.

Near Threatened	
HB:	M 150–170 cm (59–67")
	F 110–130 cm (43–51")
Ht:	M 95–105 cm (37–41")
	F 90–100 cm (35–39")
Tail:	25–40 cm (10–16")
Wt:	M 90–110 kg (200–240 lb)
	F 80–95 kg (180–200 lb)

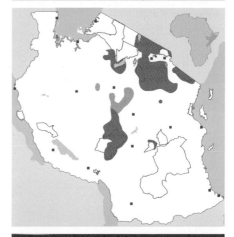

Subspecies
T. i. australis: only subspecies found in Tanzania.

Similar species
Greater Kudus (*page 184*) are much larger, have fewer white stripes on the body and lack the two distinctive white marks under the neck; males also have a distinct mane on the underside of the neck (see comparative photographs, *page 268*).

Ecology and social behaviour
Lesser Kudus are found principally in dense thicket and bushland, usually in areas with less than 650 mm (26") of annual rainfall. They are active throughout the day and night, feeding mainly on leaves, shoots, fruits and seedpods, and occasionally grass. They live singly or in small, often single-sex, groups of 3–6 animals. Adult males are generally solitary. Female groups can be highly stable over time, and are usually only joined by males for breeding. Neither sex is territorial and both have small home ranges of 0·5–5·0 km² (0·2–2·0 mi²). The home ranges of several individuals, of either sex, frequently overlap.

Distribution in Tanzania
Closely associated with *Acacia–Commiphora* bushland. In the north, Lesser Kudus range from Lake Natron to the lower western and northern slopes of Mount Kilimanjaro. The Lake Natron population is also contiguous with the population in Tarangire NP, via Lolsimongori Mountain and Manyara Ranch. They occur across much of the Maasai Steppe

Where to look
Lesser Kudus can be easily seen on Manyara Ranch in the thicker bush areas in the centre of the ranch. Another good location is Ndarakwai Ranch and the Enduimet WMA in West Kilimanjaro. In Mkomazi NP, they are frequently seen in small groups on the road from Zange to Kamakota. They are less commonly seen in Tarangire NP, although the road south of Silale Swamp to Loiboserit is a good place to try. In Ruaha NP, they are regularly seen on the upper Mwagusi Drive, particularly in the thick riverine bush between Mbagi and Mdonya Juu.

and have been recorded from Nyumba ya Mungu dam and Kitwai in the eastern part of the Steppe. They are also present in Maswa GR, southwestern Serengeti NP and Ngorongoro CA, and the Yaeda Valley. There are possible records from the bushland areas bordering the Wembere Wetland, and from Swagaswaga GR. In Mkomazi NP

Lesser Kudus are distributed throughout the National Park. They range throughout the *Acacia–Commiphora* bushland in the Ruaha–Rungwa ecosystem as far south as the Usangu Wetland, which is the southernmost end of the species' range in Africa. They are also known from the wooded lowlands in Udzungwa NP.

Population size and conservation status
Lesser Kudus are common in several areas in Tanzania, although numbers and population trends are not known. There are about 6,000 in Mkomazi NP, and they are also numerous in the dense thickets of West Kilimanjaro and common in bushland around Lake Natron, particularly around Gelai Mountain. They are common south of Tarangire NP, in the Makame WMA and probably still common in areas of thick bush across the Maasai Steppe. Also common in parts of Maswa Makao, although numbers in the Yaeda Valley are now low. In the Ruaha–Rungwa ecosystem they are uncommon. Hunting and habitat loss are the main threats to this species, which has disappeared from a number of areas including Shinyanga and large parts of the land between Tarangire NP and the Ruaha ecosystem.

Lesser Kudu
MAIN PHOTO: male (Kenya); INSET: female (Kenya)

Greater Kudu

Tragelaphus strepsiceros

SWAHILI: Tandala Mkubwa

A very large, long-legged antelope. Females and young males have a tawny-brown body, becoming grey-brown or grey in older males. Both sexes have a grey neck. There is a distinct hump on the shoulders, and a mane that runs from the back of the head to the base of the shoulders. Mature males have a long mane running along the underside of the neck. There are 4–12 white stripes on the body running from the back down to the belly. The black-tipped tail, that reaches almost to the hock, is the same colour as the body on the upper side and white on the underside. Males have huge spiraled horns that can reach 157 cm (62") in length. Females do not have horns.

Similar species
The Lesser Kudu (*page 182*) is significantly smaller and has two distinctive white marks beneath the neck; males of that species also have no mane on the underside of the neck and are a slate grey colour (see comparative photographs, *page 268*).

Ecology and social behaviour
Preferred habitat is bushland, dense thicket and savanna woodland; forest and open grassland is avoided. Greater Kudus feed mainly on browse, seldom eating grasses, and can be largely water-independent. They are both diurnal and nocturnal, becoming more nocturnal in areas where there is human disturbance. Greater Kudus are social animals, living in small matriarchal herds of 3–10 individuals (occasionally up to 25) comprising females and their young, which may be accompanied by an adult male. Males are either solitary or form temporary bachelor herds, usually associating with the female groups for an extended period only when rutting. Female home range size in the Kruger NP (South Africa) is 4–25 km² (1–10 mi²) and up to 50 km² (20 mi²) for males, although there is significant overlap between home ranges of both sexes.

Least Concern	
HB:	M 204–245 cm (80–96")
	F 186–217 cm (73–85")
Ht:	M 140–150 cm (55–59")
	F 120–130 cm (47–51")
Tail:	37–51 cm (15–20")
Wt:	M 190–340 kg (420–760 lb)
	F 120–210 kg (260–460 lb)

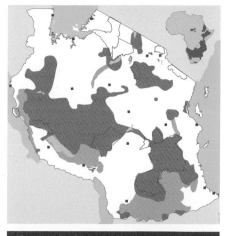

Where to look
Frequently seen in Ruaha NP, particularly in the Kimilimitonge Hill area, and can also be easily observed around the Sangaiwe Hills in Tarangire NP and, less commonly, around Gursi swamp in western Tarangire NP.

Distribution in Tanzania
The Greater Kudu is widely distributed throughout Tanzania. It occurs in areas of dense bush and thicket in Tarangire NP, the Maasai Steppe, Lake Natron, Maswa GR, southwestern Serengeti NP and Ngorongoro CA, and in the Yaeda Valley; the Yaeda population may still extend into the Wembere Wetland. In western Tanzania, it is found in the Moyowosi–Kigosi, Katavi–Rungwa and Ruaha–Rukwa ecosystems. It is likely to occur in miombo woodland in eastern Mahale NP. There are still populations in areas of thick bushland in Singida region, in Wami–Mbiki WMA and western Sadaani NP. In southern Tanzania it is found in Mikumi NP and the

Selous ecosystem. This is a resilient species and often survives in unprotected areas where other large ungulates have been extirpated.

Population size and conservation status

There are no accurate population figures for the Greater Kudu in Tanzania. Densities are generally low and nowhere do they reach those recorded in southern Africa. The largest populations occur in the Selous GR and Ruaha–Rungwa ecosystems, each probably with several thousand animals. This species is common in parts of western Tanzania, including Ugalla and Lukwati GRs, throughout much of the Ruaha–Rungwa ecosystem, part of the Selous GR, and Swagaswaga and Lukwika GRs. It is uncommon in Sadaani NP, most of the Tarangire ecosystem, the western Serengeti ecosystem and the Yaeda Valley, and uncommon or rare around Lake Natron and the Moyowosi–Kigosi GRs. The main threat to the Greater Kudu is poaching for meat, particularly outside protected areas. Rinderpest outbreaks have greatly reduced populations in Kenya, although this disease is not believed to have affected populations in Tanzania.

Greater Kudu
MAIN PHOTO: male (Botswana); INSET: female (Kenya)

Common Eland
Tragelaphus oryx

Cape Eland

SWAHILI: Pofu

The second-largest antelope in Africa (the Giant Eland *Tragelaphus derbianus*, from West and Central Africa, and South Sudan, is the largest). The body colour ranges from reddish or tawny-brown to dark grey or blue-grey in older males. Both sexes have a dewlap (particularly prominent in bulls). The white stripes that run down from the back onto the flanks vary in number (2–15) and prominence between individuals. Both sexes have long horns with one or two tight corkscrew spirals starting at the base. Male horns are shorter (54 cm | 21" long) and thicker than female horns (60 cm | 24" long). The largest-horned individuals are found in the Selous, where horn lengths of 111 cm (44") have been recorded. The tail has a long, bushy black tassel at the tip.

Subspecies
T. o. pattersonianus: only subspecies found in Tanzania.

Similar species
Unlikely to be mistaken for any other mammal.

Ecology and social behaviour
Common Elands are found in a wide variety of habitats including grasslands, miombo woodland, agricultural land and montane highlands. They avoid thick forests and on Mount Kilimanjaro have even been recorded at the edge of the scree at an altitude of 4,600 m (15,000 ft). They live in single-sex or mixed groups averaging 3–12 animals, although aggregations of 300–500 (and sometimes 1,000) individuals are common, particularly during the wet season. Groups are dynamic, changing frequently in size and composition, and may comprise solely juveniles and calves. Common Elands are highly migratory, covering large distances in search of forage, with home range sizes varying from 50–400 km² (20–150 mi²). They are active both day and night and feed on grasses.

Least Concern	
HB:	220–263 cm (87–104")
Ht:	125–180 cm (49–71")
Tail:	54–75 cm (21–30")
Wt:	350–600 kg (770–1,320 lb)

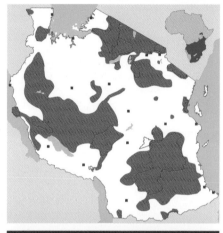

Where to look
Common Elands can be readily seen in the Serengeti NP and Ngorongoro CA, particularly within the Ngorongoro Crater and on the short-grass plains spanning the two protected areas. Large herds can be seen in the north of Tarangire NP during the dry season. In Ruaha NP they can be seen around Kimirimatonge Hill and Little Serengeti, while in the Selous they are frequently seen around Lake Manze.

Distribution in Tanzania
Formerly found throughout Tanzania, Common Eland is still widespread although now primarily restricted to protected areas. In the north, it occurs throughout the Serengeti, Tarangire and Mkomazi ecosystems and from Lake Natron across to West Kilimanjaro. It occurs on the northern slopes of Mount Meru, although it has not been recorded in Arusha NP in recent years, and is also found in the upper forest and lower heather zone on the northern and northwestern slopes of Mount Kilimanjaro. There are populations in

Sadaani NP, the Ruaha–Rungwa ecosystem, Mahale and Katavi NPs, Moyowosi–Kizigo GRs, Suledo Forest, Wami–Mbiki WMA and throughout the Selous ecosystem. There are a few records from southern Ugalla GR, where the species is now rare. It also occurs in the far northwest in the Burigi– Biharamulo GRs and Ibanda–Rumanyika GRs.

Population size and conservation status
Aerial counts in the Serengeti ecosystem suggest a population of 20,000–35,000 animals, making this the largest population in Africa. Other significant populations occur in the Selous ecosystem with 3,500 individuals, the Ruaha ecosystem with 2,000–3,000 individuals, and the Katavi and Tarangire ecosystems, each with approximately 1,000–2,000 individuals. Common Elands are highly mobile and often migrate long distances, making them vulnerable to hunting when protected areas are not large enough to encompass their movements. Their large size and prized meat makes them a favoured target of bushmeat hunters across their range. However, as they are naturally shy and often run from vehicles at a great distance, they are more difficult to hunt than other species of large ungulate. The population in Tanzania is declining outside protected areas.

Common Eland
TOP: male, Serengeti NP; BOTTOM: females with calves, Ngorongoro CA

Bushbuck

Tragelaphus scriptus

SWAHILI: Ponqo

A small antelope with a wide variety of coat colours and patterning. Males range from red-brown to almost black, with the pelage becoming progressively darker with age. Females are usually red. Both sexes have a white patch on the throat and also at the base of the neck. Some individuals have distinct white stripes on the back and white spots on the flank, though in others these markings are faint or absent. There is often a black or dark ring around the lower neck and a white dorsal crest. The short, bushy tail is the same colour as the body on the upper side and white on the underside. Only males have horns (25–47 cm | 10–19" long), which are nearly straight with one or slightly more than one spiral.

Least Concern		
HB:		M 117–142 cm (51–67")
		F 114–132 cm (51–63")
Ht:		M 64–87 cm (25–34")
		F 60–71 cm (24–28")
Tail:		19–25 cm (7–10")
Wt:	M 30–55 kg (66–121 lb)	F 24–34 kg (53–75 lb)

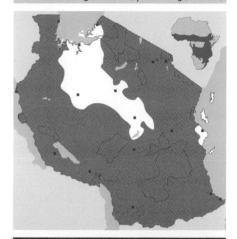

Subspecies
T. s. fasciatus: northeast coastal forests; males are grey-ochre, occasionally with distinct white longitudinal stripes.

T. s. dama: western Tanzania; males are small, mostly red, with distinct white spots on the rump.

T. s. delamerei: central and southern Tanzania; males are large and dark brown above.

Similar species
Female Sitatunga (*page 190*) look very similar but are slightly larger with a shaggier coat, have no grey on the neck and often have more prominent white dorsal stripes (see comparative photographs, *page 266*).

Ecology and social behaviour
Bushbucks occur in any area with dense cover and permanent water, including bushland, woodland, forest and agricultural land. They are mainly browsers that feed on leaves and shrubs but will also eat grass and fruits. They are solitary and non-territorial, although will sometimes form temporary associations with other individuals, usually relatives. Home ranges of both sexes may overlap extensively; in Nairobi NP (Kenya), six males and six females were found to share the same area of bushland. Home ranges in

Where to look
Easily seen in many National Parks. A reliable place to look is the Serengeti Ndogo in Arusha NP, a small, open patch of grassland just north of the main Ngurdoto Gate. In Mahale NP they are frequently seen on the beaches around the lodges and in Ruaha and Serengeti NPs they are commonly encountered along the main rivers in the early morning and late afternoon.

East Africa vary from 2–35 ha (5–85 acres). They are active at all hours of the day, with activity peaks between 6:00–9:00 a.m. and 7:00–10:00 p.m.

Distribution in Tanzania
The Bushbuck is one of the most widely distributed ungulates in Tanzania, occurring in all of the mainland National Parks and Game Reserves in the country. The species has been camera trapped in more locations than any other species of mammal in Tanzania. Its ability to withstand heavy hunting pressure

allows it to live in areas of high human density, including on the outskirts of major cities such as Arusha.

Population size and conservation status
The Bushbuck is probably one of the most abundant ungulates in Tanzania. Camera trap surveys recorded extremely high densities in the forests of Gelai Mountain, and it is also abundant in Arusha NP and in Mbarangandu WMA in the southern Selous ecosystem. The Bushbuck is common in Ngorongoro CA, and Kilimanjaro, Sadaani, Mahale, Mikumi and Rubondo NPs. In suitable habitat, it can occur at densities of up to 26 animals per km^2 (68 animals per mi^2). The main threat to this species is habitat loss.

Bushbuck
TOP: male ssp. *dama* (Uganda); BOTTOM LEFT: male ssp. *delamerei*, Arusha NP (Tanzania);
BOTTOM RIGHT: female ssp. *delamerei*, Kilimanjaro NP (Tanzania)

Sitatunga

Tragelaphus spekii

A medium-sized antelope. Males are dark brown, while females can range from light brown to deep red in colour. Both sexes have two white patches on their neck and males have white chevrons on the face. Some individuals have distinct white stripes on the back and flanks, while in others these markings are indistinct or missing entirely. The hair is long and oily, giving the animal a shaggy appearance, and older males may have a mane. Only males have horns (45–76 cm |18–30" long) with one-and-a-half or two-spiral turns. The hooves are long and widely splayed as an adaptation to living in swamps.

Subspecies
T. s. spekii: only subspecies found in Tanzania.

Similar species
The closely related Bushbuck (*page 188*) is very similar both in colour and markings, but is smaller, has shorter body hair, lacks splayed hooves and has a grey neck or grey collar. Male Sitatungas also have longer horns (see comparative photographs, *page 266*).

Ecology and social behaviour
A swamp specialist found only in permanent marshes and wetlands. Mostly diurnal, they are most active in the morning and late afternoon. They usually occur in the deepest part of the swamp, where they wade through water channels to feed; in areas with little human disturbance they will also feed along lake shores or in forest wetlands. Their long hooves give them a clumsy gait on land. They are excellent swimmers and, when threatened, can submerge so only their eyes and nostrils are visible above water. Reeds, sedges and grasses form the bulk of their diet. Sitatungas live alone or in small groups of two to four females or one male and several females. Home ranges average 2 km² (1 mi²).

Distribution in Tanzania
Sitatungas are mostly restricted to large wetland areas of western Tanzania. They occur in the Ibanda–Rumanyika and

Least Concern	
HB:	M 150 170 cm (59–67")
	F 135–145 cm (53–57")
Ht:	M 88–125 cm (35–49")
	F 75–90 cm (30–35")
Tail:	M 14–35 cm (6–14")
	F 17–37 cm (7–15")
Wt:	M 70–125 kg (150–275 lb)
	F 50–57 kg (110–125 lb)

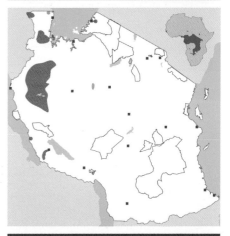

Where to look
Rubondo NP is the best place to see Sitatungas in Tanzania. They are often observed feeding in the forest in the vicinity of the bungalows and airstrip at Kageye or around Nhoze hide, while a boat ride around Rubondo Island offers good opportunities to see them along the lake shore.

Burigi–Biharamulo GRs, and throughout the large Moyowosi–Malagarasi Wetland, as far south as the Luganzo and Msima Game Controlled Areas. In the past there were many small populations on the Ufipa Plateau; most of these have disappeared, although there are still scattered populations in the Kalambo River watershed, including in the Lichwe Valley in Sumbawanga and on Kalambo Ranch. A population at Mbangala on the south end of Lake Rukwa has now disappeared. They are found in Rubondo NP and there is a small population in the Masura swamp near Musoma on the eastern shore of Lake Victoria. There are recent records from near Kipili village on Lake Tanganyika.

Population size and conservation status

The largest population of Sitatungas is in the Moyowosi–Malagarasi swamp, an area of 21,000 km² (8,100 mi²). Aerial counts in 2001 suggested a total of 1,670 animals in the Moyowosi GR, with another 330 in Kigosi GR, Lake Nyamagoma and Lake Sagara areas. These figures are likely to be underestimates as Sitatungas are secretive, and often shelter

during the heat of the day, making it difficult to count them from the air. In suitable habitat, such as in Akagera NP (Rwanda), densities of up to 64 animals per km² (166 per mi²) have been recorded. They are common in Ugalla Niensi Open Area and abundant in Rubondo NP. In Burigi–Biharamulo GRs numbers have been significantly reduced due to over-hunting and they are now uncommon. Sitatungas are easily hunted or snared because they regularly use the same favoured river channels and pathways. As a result, the species has been extirpated from several areas in Tanzania.

Sitatunga
TOP: male (Kenya);
BOTTOM: female (Kenya)

Suni

Neotragus moschatus

Least Concern	
HB:	55–61 cm (22–24")
Ht:	33–35 cm (13–14")
Tail:	11–13 cm (4–5")
Wt:	4–9 kg (9–20 lb)

A very small antelope with a hunched stance. It ranges in colour from light brown to dark or grey-brown above and white or pale grey below. The lower parts of the legs are rufous. Individuals in montane areas are darker than those from the coast. The tail is relatively long and bushy, white underneath with the upper side the same colour as the body. Only males have horns (6–9 cm | 2–4" long), which are ringed for three-quarters of the length from the base. The large pre-orbital gland is straight.

Subspecies

N. m. moschatus: lowland areas of east and southern Tanzania; light brown.

N. m. kirchenpaueri: mountains in northern Tanzania, Eastern Arc and Livingstone Mountains; much darker than lowland animals.

Similar species

The Blue Duiker (*page 194*) is a darker colour and the tail has a central black stripe bordered with white. The Suni's tail is bushier and brown above, and is flicked from side to side, rather than up and down as in the Blue Duiker. The Kirk's Dik-dik (*page 208*) has a white ring around the eye and is absent from forest habitat (see comparative photographs, *page 265*).

Ecology and social behaviour

Suni inhabit areas of dense undergrowth including thickets, coastal and montane forests, and dense bushland; they also readily colonize secondary thicket and forest. They are typically found in pairs, although several females may overlap with the range of one male. Males occupy territories of approximately 3 ha (7 acres). Suni are active throughout the day and night with activity peaks between 6:00–8:00 a.m. and 6:00–8:00 p.m. An unspecialized feeder, they browse on a wide range of plants and will also eat fruits, fungi and sometimes grass roots. Suni often zig-zag rapidly when fleeing, sometimes emitting a high-pitched double-scream.

Where to look

Often seen in Arusha NP during the early morning or late afternoon, especially the forested sections between the old museum to the Momella gate, along the main road between the Ngongogare gate and Momella gate, and, less commonly, on the road up to the Mount Meru crater. In Ngorongoro, try the grounds of the Serena hotel. They are also occasionally seen at the Selous Mbega camp.

Distribution in Tanzania

Suni are widely distributed in east, south, and parts of northern Tanzania, and on the islands of Zanzibar and Mafia. In coastal areas and southern Tanzania they are found in lowland forest and scrub, whereas further inland they are generally restricted to higher elevation montane forest. Found throughout the Eastern Arc Mountains, including the Mahenge Mountains and Malundwe Mountain in Mikumi NP. They are also probably present in the Livingstone Mountains. They occur sporadically in areas of thick bush in the Selous ecosystem, although the extent of their distribution there is unclear. In northern

Tanzania they are found on Kilimanjaro, Meru, Monduli, Burko and Longido Mountains, and in the Ngorongoro Crater highlands. They occur in the Nou FR, although not in the nearby Ufiome Forest. A population was introduced to Rubondo NP.

Population size and conservation status
Abundant in the mountain ranges in northern Tanzania, such as Ngorongoro Crater, Mount Meru, and Mount Kilimanjaro. The population of Suni on Mount Kilimanjaro has grown markedly since the forest was upgraded from

a Forest Reserve to a National Park in 2005. It is also common in Zoraninge Forest in Saadani NP, and in many of the forests in the Udzungwa Mountains. On Zanzibar, the population in 1996 was estimated at 20,000, with the highest densities located in Michamvi, Mtende, Makunduchi and Chaka FRs. In the Selous ecosystem they are found in low numbers and generally restricted to areas of thicker bush. Over-hunting has reduced populations in many coastal forests, but this species has the capacity to increase very rapidly with effective protection.

Suni
TOP: male ssp. *kirchenpaueri*, Arusha NP; BOTTOM: female ssp. *moschatus*, Zanzibar

Blue Duiker

Philantomba monticola

SWAHILI: Paa Chesi, Ndimba

A very small antelope ranging in colour from light brown to dark blue-grey on the back and white or whitish-grey on the belly. The short tail has a white underside and an upper side with a central black stripe flanked with white on the edges and tip. Males always have horns (2–4 cm | 1–2" long), which are lightly ringed at the base; females may have horns. The pre-orbital gland curves downwards forming a crescent-shape.

Subspecies

P. m. lugens: Southern Highlands and Mahale; dark blue-grey upperparts and whitish-grey underparts, individuals can be very dark or entirely melanistic.

P. m. schusteri: Eastern Arc Mountains; fawn-grey, although individuals can be very dark.

P. m. sundevalli: coastal Tanzania and islands; grey or grey-brown.

P. m. musculoides: northwest Tanzania; light brown, grey-brown to deep blue-grey.

Similar species

Most likely to be confused with the Suni (*page 192*), which is similar in size and appearance. The Suni has a paler coat, larger ears, and the tail is bushy, uniformly brown above and with no white stripe down the centre (see comparative photographs, *page 265*).

Ecology and social behaviour

Found in a range of habitats that offer plenty of cover, including riverine forests, gallery forests, dense bushland, agricultural land and coastal scrub. They live in monogamous-bonded pairs occupying small territories (2·5–4·0 ha | 6–10 acres). Their diet consists mostly of fallen fruit, flowers and leaves. Blue Duikers are diurnal and crepuscular with peaks of activity in the early morning and late afternoon.

Distribution in Tanzania

Blue Duikers have a scattered distribution on mainland Tanzania, and are also present on the islands of Zanzibar, Mafia and Pemba.

Least Concern	
HB:	55–66 cm (22–26")
Ht:	31–38 cm (12–15")
Tail:	7–9 cm (3–3·5")
Wt:	4·0–6·5 kg (9–14 lb)

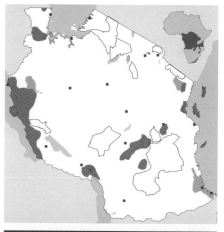

Where to look

This species can be seen along the forest paths around the bungalows and lodges in Mahale National Park, although it is shy and sightings are often fleeting. Try walking very quietly along the trails or sitting in one place for a while.

They are well distributed in pockets of forest throughout the coastal region including Sadaani NP and in Mtwara Region. Although recorded in the Mahenge Mountains to the west of the Selous GR, there is no evidence of them occurring in the Selous GR itself. In western Tanzania they are restricted to densely forested areas west of Lake Victoria, including Burigi–Biharamulo GRs and Minziro FR, and along the eastern shores of Lake Tanganyika, including Lwafi GR and Gombe and Mahale NPs, inland as far east as Issa near Ugalla GR. They are also found in the Uluguru and Udzungwa Mountains, and the East Usambara lowlands, although records from the West Usambaras need to be verified. In the Southern Highlands they occur on Mount Rungwe, and are also found in Ufipa and Ukinga. Blue Duikers are absent from the northern and central parts of the country and from most low-lying inland areas in south and central Tanzania. In Zanzibar, they occur in the Jozani Chwaka Bay NP, and Ukorongoni, Mtule, Muongoni and Mtende Forest Reserves.

Population size and conservation status
Abundant in Mahale NP: over one-third of all camera trap photographs obtained during a survey were of this species. Also common in the forests of Burigi–Biharamulo GRs and in dense, undisturbed thicket on Zanzibar. Blue Duikers are uncommon in Saadani NP, most coastal forests, the Southern Highlands and the Eastern Arc Mountains. They are rare in Udzungwa NP and the surrounding forests. In areas where both Suni and Blue Duikers co-exist, Suni are usually significantly more common for reasons that are unclear. Habitat loss and unregulated hunting within forested areas poses the main threat to this species, although populations are capable of recovering quickly if offered adequate protection.

Blue Duiker
TOP: camera trap photo, female ssp. *lugens*, Mahale NP;
BOTTOM LEFT: camera trap photo, female ssp. *musculoides*, Burigi GR;
BOTTOM RIGHT: camera trap photo, male ssp. *schusteri*, dark variant, Uluguru Mountains

Bush Duiker

Sylvicapra grimmia

Common Duiker, Grey Duiker

SWAHILI: Nsya

A medium-sized duiker with a leaner build and a longer body than the forest duikers. Coat colour differs significantly by region. In the east and south of the country, most individuals are yellow-brown or grey-brown, while in the west (particularly around Ugalla, Moyowosi and Burigi GRs), they are often tawny or rufous. On Mount Kilimanjaro the coat is a dense grizzled grey-brown. Coat length is longest in montane forms. The underbelly is white, but can be flecked with grey; the tail is black on the upper side and white underneath. There is usually a tuft on the top of the head that ranges in colour from tawny to black and a prominent black stripe that typically runs from between the eyes down to the muzzle. In some individuals this stripe can extend as far up as the tuft. The forelegs are striped black or brown. The pre-orbital glands are usually highly visible. Only the males have horns (8–14 cm | 3–6" long).

Subspecies

S. g. hindei: northeastern Tanzania.

S. g. ssp. nov.: Mount Kilimanjaro.

S. g. orbicularis: rest of the country.

Similar species

The Steenbok (*page 206*) and Sharpe's Grysbok (*page 204*) both have shorter bodies, very small tails and lack the black facial stripe and black stripe down the tail. The Natal Red Duiker (*page 200*) is smaller and has a distinctive red coat. The Oribi (*page 218*) has a more upright stance, no black on the face, has a black pre-orbital patch and is generally found in open grassland (see comparative photographs, *page 265*).

Ecology and social behaviour

Bush Duikers utilize a wide range of habitats including bushland, savanna, woodland, agricultural areas and above the treeline in the heather zone and alpine moorland up to an altitude of 4,600 m (15,000 ft) on

Least Concern	
HB:	70–115 cm (28–45")
Ht:	45–70 cm (18–28")
Tail:	11–19 cm (4–7")
Wt:	10–25 kg (22–55 lb)

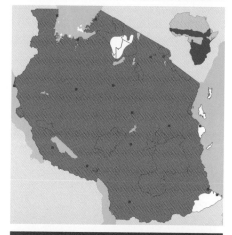

Where to look

This species is easy to see at Simba Farm on the lower slopes of West Kilimanjaro and above the tree line on the road leading up to the Shira Plateau in Kilimanjaro NP. It can also be found in bushland at the edge of swamps in Katavi NP.

Mount Kilimanjaro. They are absent from forests and open grasslands with little cover. Their diet includes leaves, fruits and shoots, with invertebrates and occasionally young birds also being eaten. Bush Duikers are primarily solitary, although sometimes seen in pairs. The territories of several females usually overlap with one male, and sometimes with those of other females, while male territories seldom overlap. Territory sizes in Uganda average 6 ha (15 acres). This species is both diurnal and nocturnal, but in areas where they are regularly disturbed they become more active at night.

Distribution in Tanzania

The Bush Duiker is one of the few ungulates that can survive in areas with relatively intensive human agriculture, and is widespread in Tanzania. It is found in all mainland National Parks except for Rubondo NP.

Population size and conservation status
The Bush Duiker is one of the most common and widespread ungulates in Tanzania. Camera trap surveys have shown it to be very common in many protected areas, including Moyowosi, Burigi–Biharamulo and Ugalla GRs in the west, Swagaswaga GR in north-central Tanzania, the Muhuwesi FR in the southern Selous ecosystem, and on the high moorland on Mount Kilimanjaro, where camera trapping rates were second

only to Suni (*page 192*). The Bush Duiker was also among the most frequently recorded animal species in the Lukwika–Lumesure and Mbangala GRs on the border with Mozambique. It is, however, uncommon in several of the northern National Parks, including Arusha and Tarangire and the Ngorongoro CA, and absent from most of the Serengeti NP plains where the habitat is too open for its liking. A very resilient species, the Bush Duiker is able to withstand heavy hunting pressure and are often found close to human settlement, including on the outskirts of Arusha.

Bush Duiker
TOP: male (Namibia);
BOTTOM LEFT: camera trap photo, male ssp. nov. from Mount Kilimanjaro showing characteristic dense coat;
BOTTOM RIGHT: camera trap photo, female ssp. *orbicularis*, Swagaswaga GR

Ader's Duiker

Cephalophus adersi

SWAHILI: Paa Nunga

A medium-sized duiker with a reddish-brown body and legs, and a white belly. A white band, the size of which varies between individuals, runs across the rump behind the tail. Most individuals have speckled white-and-yellow markings on the front legs. The slender tail has a small white tuft at the tip. Both sexes have short horns (Male 4·6 cm | 1·8", Female 2·8 cm | 1·1" long) that are surrounded by distinct red tufts.

Similar species
The Natal Red Duiker (*page 200*) has a red, rather than white, belly and lacks both the white stripe across the rump and speckling on the legs.

Ecology and social behaviour
Ader's Duikers inhabit tall, undisturbed coral rag thicket dominated by *Mystroxylon* and *Diospyros* tree species, but are occasionally found in secondary thicket. They are browsers that feed on leaves, seeds and fruits. Predominantly diurnal and crepuscular, they are usually found singly or in pairs.

Distribution in Tanzania
Known only from a few locations on Zanzibar, with the main populations occurring in the Kiwengwa Forest, the Jozani Chwaka Bay NP and the Mtende–Kichongoni thicket. Between 2000–2005, a few individuals were introduced to Chumbe and Mnemba Islands. There are reports of a small population on the mainland, south of Dar es Salaam, but as yet there are no confirmed records from this area.

Population size and conservation status
The population of Ader's Duikers on Zanzibar has declined rapidly in recent decades, from approximately 5,000 individuals in 1982 to only 600 in 1999. There have been no recent counts, and numbers are thought to be very low. The highest densities are found in Mtende Forest in the south of the Island. In February 2000, five Ader's Duikers were introduced to Chumbe Island, joining a female that had been moved there three

Critically Endangered	
HB:	65–78 cm (26–31")
Ht:	38–44 cm (15–17")
Tail:	6–14 cm (2–6")
Wt:	7–12 kg (15–26 lb)

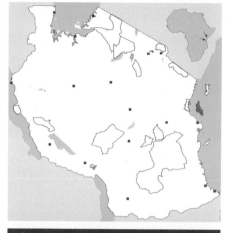

Where to look
With patience and luck, Ader's Duikers can be seen in the Mtende Forest in the south of Zanzibar. Trips can be arranged with the Mtende village leaders, who will take small groups to areas frequented by the duikers in the coral rag thicket. Because the vegetation is very dense, it is best to sit quietly in one place and wait for them to pass. Ader's Duikers can also be easily seen on Mnemba Island, although the Island is privately owned and accessible only to guests of the lodge.

years earlier; this population appears to be increasing slowly. A further five individuals were introduced onto Mnemba Island in 2005 and these are breeding well, with the population now up to 18 animals. However, Mnemba Island is small (11 ha | 27 acres) and has limited potential for further population growth. Ader's Duikers are protected in Jozani Chwaka Bay NP, but much of the vegetation in the National Park is unsuitable habitat and the National Park supports less than 10% of the total Zanzibar population. The stronghold for this species is the Boni–Dodori Forest in northeast Kenya, where camera trapping surveys have shown it to be abundant. Hunting and habitat destruction have had a severe impact on Ader's Duiker numbers; its meat is prized for its taste and the large increase in the human population on Zanzibar has led to rapid deforestation and loss of old-growth vegetation, a critical component of the habitat this duiker requires.

Ader's Duiker
TOP: female, Zanzibar; BOTTOM: male, captive individual, Zanzibar

Natal Red Duiker

Cephalophus natalensis

Red Duiker

SWAHILI: Kiduku, Funo

A medium-sized duiker. Both sexes have short, conical, ringed horns (Male 4–10 cm | 1·5–4·0"; Female 2–4 cm | 1–2" long), although female horns are often concealed by their crest.

Subspecies

C. n. robertsi: southern Tanzania along the Ruvuma River; the upperbody is a uniform rufous-red and the underbelly is a paler tawny-red. May have some black on the front and inner sides of the legs.

C. n. harveyi: Harvey's Duiker occurs in north, east and central Tanzania; deep red on the back and haunches, mostly black on the lower part of the legs and a black nape that extends down to the shoulders and neck in some individuals. Has a distinct black stripe running from the forehead to the nose.

Note: There is considerable debate over the status of the Harvey's Duiker, with some authorities listing it as a separate species; further research is required to determine its status. The animals in the Selous Game Reserve have characteristics of both subspecies, indicating that this is an area of hybridization.

Similar species

Ader's Duikers (*page 198*) have a white stripe across the rump. Sharpe's Grysboks (*page 204*) are mostly nocturnal and have distinctive white flecks in their fur. Bush Duikers (*page 196*) have a longer body and a black stripe down the tail (see comparative photographs, *page 265*). Sightings of **Weyns's Duikers** *Cephalophus weynsi lestradei* were reported from Mahale and Gombe forests in the 1950s, but there have been no recorded sightings since then; they are larger than Natal Red Duikers and have a dark, mostly grey-brown body.

Ecology and social behaviour

These duikers are found in a variety of habitats including coastal bushland, thicket, secondary forest and montane forest ranging from sea level up to an altitude of 2,400 m (7,900 ft). They are secretive animals, which will often

Least Concern	
HB:	80–95 cm (31–37")
Ht:	38–47 cm (15–19")
Tail:	8–15 cm (3–6")
Wt:	9–13 kg (20–29 lb)

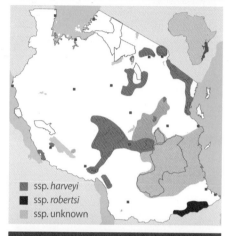

- ssp. *harveyi*
- ssp. *robertsi*
- ssp. unknown

Where to look

Regularly seen in Arusha NP on the Ngurdoto Crater road. Sometimes found on the road leading up to the Shira Plateau on Mount Kilimanjaro, particularly in the transition zone between the forest and the heather zone. Occasionally seen at the Mbega Forest Camp in the Selous GR.

run and dive into thick cover when disturbed, sometimes emitting a loud alarm whistle. They are diurnal and mostly solitary or in pairs. Home ranges are typically 2–15 ha (5–40 acres). Their diet consists mainly of leaves and fruits and their distribution is limited by their need for access to permanent water.

Distribution in Tanzania

Widely distributed across most of northern, central and southern Tanzania. Found in many National Parks including Arusha, Kilimanjaro, Manyara, Mkomazi, Saadani, Udzungwa, Mikumi and Ruaha. They are distributed throughout the Eastern Arc Mountain range, except for the Uluguru

Mountains where they have now disappeared. There are populations in the Livingstone Mountains and Loasi–Kalambo FRs and a record from Kwimba Mountain from the mid-1990s. In northern Tanzania, these animals occur on the mountains of Meru, Monduli, Burko and Ufiome, with scattered populations in dense thicket on the south Maasai Steppe. They are also found in Swagaswaga and Kizigo GRs. Distribution is sporadic in the Selous ecosystem, with areas of concentration in dense '*msitu*' thicket. A typical ssp. *robertsi* form is found in the far south in Lukwika–Lumesule GR and Mbangala FR.

Population size and conservation status
Abundant in Arusha NP and in Ufiome FR south of Babati, and common in Swagaswaga GR, in the Zoraninge Forest in Saadani NP, in parts of Udzungwa NP, on the upper slopes of Kilimanjaro NP and in the thicket areas of Mkomazi NP. They are also common in Forest Reserves adjacent to the Mozambique border including Mbangala FR and Lukwika GR, although they are uncommon in Mikumi NP and rare in Manyara and Ruaha NPs, and are uncommon or rare across most of the Selous GR. Populations outside protected areas are threatened by snaring and hunting with dogs.

Natal Red Duiker
TOP: male ssp. *harveyi*, Saadani NP; BOTTOM LEFT: camera trap photo, male ssp. *robertsi*, Lukwika GR; BOTTOM RIGHT: camera trap photo, male ssp. *harveyi*, Ufiome FR

E Abbott's Duiker   *Cephalophus spadix*

SWAHILI: Minde

A large duiker with a dark brown, purple-black or black body. The inner sides of the upperparts of the legs, and occasionally the belly, are red. The face and neck are lighter in colour than the rest of the body. It has a white upper lip and a distinctive and prominent red crest on the top of its head. Both sexes have smooth horns (8–12 cm | 3–5" long).

Similar species
The Natal Red Duiker (*page 200*) is much smaller and is a distinctive red colour.

Ecology and social behaviour
This is strictly a forest species. On the northern slopes of Mount Kilimanjaro it favours steep-sided valleys with dense vegetation cover, and has also been reported from the heather zone at an altitude of 2,700 m (8,850 ft) and in open grassy glades within the forest. In the Udzungwa Mountains it favours wetter, more swampy areas. It is primarily nocturnal although is also active at dawn and dusk. It is believed to be solitary and is primarily a fruit-eater, although a camera trap picture shows an individual in the Udzungwa Mountains eating a frog.

Distribution in Tanzania
The Abbott's Duiker is endemic to Tanzania. It was formerly found in the Eastern Arc Mountains and parts of northern Tanzania, but has now disappeared from the Uluguru, East Usambara, Pare and Nguru Mountains, and from the Mfrika Scarp. The population in the Nou FR near Babati was last recorded in 1951 and may now be extinct. The last recorded sighting in the West Usambaras was in the early 2000s and its current status there is unknown. The species is currently known from Mount Kilimanjaro, the Udzungwa Mountains, the Southern Highlands and the southern Rubeho Mountains. It occurs in many of the forests within the Udzungwa Mountains, including Luhombero–Ndundulu, Mwanihana, Iwonde and Matundu, as well as the Uzungwa Scarp, Kising'a–Rugaro, Nyumbanitu, New Dabaga–Ulang'ambi

Endangered	
HB:	100–135 cm (39–53")
Ht:	66–74 cm (26–29")
Tail:	11–14 cm (4–5·5")
Wt:	50–58 kg (110–128 lb)

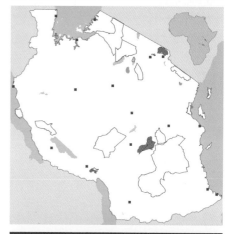

Where to look
There are no reliable sites for seeing Abbott's Duiker. They may occasionally be seen in Matumbu and Ndundulu Forests (Udzungwa Mountains) by walking very quietly through the forest at dusk and dawn. However, the logistics of getting to these sites are best organized through a safari company. On Mount Kilimanjaro they are very occasionally observed in the forest on the Machame route and at night or early morning on the farms adjacent to the forest on the slopes of West Kilimanjaro.

and Ukami Forests. Its current status in the Kiranzi–Kitungulu Forest is unknown. In the Southern Highlands it is known from Mount Rungwe, the Livingstone Forest in Kitulo NP and the Ndukunduku Forest on the southeast border of Kitulo NP. A previously unknown population was discovered in Ilole Forest in the southern Rubeho Mountains in 2006.

Population size and conservation status
The main stronghold for this species is in the Mwanihana, Luhomero–Ndundulu and

Ukami Forests of the Udzungwa Mountains, where it is locally common and has been recorded at densities of approximately 1 individual per km² (3 individuals per mi²). It is scarce in Nyumbanitu Forest and rare in the other Udzungwa Forests. It is very rare in the Southern Highlands, with an estimated total of 40 individuals on Mount Rungwe and in the Livingstone Forest, while a population recently discovered in Ilole Forest in the southern Rubeho Mountains may have a further 50 individuals. Numbers on Mount Kilimanjaro are not known, although it is likely that the population there is growing due to better protection of the Kilimanjaro forest since its incorporation into the Kilimanjaro National Park in 2005. This species is an attractive target for hunters because of its large size, and it is easily snared due to its consistent use of the same pathways.

Abbott's Duiker
TOP: male, Udzungwa Mountains; BOTTOM: camera trap photo, female, Udzungwa Mountains. There are very few photographs of this species in the wild.

Sharpe's Grysbok

Raphicerus sharpei

SWAHILI: Dondoro

Least Concern	
HB:	60–85 cm (24–33")
Ht:	50 cm (20")
Tail:	4·5–7 cm (2–3")
Wt:	6·5–11 kg (14–24 lb)

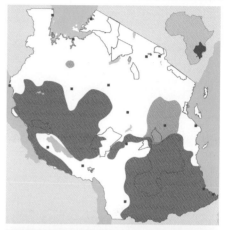

A small, stocky antelope with a rufous-brown coat that is flecked with distinctive white hairs. The throat, neck and underparts are white. The short tail has a rufous-brown upper side, a white underside, and is flanked by long hairs extending down the rump. Only the males have horns, which are very short (3–4·5 cm | 1–1·8" long) and smooth.

Similar species

The Steenbok (*page 206*) is a similar size, but is less stocky, has proportionately longer legs and larger ears, and lacks the white coat hairs. The Steenbok occurs in *Acacia* grasslands while the Sharpe's Grysbok is a miombo woodland species. The Bush Duiker (*page 196*) is larger, has a black stripe down the face, and a longer tail. When disturbed, the Bush Duiker bounds away through the vegetation whereas the Sharpe's Grysbok runs low to the ground. The Natal Red Duiker (*page 200*) has red, rather than white, underparts and has a longer tail (see comparative photographs, *page 265*).

Ecology and social behaviour

Sharpe's Grysboks are closely associated with miombo woodland, preferring areas with thick ground cover and scrub, but occasionally on cultivated land. They are mostly nocturnal, but are sometimes active during the early morning and late afternoon, particularly in overcast conditions. One was camera trapped at noon in southern Tanzania. Males and females form monogamous pairs that defend a territory, but they are generally seen alone, except during the mating season. They feed mostly on browse, particularly leaves and buds, but also eat fruits, seeds and grass.

Distribution in Tanzania

The Sharpe's Grysbok is widely distributed in miombo woodland in southern and western Tanzania. It probably occurs more widely than records suggest, as being largely nocturnal it is easily overlooked. It is found in the miombo woodland areas of the Ruaha–Rungwa ecosystem, around Iringa, in Katavi NP and the Ugalla area as far north as Luganzo;

Where to look

The Sharpe's Grysbok is not easy to see because of its nocturnal habits. It is sometimes observed on the road between Manyoni and Rungwa GR. It is also very occasionally seen in the miombo woodland areas of Katavi and Ruaha NPs, particularly in the early morning and late afternoon. It bolts easily when disturbed, running low to the ground and darting into thick cover, so most views of this species are of a red rump disappearing into a thick bush.

however, there are no records from the Moyowosi ecosystem. It is also known from the eastern section of Mahale NP. It occurs throughout the Selous ecosystem, including parts of the Kilombero Valley, and in Lukwika–Lumesule GR and Magwamila along the border with Mozambique. There are also historic records from around Kilwa and Liwale Districts on the coast. There is apparently suitable miombo woodland habitat around Morogoro as far south as the Nguru Mountains, although there are no records from this area.

Population size and conservation status

There are no density figures for Sharpe's Grysbok in Tanzania. It is common in the west of the country, particularly the area between Rungwa GR and Lake Rukwa, Katavi NP and Ugalla GR and around the Itigi thicket. It is uncommon in Ruaha NP and Muhezi and Kizigo GRs.

Densities across much of the Selous GR are low; it is rare in the photographic block of the Game Reserve, although occurs more frequently in the thicker bushland in the south. Hunting with dogs and snares outside protected areas poses a threat to this species, but there are still healthy populations around the country.

Sharpe's Grysbok
TOP: male, location unknown; BOTTOM LEFT: camera trap photo, male, Mlele FR (Tanzania); BOTTOM RIGHT: camera trap photo, male, Ugalla GR (Tanzania)

Steenbok

Raphicerus campestris

SWAHILI: Isha

A small, slender antelope with a smooth, rufous or rufous-brown coat and white underparts. The long, slender legs have rufous outer sides, and inner sides that are white above the knee. The ears are very large. There is white on the lower muzzle, the inside of the ears and around the eyes, and a triangle of black above the nose. Only the male has horns (7–11 cm | 3–4" long), which are nearly vertical and ridged only at the base. The tail is very short.

Least Concern	
HB:	72–87 cm (28–34")
Ht:	45–60 cm (18–24")
Tail:	5 cm (2")
Wt:	9–13 kg (20–29 lb)

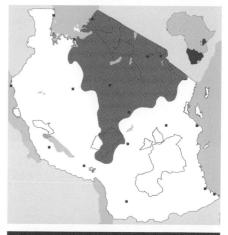

Similar species
Kirk's Dik-diks (*page 208*) are much smaller and have a longer, flexible nose. Oribi (*page 218*), whose range overlaps in parts of the Ruaha–Rungwa ecosystem and in northern and northwestern Serengeti, are slightly larger with a longer neck and a distinctive black spot below the ear. Sharpe's Grysboks (*page 204*) have shorter legs, more rounded hindquarters, smaller ears and white hairs in their coat. Sharpe's Grysboks inhabit miombo woodland while Steenboks are found in grassland and *Acacia* woodland; their ranges are only known to overlap in the Ruaha–Rungwa ecosystem, although they are likely still to be separated by their habitat preferences. Bush Duikers (*page 196*), which can also have a reddish coat, have a much longer tail and a prominent black stripe down the face (see comparative photographs, *pages 265*).

Ecology and social behaviour
Steenboks are active both during the day and night and are either solitary or found in pairs. Their preferred habitat is grassland, interspersed with open bush and open woodland, but they also frequently inhabit farmland and occasionally occur in semi-urban environments. They avoid thick woodland and forest. Steenboks feed on both grass and browse and can be water-independent. They live in monogamous pairs that share a territory of 5–60 ha (10–150 acres). Pairs commonly move and rest separately, although usually stay within 200–300 m (650–1,000 ft) of each other.

Where to look
Easily seen around Ndutu in the *Acacia* woodland on the road to Makao and the road towards Big Marsh. In Tarangire NP it is often seen on the Lemiyon road in late afternoon and early morning. It can also be reliably seen at night on Simba Farm or Ndarakwai Ranch in West Kilimanjaro.

Distribution in Tanzania
This species is closely linked with *Acacia–Commiphora* bushland and is absent from most of southern and western Tanzania. It is found throughout the Serengeti ecosystem to Mkomazi NP, including West Kilimanjaro, Kilimanjaro and Tarangire NPs, and occasionally in the grassland in northern Arusha NP. It is also known from the Yaeda Valley and the Wembere Wetland. It occurs throughout the Maasai Steppe and extends to Ruaha NP. In the 1970s there was a population at the base of the Ufipa escarpment, although it has not been recorded there recently.

Population size and conservation status

There is a large population of Steenbok in northern Tanzania. The species is most common in the Serengeti ecosystem, including Maswa GR and Loliondo, in the Yaeda Valley, Tarangire NP, the low-lying land around Gelai and Kitumbeine Mountains, in the grasslands north of Arusha NP, and on the western slopes of Mount Kilimanjaro. It is also common in parts of the Maasai Steppe. It is fairly common in Mkomazi NP and uncommon in the Ruaha ecosystem. The main threats to Steenboks are habitat loss and illegal hunting, although populations are stable inside most protected areas.

Steenbok
TOP: male, Ngorongoro CA (Tanzania); BOTTOM: immature male (Kenya)

Kirk's Dik-dik   *Madoqua kirkii*

SWAHILI: Digidigi

A small, slender antelope with long, dainty legs and large eyes and ears. The nose is pointed and very flexible, and can be greatly elongated to protrude over the lower lip. The coat is grizzled grey on the neck, back and haunches, and reddish on the sides, face and legs. The chin and belly are white and there is a white ring around the eye. There is a crest of hair on the crown, and the male has short, straight horns that are heavily ridged (6–10 cm | 2–4" long).

Subspecies in Tanzania

M. k. kirkii: Kirk's Dik-dik, lowland areas east of Ruvu River to Usambara Mts, including Mkomazi NP; sides are grey, rufous only on rump and back.

M. k. cavendishi: Cavendish's Dik-dik, Mount Kilimanjaro to eastern Lake Victoria, including the Serengeti ecosystem south to Lake Eyasi; males and females are the same size and have rufous sides.

M. k. thomasi: Thomas's Dik-dik, central Tanzania; females are larger than males and have rufous sides.

Note: Some authorities consider these three subspecies to be separate species, forming part of a Kirk's Dik-dik species complex.

Similar species

Steenboks (*page 206*) are significantly larger, have a reddish coat, a smaller, shorter nose, and larger ears. Suni (*page 192*) are uniformly coloured, and are typically found in denser vegetation (see comparative photographs, *page 265*).

Ecology and social behaviour

Kirk's Dik-diks are found in savanna grassland, bushland, open woodland and thicket, with preferred habitat being a combination of thicket and open areas with a well-developed shrub layer. They feed mostly on shrubs, trees and seeds, although will also eat grass and herbs, and are water-independent. Kirk's Dik-diks live in pairs, and often bond with the same partner for

Least Concern	
HB:	54–71 cm (21–28")
Ht:	30–44 cm (12–17")
Tail:	3–7 cm (1–3")
Wt:	2·6–6·4 kg (6–14 lb)

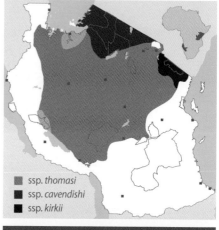

■ ssp. *thomasi*
■ ssp. *cavendishi*
■ ssp. *kirkii*

Where to look

Easily seen in Tarangire and Mkomazi NPs, around the lakes in Arusha and Manyara NPs, and the River Drive in Ruaha NP.

life, although a second adult female will occasionally share the territory of one male in areas of high density. Adult pairs are typically accompanied by one or two juvenile offspring, which remain with the parents for 7–12 months. Pairs defend a territory, ranging from 5–35 ha (10–85 acres). Family members use regular dung middens that are usually located on the boundaries of their territory. Kirk's Dik-diks are active throughout the day and at night.

Distribution in Tanzania

Kirk's Dik-diks are distributed across northern and central Tanzania, but absent from the south, parts of the west, and the coastal areas. They are found in all of the northern National Parks as well as Ruaha NP. The southern distribution extends to the Mpanga–Kipengere GR, and there is a population in the low-lying areas of Udzungwa NP, although they are absent from Mikumi NP and the Selous ecosystem. They are sparsely distributed in western Tanzania, including Ugalla and Burigi–Biharamulo GRs, and possibly Katavi NP, and still occur in pockets of scrub bushland and agricultural land throughout Shinyanga and Tabora regions. Kirk's Dik-diks can be found on the outskirts of large cities such as Arusha.

Population size and conservation status
Density estimates in northern Tanzania range from 3–60 animals per km² (8–165 animals per mi²). They do well in areas that have been overgrazed by livestock or cleared by humans, and are particularly abundant in drier parts of the country including the Yaeda Valley, Lake Natron, West Kilimanjaro, and Mkomazi and Tarangire NPs. They are also common in parts of the Serengeti ecosystem and the Rungwa–Ruaha ecosystem. Kirk's Dik-diks are less frequent in miombo habitat, although they are fairly common in Ugalla GR and parts of Chunya District. They are uncommon in Piti, Kigosi and Burigi–Biharamulo GRs. Although widely hunted, this species can survive in areas close to human settlement and numbers across much of the country are probably stable.

Kirk's Dik-dik
TOP LEFT: female ssp. *cavendishi*, Tarangire NP;
TOP RIGHT: male ssp. *thomasi*, Ruaha NP;
BOTTOM: camera trap photo, male ssp. *kirkii*, Mkomazi NP

Klipspringer

Oreotragus oreotragus

SWAHILI: Mbuzi Mawe

A small, stocky, antelope with a rounded back and a dense, coarse coat that has a grizzled, 'salt-and-pepper', appearance. There is much individual variation in colour, although they are generally russet or yellowish on the sides, neck and face, and grey on the legs, back and haunches. The underside is white. The horns are vertical, ridged at the base and smooth at the tip (8–15 cm | 3–6" long). The presence of horns in females varies by subspecies. The Klipspringer walks on the tips of its hoofs and has a very upright stance.

Subspecies

O. o. schillingsii: west and northern Tanzania; females often have horns.

O. o. aceratos: southern Tanzania south of the Rufiji River; females lack horns.

Similar species

The Mountain Reedbuck (*page 220*) occurs in similar habitats, but is larger, usually found in larger groups, and has a distinctive long tail with white beneath.

Ecology and social behaviour

Klipspringers inhabit rocky terrain, including small hills, rock kopjes, mountain slopes and escarpments. They live in monogamous pairs or family groups of 4–5 individuals, comprising two adults and their young. They defend small territories that vary in size from 8–50 ha (20–120 acres), which tend to be larger in areas with lower rainfall. Males will often stand motionless on a high rock keeping watch for predators or rivals, adopting a characteristic position with all four feet bunched close together under the body. When alarmed, they can leap from boulder to boulder with great agility. Mostly diurnal, Klipspringers have activity peaks in early morning and late afternoon, and feed on herbs, leaves, flowers and fruits.

Distribution in Tanzania

Widely distributed in mainland Tanzania, Klipspringers are found in all mainland National Parks, except for Gombe, Rubondo,

Least Concern	
HB:	75–100 cm (29–39")
Ht:	43–60 cm (17–24")
Tail:	6–10 cm (2–4")
Wt:	M 9·0–11·6 kg (20–26 lb)
	F 10·5–16·0 kg (23–35 lb)

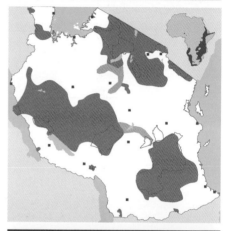

Where to look

Klipspringers are commonly encountered in the Serengeti NP in the hills of the Mbuzi Mawe camp (north of Seronera) and on many kopjes in northern Serengeti NP, including around Lobo Lodge. They are also frequently seen along the escarpment in Manyara NP. In Ruaha NP they can be seen at Kimirimatonge Hill.

Sadaani, Mikumi and possibly Udzungwa where interviews with local villagers suggest they may be present. There are historical records from the Livingstone Mountains, although there have been no recent sightings in the area. There are also historical records from parts of Singida Region, where the species may still be present.

Population size and conservation status

There are no population estimates for this species and the status of the Tanzanian population is unclear. Klipspringers are restricted to rocky areas, and may be locally common in suitable habitat within a small section of a National Park, but otherwise absent from the rest of the National Park. They are common in areas of favourable habitat across much of western Tanzania, in the Serengeti ecosystem, Lake Natron and the surrounding mountains, and Manyara NP. This species is uncommon in Tarangire and Ruaha NPs and much of the Selous GR, mainly because of limited habitat, and is rare in Arusha and Kilimanjaro NPs. Klipspringers are less susceptible than most other ungulates to habitat loss, although localized populations are often small and vulnerable to extinction by hunting.

Klipspringer
TOP: male ssp. *schillingsii*, Serengeti NP (Tanzania); BOTTOM: female ssp. *schillingsii* (Uganda)

Thomson's Gazelle

Eudorcas thomsonii

SWAHILI: Swala Tomi

A small gazelle with a sandy-rufous coloured back and a prominent black horizontal band along the side with paler brown above and a white belly. The rump is white, bordered by thin black stripes. The tail is entirely black. The face has a rufous blaze running from the horns to the nose and bold lateral black and white stripes below the eyes. Males have strongly ridged, slightly rear-curving horns that bend forward at the tip (30–45 cm | 12–18" long). Females have very small, thin and straight horns (8–15 cm | 3–6" long).

Near Threatened	
HB:	92–107 cm (36–42")
Ht:	58–70 cm (23–28")
Tail:	20–28 cm (8–11")
Wt:	M 17–25 kg (37–55 lb) | F 13–20 kg (29–44 lb)

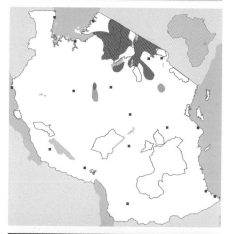

Similar species
The Grant's Gazelle (*page 214*) is larger and has a white rump patch that extends above the tail (see comparative photographs, *page 266*).

Ecology and social behaviour
Thomson's Gazelles are mostly found in open grassland with short grasses and occasionally in farmland; they usually avoid tall grasses and bushland except during migration. They feed predominantly on grass, supplemented with occasional browse. In the Serengeti NP they follow similar seasonal movements to the migratory Common Wildebeest (*page 238*) and Plains Zebra (*page 170*) populations, but they remain longer on the open plains in the wet season and do not migrate as far north (*i.e.* not into the Maasai Mara in Kenya) during the dry season. Female Thomson's Gazelles move together in unstable, loosely knit aggregations of up to 200 individuals. Male Thomson's Gazelles form small territories of 1–3 ha (3–8 acres) or live in bachelor herds. During migrations these social groupings generally break down and several thousand individuals may move together in a loose association.

Distribution in Tanzania
Thomson's Gazelle is restricted to a narrow area of northern Tanzania. It is found throughout the Serengeti ecosystem, with the largest numbers concentrated on the short-grass plains. There is a small population in the Yaeda Valley and in the Wembere Wetland, although the full extent of its

Where to look

Sightings of this species are guaranteed throughout the year on the short- and long-grass plains of the Ngorongoro CA and the Serengeti NP, as well as within the Ngorongoro Crater itself. Scattered individuals are occasionally seen in the open plains south of Lake Natron.

distribution in the Wembere is not known. A population that formerly occurred in Shinyanga has now disappeared. It is also found on the open grass plains of Manyara NP, Manyara Ranch, occasionally in the very northern tip of Tarangire NP, and from Mto wa Mbu village up to Lake Natron. It occurs widely on the Simanjiro plains to the east of Tarangire NP and across much of West Kilimanjaro, where high cattle densities create the species' preferred short-grass feeding conditions. There are former hunting records from the Kitwai Plains but its current status there is unknown.

Population size and conservation status

The largest concentration of Thomson's Gazelles occurs in the Serengeti ecosystem, although numbers there have fallen from approximately 600,000 in 1970 to 328,000 in 1996. This decline is probably linked to the increase in the number of Common Wildebeest, which are competitors for food, although the gazelle population now appears to have stabilized. Numbers in other parts of their range are much lower.

An aerial count in 2010 recorded 345 individuals around Lake Natron and 213 individuals in West Kilimanjaro, where they are becoming increasingly uncommon. There is a small population on Manyara Ranch, while the population in the Simanjiro plains probably numbers in the low hundreds. There are no figures for the Wembere Wetland population, which is believed to be small and declining. The main threat to the Thomson's Gazelle is poaching outside protected areas.

Thomson's Gazelle
TOP: male (Kenya); BOTTOM: female with newborn calf, Ngorongoro CA (Tanzania)

Grant's Gazelle

Nanger granti

SWAHILI: Swala Granti

A large gazelle with a light tan back and white underbelly. Younger animals and females typically have a horizontal black or brown band running along the flank, although this feature is absent in adult males. There are two prominent white stripes running down the face from above the eye to the nose, and a black ridge above the nose. The white colouring on the rump extends both below and above the tail, and is often bordered by black stripes. The tail is white with a black tassel at the tip. Males have large, heavily ridged horns (50–77 cm | 20–30" long); horns of females are noticeably shorter (35–45 cm | 14–18" long) and thinner.

Subspecies

G. g. robertsi: west of East African Rift wall; horns splay sharply outwards and slightly backwards about one-third of the length from the base. Black side-stripe on females often faint or absent.

G. g. granti: east of East African Rift wall; horns have a lyrate shape, gradually curving outwards and then sharply inwards at the tip.

Similar species

Female Grant's Gazelles can be mistaken for male Thomson's Gazelles (*page 212*). However, Thomson's Gazelles have no white above the tail, are slightly smaller, and the horns curve backwards rather than straight upwards (see comparative photographs, *page 266*).

Ecology and social behaviour

Grant's Gazelles are found in open savanna grassland, open bushland and woodland, and semi-desert scrub. They feed on both browse and grasses, and are largely water-independent. They typically move in herds of about ten females and fawns controlled by a dominant male, or in larger mixed sex herds of 40+ animals. Larger, temporary aggregations of up to 400 animals occasionally occur. Males are sometimes territorial, particularly during the wet season when they may establish territories of 2·5–10 km² (1–4 mi²). Younger

Least Concern	
HB:	M 135–160 cm (53–63")
	F 120–140 cm (47–55")
Ht:	M 85–94 cm (33–37")
	F 75–83 cm (30–33")
Tail:	25–35 cm (10–14")
Wt:	M 55–80 kg (121–176 lb)
	F 35–50 kg (77–110 lb)

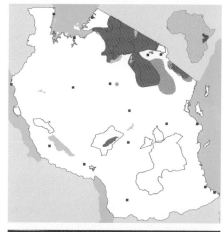

Where to look

Grant's Gazelles can be reliably seen throughout the year around Ndutu, Naabi Hill and Seronera in the Serengeti ecosystem. In Tarangire NP, small groups are commonly observed on the open plains a few kilometres south of the main bridge. In Ruaha NP they are frequently seen along the River Drive.

males often form bachelor groups. Grant's Gazelles in the Serengeti are migratory, usually occupying the short-grass plains in the dry season and the woodlands in the wet season.

Distribution in Tanzania

Grant's Gazelles are concentrated in the north of the country with the exception of one small, isolated population along the Ruaha River in Ruaha NP. They are widely distributed in the Serengeti ecosystem, Lake Natron, West Kilimanjaro, Mkomazi NP and most of the Tarangire ecosystem, including Tarangire NP and occasionally Manyara NP. They extend across much of the Maasai Steppe as far south as the Kitwai plain. There is a record from 2010 from Ngori, east of Singida.

Population size and conservation status

The largest population of Grant's Gazelle in Africa is in the Serengeti ecosystem, with counts suggesting 35,000–55,000 animals. Most of these are concentrated on the short-grass plains of Ngorongoro CA and Serengeti NP, and in central Loliondo, with smaller numbers occurring in the western Serengeti. A count in the Tarangire ecosystem in 2011 recorded 4,300 individuals, mostly concentrated in the Simanjiro Plains and the open grasslands north of Mto wa Mbu village, with small numbers in Tarangire NP. In 2010, 905 Grant's Gazelles were counted in the Lake Natron area and 136 across West Kilimanjaro, and a further 440 were recorded in Mkomazi NP. The species is uncommon in Ruaha NP and habitat loss and poaching has reduced populations in West Kilimanjaro and the Maasai Steppe. Fortunately, the largest concentration, on the plains of the Serengeti and Ngorongoro CA, is well protected and the overall population is stable.

Grant's Gazelle
TOP LEFT: male ssp. *robertsi*, Ngorongoro CA; TOP RIGHT: male ssp. *granti*, Tarangire NP; BOTTOM: female and calf ssp. *robertsi*, Ngorongoro CA

Gerenuk

Litocranius walleri

Walller's Gazelle

SWAHILI: Swala Twiga

A tall gazelle with a reddish-brown 'saddle', light brown sides and legs, and a white belly. The tail is of medium length, sparsely haired, brown on the upper side and bare on the underside, with a small black tuft at the tip. The neck and legs are extremely long, giving rise to its Swahili name, which means 'giraffe gazelle'. It has a long, thin face, large ears and white ring around the eye. Only the males have horns (32–58 cm | 13–23" long), which are 'S'-shaped and heavily ridged.

Near Threatened	
HB:	140–160 cm (55–63")
Ht:	M 90–105 cm (35–41")
	F 80–100 cm (31–39")
Tail:	22–35 cm (9–14")
Wt:	M 35–52 kg (77–114 lb) | F 30–45 kg (66–99 lb)

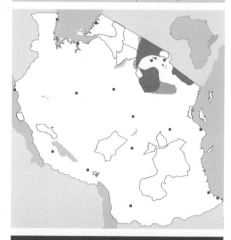

Subspecies

L. w. walleri: only subspecies found in Tanzania.

Similar species

This species is easily distinguished from other gazelles by its long neck.

Ecology and social behaviour

The Gerenuk occurs in arid, open or semi-open bushland, in areas with less than 600 mm (24") of annual rainfall, being able to survive with little or no water. It is diurnal and exclusively a browser, feeding mainly on leaves and shoots, frequently standing on its hind legs to reach higher vegetation. Adult males are territorial with a home range of 0·8–3 km² (0·3–1 mi²) and usually solitary. Social groupings can be single-sex or mixed-sex, with group sizes varying from 2–10 individuals.

Distribution in Tanzania

The Gerenuk is restricted to areas of arid bushland and thicket in the north of the country. It occurs across a swathe of land stretching from the eastern shores of Lake Natron to the lower western slopes of Mount Kilimanjaro, and south as far as the northern slopes of Mount Meru. It is distributed throughout Mkomazi NP and in the drier parts of the Tarangire ecosystem, including the southern half of Tarangire NP, the Mkungunero GR and the Maasai Steppe as far south as Kitwai. There is also a population in the Lalatema Mountains.

Where to look

Gerenuks can be reliably seen in West Kilimanjaro, particularly in the Enduimet WMA or around Ndarakwai Ranch. They are also regularly seen from the main road between Arusha and Namanga, just south of Longido town, and on the dirt road between Longido and Gelai towns. They are not as easily seen in Mkomazi NP because of the comparatively thick bush, although a good place to try is the area between Ndea to Kamakota Hills in the northwest of the National Park.

The extent of its distribution in the eastern section of the Maasai Steppe is unclear.

Population size and conservation status

Ground counts in Mkomazi NP in 1996 suggested a minimum population of 930 individuals but this is probably an underestimate. There are no accurate figures for other areas, although Gerenuks are common in parts of the Lake Natron area, particularly around Gelai and between Kitumbeini and Longido Mountains.

They are also fairly common throughout West Kilimanjaro, particularly in the wooded savannas and the edges of the open plains. Gerenuks formerly occurred in reasonable numbers in the Makame depression, although the population has declined in recent years due to over-hunting and they are now uncommon there. The main threat to this species is uncontrolled hunting, and to a lesser degree agricultural expansion in the southern Maasai Steppe, although most of its range is too arid to sustain agriculture.

Gerenuk
TOP LEFT: male (Kenya);
TOP RIGHT: male feeding by standing on hind legs (Kenya);
BOTTOM: female, Tarangire NP (Tanzania)

Oribi

Ourebia ourebi

A small, graceful, long-legged antelope with a long neck, a tan coat with a white underbelly, large ears, and a conspicuous black glandular spot below the ear. There is a small white patch on the rump on either side of the tail. The tail has a white underside, and the colour of the upper side varies between subspecies. Only males have horns, which are heavily ringed at the base and average 10–12 cm (4–5") long; they can reach 16 cm (6") in length in the Serengeti population. Females are on average 2 kg (4 lb) heavier than males.

Subspecies

O. o. hastata: west and southern Tanzania; tail has black upper side.

O. o. cottoni: Serengeti NP only; tail has tan-brown upper side, white underside.

Similar species

Bohor Reedbuck (*page 224*) and Southern Reedbuck (*page 222*) are larger, have a longer, thicker coat, and a longer tail that extends below the rear haunches. In both these species, the separation between the dorsal coat and the white underbelly is less distinct than in the Oribi. Male reedbucks have curved rather than straight horns. Steenboks (*page 206*) have shorter necks and lack a black spot beneath the ear (see comparative photographs, *page 267*).

Ecology and social organization

Oribi live in flat or hilly open grasslands and floodplains, favouring recently burned areas, and in open, dry swamp areas within miombo bushland. They are primarily grazers, although will eat browse during the dry season. They are active both during the day and at night. Oribi live in pairs or in small groups of three to six individuals, with males maintaining a territory of approximately 60 ha (150 acres) that is occupied by one or two females and their young. Dominant males will occasionally tolerate one or more other males in their territory. They can run extremely fast and often produce several short, loud whistles when alarmed.

Least Concern	
HB:	93–112 cm (38–45")
Ht:	60–69 cm (23–29")
Tail:	7–11 cm (3–4")
Wt:	15–21 kg (33–46 lb)

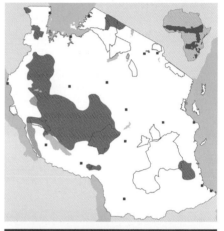

Where to look

Oribi are very common in the northern Serengeti, and are easily seen in the open grassland areas in the vicinity of Lobo Lodge. The open grasslands and swamps interspersed in the miombo woodland on the plateau area of Ruaha NP is also a good place to look for them.

Distribution in Tanzania

There are three main populations of Oribi in Tanzania: in the west, east, and north of the country. In the west, their range extends from Kitulo NP north to the Ugandan border, including Ruaha and Katavi NPs. They may still occur in the Kalambo–Loasi watershed. Another population in the southeast ranges from the eastern section of the Selous GR (in the Matandu River area), south into Lindi Region. This species was formerly known from Masasi District close to the border with Mozambique, but there have been no recent records from that area. The third population occurs in the northern Serengeti, including Ikorongo and Grumeti GRs and the western parts of Loliondo.

In Serengeti NP, its distribution starts very abruptly a few kilometres south of Lobo Lodge and continues to the Kenya border.

Population size and conservation status
The population in the northern Serengeti has been increasing rapidly during the past 20 years and now probably exceeds 7,000 individuals. It is also fairly common across many parts of western Tanzania, including Ugalla and Moyowosi GRs, and between Lake Rukwa and the Rungwa–Kizigo GRs.

It is common in grasslands in miombo areas of western Ruaha NP. Little is known about the status of the southeastern population, although it is probably uncommon and thought to be declining as a result of being hunted for bushmeat. The Oribi has disappeared from many areas around Lake Victoria as a result of habitat loss and hunting, although their great speed makes them less susceptible to hunting with dogs than other small ungulates.

Oribi
TOP LEFT: male ssp. *hastata*, Ugalla GR;
TOP RIGHT: male ssp. *cottoni*, Serengeti NP;
BOTTOM: female ssp. *cottoni*, Serengeti NP

Mountain Reedbuck

Redunca fulvorufula

SWAHILI: Tohe Milima

A medium-sized antelope with a soft, woolly coat. The fur is grey above, contrasting sharply with the bright white underside; the neck, forehead and back of the ears are brown. The tail is very bushy, grey-brown on the upper side, white underneath and with a white tip. There is a black glandular patch below the ear. Only males have horns, which are short (10–18 cm | 4–7" long) and curve forward at the tip.

Subspecies
R. f. chanleri: only subspecies found in Tanzania.

Similar species
The Bohor Reedbuck (*page 224*) has a light brown rather than grey coat, and is generally found in grasslands, not hilly areas (see comparative photographs, *page 267*).

Ecology and social behaviour
Found on mountain ridges, grassy hills and rocky slopes with scattered trees and bushes where there is permanent water. It is exclusively a grazer, feeding on soft green grasses and avoiding dry stems. Mountain Reedbucks live in small family groups of three to ten individuals, with female territories overlapping with those of territorial males, which are solitary. Male territory sizes are approximately 28 ha (70 acres), while female home ranges average 57 ha (140 acres). They are both nocturnal and diurnal, with activity peaks during cooler periods.

Distribution in Tanzania
The Mountain Reedbuck has a very restricted distribution in Tanzania, and is now only found in a narrow belt of land between the Serengeti NP, Mount Kilimanjaro and Tarangire NP. It is widespread in the hills and rocky outcrops in the Serengeti ecosystem, including the Kuka, Ngare Nanyuki and Nyamaluma Hills within Serengeti NP, in Grumeti GR and in the hilly areas of western Loliondo. It is also found on Lolsimongori, Monduli, Burko and Gelai Mountains.

Least Concern	
HB:	120–145 cm (47 57")
Ht:	72–84 cm (28–33")
Tail:	17–26 cm (7–10")
Wt:	22–37 kg (48–81 lb)

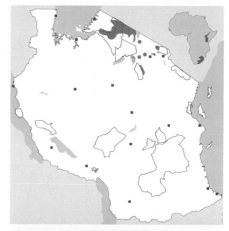

Where to look
Small groups may be observed on the lower slopes of the Kuka Hills, just north of the Kleins Camp gate in northeastern Serengeti NP, and in the hills in the adjacent Loliondo area. They are also occasionally seen on Ndarakwai Ranch in West Kilimanjaro.

Small populations exist on several of the mountains east of Tarangire NP, including Oldonyo Sambu, Oldonyo Ngahari, Lorkiman and possibly Lolkisale. It was last seen in Tarangire NP in 1993 but may still occur as a vagrant in the area. There are a few scattered populations in West Kilimanjaro, notably in the Larkarian Hills and in the hills just west of Ngare Nairobi.

Population size and conservation status
There is no information on the number of Mountain Reedbucks in Tanzania, although the population is declining. The highest numbers are found in Loliondo and Serengeti NP, where it is still relatively common in

suitable habitat. It is also relatively common in parts of the Lake Natron area, and on Lolsimongori and Monduli Mountains. During the past 40 years it has disappeared from Mount Hanang, Lake Jipe, the North Pare Mountains, and even from well-protected National Parks including Arusha and probably Manyara. The species was formerly commonly seen inside the Ngorongoro Crater and around the Crater rim, but it has not been recorded there for many years and is now very rare in the Ngorongoro Conservation Area. Because this species typically occurs at low densities in isolated populations, it is particularly vulnerable to local extinction from poaching, habitat loss or stochastic events. The Mountain Reedbuck should be considered locally 'Vulnerable' in Tanzania.

Mountain Reedbuck
TOP: male ssp. *chanleri* (Kenya);
BOTTOM: female (South Africa)

Southern Reedbuck

Redunca arundinum

SWAHILI: Tohe Ndope

A medium-sized antelope. Dorsal colour ranges from light yellow-brown to grey-brown or dark brown. The chin and throat are paler and the underparts are white. There are black stripes running down the front of the forelegs. The coat is fine, almost woolly. The tail is very bushy and reaches halfway down the hock; it is white underneath and the same colour as the coat on the upper side. Both sexes have a black glandular patch below the ear. Only the males have horns (30 cm | 12" long), which curve backwards then forwards in a gentle arc.

Subspecies
R. a. occidentalis: only subspecies found in Tanzania.

Similar species
The range of the Bohor Reedbuck (*page 224*) overlaps with the Southern Reedbuck in several places in Tanzania and the two species look similar at a distance. The Bohor Reedbuck is a smaller animal and has a yellowish or tan pelage, whereas the Southern Reedbuck is a duller grey-brown colour with a slightly longer, bushier tail. The horns of male Bohor Reedbucks are shorter and distinctly hooked at the tip, while those of the Southern Reedbuck are more widely splayed at the base, giving them the profile of a small Waterbuck (*page 228*). The white, new growth at the base of the horn is more pronounced in the Southern Reedbuck (see comparative photographs, *page 267*).

Ecology and social behaviour
Southern Reedbucks are found in valleys and glades with tall grass in miombo woodland, always close to permanent water. They also occur in upland grasslands with some woody or rocky cover, being replaced by Bohor Reedbuck as the habitat changes to open grasslands and floodplains. They are diurnal and form monogamous pairs, although are often seen singly or in small family parties of females with young. Larger groupings are rare. Home ranges vary from 5–120 ha (12–300 acres). They are predominantly

Least Concern	
HB:	120–160 cm (47–63")
Ht:	80–95 cm (31–37")
Tail:	20–30 cm (8–12")
Wt:	M 43–68 kg (95–150 lb)
	F 32–50 kg (70–110 lb)

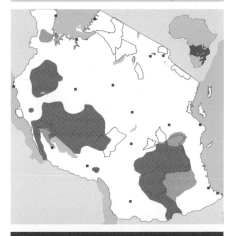

Where to look
In Ruaha NP, Southern Reedbucks can be commonly seen in open areas in the miombo woodland to the west of the National Park, including around Magangwe, although there are few roads in this area and it is seldom visited by tourists. In Katavi NP it is occasionally seen in the miombo woodland on the road between the Ikuu Ranger Post and Sitalike.

fresh grass grazers, but will occasionally take small quantities of herbs and in some areas may browse extensively.

Distribution in Tanzania
Southern Reedbucks are found in open areas of miombo woodland throughout the south and west of the country. They occur throughout the southern Selous GR (although their presence in the photographic area is unclear) and parts of the Selous–Niassa corridor, including the Muhuwesi GR. They are also found in Kitulo NP. In Ruaha NP, Southern Reedbucks are distributed in the miombo woodland habitat, but are

replaced by the Bohor Reedbucks in the Usangu Wetland. They are present throughout the Rungwa–Kizigo GRs, in Katavi NP, and in the Rukwa, Lwafi, Ugalla, Moyowosi and Uvinza GRs, and the Sitebe–Sifuta Moutains. There are past records from the Burigi–Biharamulo GR, although the species was not recorded there during a recent survey.

Population size and conservation status

There are no accurate population estimates for this species. It is common throughout much of western and southern Tanzania including the southern Selous ecosystem, Chunya, Lukwati, Piti, Rungwa, Ugalla and Moyowosi GRs, although it is less common in Moyowosi–Uvinza. In Ruaha NP it is relatively common in the western plateau of the National Park. It occurs in low numbers in the Rukwa GR and Katavi NP and is rare in Kitulo NP. Hunting and loss of suitable habitat outside protected areas are the main threats to this species. The difficulty of distinguishing Southern and Bohor Reedbucks means there are insufficient data to determine population trends.

Southern Reedbuck
TOP: male (Zambia);
BOTTOM: female
(Mozambique)

Bohor Reedbuck

Redunca redunca

SWAHILI: Tohe, Forhi

A medium-sized antelope that is uniform reddish-yellow or straw-yellow above and white below. The upper side of the tail is the same colour as the body and the underside is white. The front legs often have a black stripe running down the front. There is a patch of bare skin below the ears, although this is not always visible. Only the males have horns that are short (21 cm | 8" long) and curve backwards and then sharply forwards, forming a distinct hook at the tip.

Subspecies
R. r. wardi: only subspecies found in Tanzania.

Similar species
The Southern Reedbuck (*page 222*) is significantly larger, has a duller grey-brown coat, and the horns of the males are widely splayed at the base and lack a hooked tip; its tail is also longer and bushier. In areas where the ranges of the two species overlap, the Bohor Reedbuck dominates on the larger floodplains and areas of large open grassland, while the Southern Reedbuck occurs mainly in small openings within the woodlands. The Mountain Reedbuck (*page 220*) has a grey body. The Oribi (*page 218*) is much smaller with a shorter tail (see comparative photographs, *page 267*).

Ecology and social behaviour
Associated with floodplains and riverine grasslands in close proximity to water. They are usually found in small groups of two to five individuals. Males defend territories that encompass the home ranges of several females. Bohor Reedbucks will also occasionally converge in large groups of over 100 animals during drought periods or in areas of freshly burned grass. Home ranges of 25–60 ha (60–150 acres) were recorded in the Serengeti NP. Bohor Reedbucks feed almost exclusively on grasses.

Least Concern	
HB:	100–135 cm (39–53")
Ht:	M 75–89 cm (30–35")
	F 69–76 cm (27–30")
Tail:	18–20 cm (7–8")
Wt:	M 40–65 kg (90–140 lb)
	F 35–50 kg (80–110 lb)

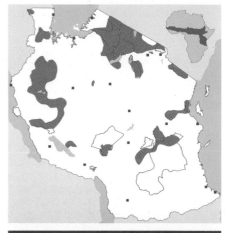

Where to look
This species is frequently seen in the Tarangire River in Tarangire NP in the dry season, along the river roads south of the main bridge. Other good places to look include along the Seronera River in Serengeti NP. Large groups of this species can be found around the National Park headquarters in Saadani NP. In Katavi NP they are easily seen in all of the large swamps.

Distribution in Tanzania
Bohor Reedbuck has a scattered distribution in northern, central and western Tanzania. They are still widespread in the west, occurring in Burigi–Biharamulo GRs, Moyowosi–Kigosi GRs, Lake Sagara, Ugalla GR, the Wembere Wetland, the Katavi NP, and in the Usangu Wetland in Ruaha NP. In the south they are found in northern Selous GR, Mikumi NP and the Kilombero Valley. There is a population along the coast in Saadani NP and in the Wami–Mbiki WMA. In the north, they occur in Tarangire and

Manyara NPs, the Ngorongoro CA, Serengeti NP, Maswa GR and Mkomazi NP. They are also found on the lower, western slopes of Mount Kilimanjaro and occasionally in the northern grasslands in Arusha NP.

Population size and conservation status
Bohor Reedbucks are very common in some protected areas in the west including Moyowosi–Uvinza GRs, Ugalla GR and Katavi NP. Ground counts suggest a population of approximately 5,000 individuals in Saadani NP. Aerial counts indicate a population of 3,000 in the Serengeti NP, while in Tarangire NP they are common along the main river. The species is uncommon in Mkomazi NP and rare in Arusha NP and the Selous GR. There is still a small but stable population in the Burigi–Biharamulo GR of around 100 individuals. Bohor Reedbucks are threatened by illegal hunting and habitat loss, in particular the loss of swamp–grasslands to agriculture or intensive grazing by livestock outside protected areas.

Bohor Reedbuck
TOP: male, Ngorongoro CA;
BOTTOM: female, Tarangire NP

225

Puku

Kobus vardonii

SWAHILI: Sheshe

A mid-sized antelope with a shaggy coat that is tan to golden-yellow above and whitish below. There is a narrow white ring around the eye and the chin and throat are pale. There are no black markings on the legs. The short and slender tail has the upper side the same colour as the body and the underside white. Territorial males often have black streaks on their lower neck, resulting from the oily secretions of their pre-orbital glands. Only the males have horns (41–55 cm | 16–22" long), which are lyre-shaped and heavily ringed.

Similar species
Female Bohor Reedbucks (*page 224*) and Southern Reedbucks (*page 222*) are a similar shape and size, but have black on the forelegs, visible black facial glands and longer, bushier tails (see comparative photographs, *page 267*). The similar **Uganda Kob** *Kobus kob thomasi* formerly occurred on both the eastern and northwestern shores of Lake Victoria but is now extinct in Tanzania as a combined result of both hunting and habitat loss.

Ecology and social behaviour
Pukus are strictly grazers and inhabit grasslands around floodplains, marshes, and rivers. They are most common in the grassy areas between rivers or floodplains and adjacent woodland, and are sometimes found in glades within open woodland. Adult males form temporary territories (averaging 4 km² | 1·5 mi²) lasting from a few days to several months, while non-territorial males live in bachelor groups of up to 40 individuals. Females live in loose associations that fluctuate in size from 6–23 animals. These female groups may traverse the territories of several males which attempt to keep the females within their territory. Pukus are both diurnal and crepuscular, with activity peaks around dawn and dusk.

Distribution in Tanzania
There are two populations of Puku in Tanzania. The largest population is concentrated around the banks of the Kilombero River in the

	Near Threatened
HB:	126–146 cm (50–57")
Ht:	73–83 cm (29–33")
Tail:	26–30 cm (10–12")
Wt:	M 67–91 kg (150–200 lb)
	F 48–78 kg (110–170 lb)

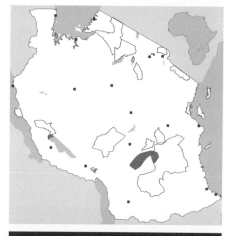

Where to look
In the wet season (November–April), Pukus can be observed on the edge of the southern floodplains below Nambinga Forest Reserve. The Forest Reserve is approximately 20 kilometres north of the town of Itete.

Kilombero Valley, a large seasonal wetland covering some 2,000 km² (770 mi²); a few individuals also extend into the western section of the Selous GR where the Kilombero River enters the Game Reserve. The second, much smaller, population is found in the Rukwa GR at the northern end of Lake Rukwa. During the mid-1960s this population was distributed widely around the lake, including an isolated population in northern Katavi NP, but has contracted significantly since then. A small population that once inhabited the northern region of Lake Nyasa was extirpated in the 1960s.

Population size and conservation status
The Kilombero Valley contains one of the largest populations of Pukus in Africa.

However, numbers have been declining steadily, from 50,000–60,000 in the 1990s, to 40,000 in 2002 and 18,000 in 2009, as a result of poaching and habitat loss. The Kilombero Valley has no official protected status and despite being designated as a Ramsar site in 2002 continues to suffer serious habitat fragmentation and overgrazing. Unless these threats are addressed, the population of Pukus in the Kilombero Valley is likely to continue to decline. The population of Pukus around Lake Rukwa was estimated at 5,000 animals in the 1960s, but rising water levels and a reduction in habitat due to livestock grazing have reduced this population to approximately 780 individuals in an area of 70 km² (30 mi²), all within the Rukwa GR. Pukus are vulnerable to hunting, particularly during the dry season when they congregate in larger herds along rivers and open areas. Poaching has been the principal reason for their extermination in much of their historical range.

Puku
TOP: male (Zambia);
BOTTOM: female (Zambia)

Waterbuck

Kobus ellipsiprymnus

Common Waterbuck and Defassa Waterbuck

SWAHILI: Kuro

A large antelope with a shaggy coat, varying in colour from dark grey to grey-brown or reddish-brown. Females are usually paler than males. The lower parts of the legs are dark brown or dark grey. There is a white collar around the throat and sides of the neck extending to the base of the ears, which are light brown above and white inside and have a black tip. The tip of the muzzle and lower lip is white and there is a white marking above the eye. The upper side of the tail is the same colour as the body, the underside is white and there is a small dark tassel at the tip. Only males have horns (64–89 cm | 25–35" long), which curve forward in a long arc, the lower three-quarters being heavily ridged. Their coats are covered with an oily secretion and they exude a strong musky scent.

Subspecies

K. e. ellipsiprymnus: Common Waterbuck, east of the East African Rift wall; distinctive white ring circling the rump.

K. e. defassa: Defassa Waterbuck, west of the East African Rift wall; the all-white rump does not extend above the base of the tail. It is usually more rufous-brown than the Common Waterbuck.

Note: The range of the two subspecies overlap in some places, including Manyara NP where individuals with intermediate characteristics have been recorded.

Similar species

Large male Southern Reedbucks (*page 222*) have a similar horn shape and can sometimes be a light grey-brown colour. This may cause confusion at distance but the reedbuck is significantly smaller and lacks a white rump.

Ecology and social behaviour

Waterbucks can be found in floodplains, grasslands and open woodlands, but always near (less than 2 km | 1·25 mi) to water. They are mainly grazers, although sometimes feed on leaves and herbs, and occasionally fruit.

Least Concern	
HB:	170–250 cm (67–98")
Ht:	120 cm (47")
Tail:	35–50 cm (14–20")
Wt:	M 190–280 kg (420–620 lb)
	F 175–200 kg (385–440 lb)

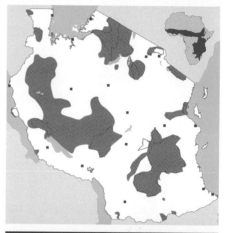

Where to look

This species is easily seen in many of the National Parks in Tanzania. The Common Waterbuck is reliably encountered in Tarangire, Arusha and Sadaani NPs,- and the Defassa Waterbuck can be seen in Ngorongoro CA and in the Serengeti, Ruaha and Katavi NPs.

Waterbucks are sociable animals, forming herds of 5–25 individuals. Larger herds occur during the wet season when food is more abundant. Males travel in bachelor herds until about 5–6 years old, when they establish firm territories (1–2 km² | 0·5–0·75 mi²). Females and their offspring form nursery herds and travel freely between territories.

Distribution in Tanzania

Waterbucks are widely distributed across protected areas in Tanzania. They occur in most of the mainland National Parks, except for Rubondo and Kitulo, and they are now extinct in Gombe NP. They are also present in most Game Reserves, although are historically absent from Swagaswaga GR.

Population size and conservation status

Aerial counts suggest there are 6,700–10,900 Waterbucks in the major National Parks and Game Reserves in Tanzania, although these numbers may be underestimates as the animals often forage or rest in dense grass or riverine woodland and can be easily missed from the air. The largest populations are in the Selous–Mikumi ecosystem with 3,500–5,000 individuals and the Serengeti ecosystem with 1,000–2,500 individuals. Other significant populations are in the Ruaha–Rungwa ecosystem (1,000), Sadaani NP (300–1,000), Tarangire ecosystem (300–500), Moyowosi GR (100–500), Katavi ecosystem (200–300) and Ugalla GR (300). There are also small populations in Burigi–Biharamulo GRs and Wami–Mbiki WMA, and there are probably at least 100 individuals in Arusha NP. Illegal hunting and habitat loss pose the main threats to this species, but numbers in most National Parks and Game Reserves are currently stable.

Waterbuck
TOP: male ssp. *ellipsiprymnus*, Arusha NP (Tanzania);
BOTTOM: female ssp. *defassa* (Kenya)

Impala
Aepyceros melampus

SWAHILI: Swala Pala

A graceful, slender antelope with a smooth, shiny coat. The upperparts are a rich reddish-brown, the lower flanks are a light tan-brown and the belly is white. There are distinctive black stripes on the back of each thigh and down the centre of the upper side of the tail that form three vertical lines when seen from behind. The edges of the tail are reddish-brown and the underside is white, the long white hairs flaring outwards when the tail is held up. The ear tips are black, and black tufts of hair cover glands on the ankles of the hind legs. Only males have horns, which are S-curved and heavily ridged (56–83 cm | 22–33" long).

Subspecies
A. m. melampus: only subspecies found in Tanzania.

Similar species
Gerenuks (*page 216*) have a similar body colour but are more slender and have much longer neck and legs. Grant's Gazelles (*page 214*) have a white belly and rump, and white markings along the sides of the face (see comparative photographs, *page 267*).

Ecology and social behaviour
Impalas favour open woodland and bushland, and generally avoid open grasslands and floodplains. In Tanzania, they are widely distributed in both *Acacia–Commiphora* woodland and miombo woodland, although they are seldom found more than a few kilometres from water. They are mainly diurnal and feed on a wide range of both grasses and browse, with the proportion of either varying by season and location. *Acacia tortilis* seedpods are frequently eaten. Female Impalas live in discrete kin-related clans of 30–120 animals with fixed home ranges, averaging 2–3 km² (1 mi²). Individuals from these clans split regularly into smaller groups of 5–35 individuals, although these can merge to form groups of over 100 animals when food is plentiful. Males disperse from the group at 6–8 months old to join bachelor

Least Concern	
HB:	120–150 cm (47–59")
Ht:	80–93 cm (31–37")
Tail:	24–33 cm (9–13")
Wt:	M 53–65 kg (120–140 lb)
	F 40–53 kg (90–120 lb)

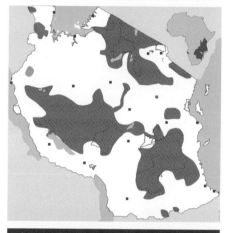

Where to look
In the northern National Parks, Impala sightings are almost guaranteed in the Serengeti, Manyara, Tarangire and Mkomazi. In the south, they are also easily seen in Mikumi, Ruaha, and Katavi NPs and the Selous GR.

herds. Territorial males will mate with any receptive females passing through their territory, and will attempt to prevent females from leaving the territory – this is usually associated with loud snorting and roaring by the male. Male territories are approximately 20–60 ha (50–150 acres).

Distribution in Tanzania
Impalas are widely distributed in Tanzania. They are historically absent from the coastal area, the eastern shores of Lake Tanganyika, and the highland areas of southwestern Tanzania. There is a population in the very south of the country in Lukwika GR, although they are absent from much of the Selous–Niassa corridor. They are also found across the Selous–Mikumi, Ruaha–Rungwa

and Katavi–Rukwa ecosystems, as well as Ugalla, Burigi–Biharamulo and Ibanda–Rumanyika GRs in the far northwest of the country. In northern Tanzania, Impalas are widespread in the Serengeti ecosystem, the Yaeda Valley, Tarangire and Manyara NPs, and occur in scattered populations from Lake Natron to West Kilimanjaro, in Mkomazi NP and across much of the Maasai Steppe, including the Suledo Forest.

Population size and conservation status
Tanzania has a large, stable population of Impala, numbering approximately 150,000

animals. The largest populations are in the Serengeti ecosystem with 70,000–90,000 individuals, and the Selous ecosystem with about 45,000 animals. Other important populations occur in the Ruaha–Rungwa ecosystem with 6,000–8,000 individuals, Tarangire with 5,000–7,000 animals, and Mkomazi NP where ground counts suggest there are at least 5,000 individuals. Ugalla GR and the Katavi–Rukwa ecosystem have populations of 2,500 and 1,400, respectively. Agricultural expansion and unregulated hunting, particularly outside protected areas, are the main threats to Impala populations.

Impala
TOP: male, Serengeti NP;
BOTTOM: female, Tarangire NP

231

Topi

Damaliscus lunatus

SWAHILI: Nyamera, Topi

A large antelope with a sloping back and a long, narrow face. The body is a glossy red-brown colour, with darker purple or purple-black markings on the upper parts of the forelegs, hindquarters, and thighs. The legs are a reddish-yellow colour below the knees. The tail, which is short and thin, is the same colour as the body at the base and has a black tassel of long hairs towards the tip. Both sexes have horns (35–56 cm | 14–22" long) that expand outwards at the base and then taper upwards and backwards. Males typically have longer horns than females.

Subspecies
D. l. jimela: only subspecies found in Tanzania.

Similar species
Both the Coke's Hartebeest (*page 234*) and Lichtenstein's Hartebeest (*page 236*) are lighter in colour, have a white rump, and lack purple patches on the flanks.

Ecology and social behaviour
Topi live in open and seasonally flooded grassland and in open, wooded grassland. They are are mostly diurnal and strictly grazers, preferring medium-height grasses. Breeding strategies for Topi vary considerably with habitat type, with some populations using a lek system, others using permanent male territories, and some a system of temporary male territories. In the Serengeti NP males defend small territories of approximately 1–4 km² (less than 1·5 mi²) and have semi-stable harems of 6–24 females and young. The dominant female will also play a role in keeping other females and males out of this territory. In some areas, large herds of up to 1,000 animals can form during the dry season.

Distribution in Tanzania
Topi are mainly restricted to northern and western Tanzania. Their stronghold is in the Serengeti ecosystem, particularly the central, northern and western sectors of the Serengeti NP, and they avoid the short-grass plains in the south. There are isolated records from

Least Concern	
HB:	190–230 cm (75–91")
Ht:	M 104–126 cm (41–50")
	F 105–118 cm (41–46")
Tail:	48–58 cm (19–23")
Wt:	M 111–147 kg (240–320 lb)
	F 90–130 kg (200–290 lb)

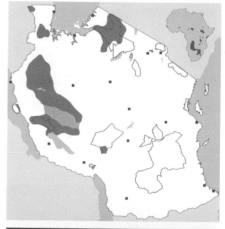

Where to look
The central and western sectors of the Serengeti NP are excellent areas to see Topi, with sightings of large numbers virtually guaranteed. In Katavi NP, single males or small groups of Topi are regularly seen on the open floodplains around the main lodges.

the very west of the Ngorongoro CA, and they are rare in Loliondo and the Maswa GR. There are populations in the Katavi–Rukwa ecosystem including Lukwati and Chunya West, and throughout the Moyowosi–Kigosi, Burigi–Biharamulo and Ibanda–Rumanyika GRs. There is also one record from the eastern section of Mahale NP. Topi formerly ranged between southern Ruaha NP and Mpanga–Kipengere GR, although they are now restricted to a small population in the Usangu plains in Ruaha NP which represents the southernmost extension of the species' distribution in Tanzania.

Population size and conservation status

The largest population of Topi in Africa occurs in the Serengeti ecosystem, where there are some 27,000–38,500 individuals. Other large populations occur in the Moyowosi–Kigosi GRs with 4,000–5,000 individuals and the Ugalla GR with 1,000–2,000 animals. There were 5,500 Topi in the Katavi–Rukwa ecosystem in 1998, although by 2009 only 560 were counted, a decline probably linked to poaching. In the Burigi–Biharamulo GRs, the Topi population has declined precipitously from over 2,000 individuals in 1990 to less than 50 in 2000 when the latest count was conducted. There are small populations in Ibanda– Rumanyika GRs, where it is easily seen. There is little information on the population in the eastern section of Mahale NP, although it is probably now rare. The population in Usangu, which now forms part of Ruaha NP, is also small. Threats include habitat loss and illegal hunting. The population in the Serengeti ecosystem is stable, while those in the west of Tanzania are declining.

Topi
TOP: male, Serengeti NP;
BOTTOM: female with calf,
Serengeti NP

Coke's Hartebeest

Alcelaphus buselaphus

SWAHILI: Kongoni

A large antelope with an elongated face and a sloping back. The body is a light brown colour above and pale below, with a white or pale rump. Both sexes have horns (38–57 cm | 15–22" long) that splay outwards before curving slightly backwards. The tail is white from the base to the mid-point and fringed with black hairs at the tip.

Least Concern	
HB:	177–200 cm (70–79")
Ht:	110–120 cm (44–47")
Tail:	45–70 cm (18–28")
Wt:	116–170 kg (250–375 lb)

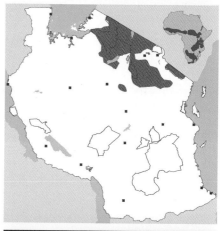

Subspecies
A. b. cokii: only subspecies found in Tanzania.

A. b. lelwel: Lelwel (or Jackson's) Hartebeest, Bukoba Region (although now extinct in Tanzania); has a reddish coat with a pale or whitish rump, and a high base to the horns (pedicel) that gives its face a very elongated appearance. Its horns (45–63 cm | 17–26" long) rise straight up and curve backwards at the tip.

Note: some authorities treat the Lichtenstein's Hartebeest as a subspecies of Coke's Hartebeest, while others consider it a full species.

Similar species
The Lichtenstein's Hartebeest (*page 236*) has a distinct red 'saddle', black on the knees and front legs, and horns that curve sharply backwards. The ranges of the two species do not overlap in Tanzania.

Where to look
Coke's Hartebeests can be reliably seen in the Ngorongoro Crater, and around Seronera and much of the central Serengeti NP.

Ecology and social behaviour
Coke's Hartebeests are found in grasslands and wooded grasslands associated with *Acacia–Commiphora* bushland, although they extend into miombo woodland at the southern edge of their range. They are mainly diurnal and strictly grazers, migrating between areas of short grass in the wet season and long grass in the dry season. Females and their young live in small family groups of 5–20 individuals. Males have small territories of 3 km² (1 mi²), often advertising their presence by standing on termite mounds; males without territories live in bachelor herds of up to 35 individuals.

Distribution in Tanzania
Coke's Hartebeests are restricted to north and central Tanzania. Their main stronghold is in the Serengeti ecosystem, with smaller populations in Tarangire NP, the Lake Natron area and Mkomazi NP. There are still a few individuals in West Kilimanjaro and occasional sightings from the Yaeda Valley. The population in Swagaswaga GR represents the southernmost edge of its distribution in Tanzania. There is no evidence of hybridization between Coke's and Lichtenstein's Hartebeests in Swagaswaga GR, despite its proximity to the population of Lichtenstein's Hartebeest in Muhezi GR.

The Lelwel Hartebeest was formerly widespread in Bukoba region and there was still a small population in the Ibanda–Rumanyika GRs in the mid-1950s. There have been no recent sightings from that area and this subspecies is now considered extinct in Tanzania.

Population size and conservation status

There are approximately 18,000 Coke's Hartebeests in Tanzania, with the largest population in the Serengeti ecosystem estimated at 16,000 individuals. Numbers in the Tarangire ecosystem have steadily declined from 4,000 in the early 1990s to around 1,100 individuals in 2011 as a result of unsustainable hunting pressure outside the National Park.

There are approximately 1,000 Coke's Hartebeests in Mkomazi NP, and the species is now rare in West Kilimanjaro. Illegal hunting outside protected areas has caused significant range contraction and declines in numbers in the past 50 years. The main threats to this species include illegal hunting and loss of habitat and migration corridors.

Coke's Hartebeest
TOP: male (Kenya);
BOTTOM: female, Ngorongoro CA

Lichtenstein's Hartebeest

Alcelaphus lichtensteinii

SWAHILI: Kongoni, Konzi

A large antelope with a sloping back and an elongated face. The body is yellow-brown, with a red 'saddle' that extends from the shoulders to the base of the tail, and the hindquarters are white. This species often rubs its face on its upper shoulder and sides, leaving a dark stain caused by the sticky black liquid from its pre-orbital glands. There are black stripes extending down the front legs. Horns (38–64 cm | 15–25" long) are present in both sexes, and bend inwards towards each other in a half-circle before curving sharply backwards at the tip.

Similar species

The Coke's Hartebeest (*page 234*) looks similar but the ranges of the two species do not overlap. The Topi (*page 232*) has a much darker, purple-brown body.

Note: some authorities consider the Lichtenstein's Hartebeest a subspecies of Coke's Hartebeest, while others consider it a full species.

Ecology and social behaviour

Lichtenstein's Hartebeest are closely associated with miombo habitat, favouring drainage-line grasslands on the edge of the woodland. They are mostly diurnal and feed predominantly on grasses, although will occasionally browse. Males are territorial with territories of approximately 3 km² (1 mi²) and appear to associate permanently with a small herd of 3–5 females and young. Territorial males will often stand on a termite mound as a form of static territorial display. Larger mixed-sex aggregations of up to 60 individuals may gather in the dry season.

Distribution in Tanzania

The Lichtenstein's Hartebeest is widespread in miombo woodland in western Tanzania, occurring in a mostly uninterrupted swathe from the Ruaha–Rungwa ecosystem to the Moyowosi–Kigosi GRs, including Ugalla GR and the Katavi–Rukwa ecosystem. There is still a small population in the Burigi–Biharamulo GR and it is also found in the eastern section

Least Concern	
HB:	160–200 cm (63–79")
Ht:	119–136 cm (47–54")
Tail:	40–50 cm (16–20")
Wt:	155–205 kg (340–450 lb)

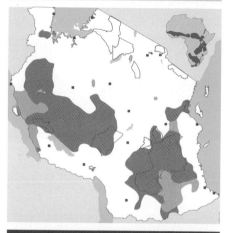

Where to look

The Lichtenstein's Hartebeest can be found in the tourist section of the Selous GR in the dry season, particularly the eastern section around Mtemere and around Lake Manze. It is also frequently seen around Mwayembe Springs in Ruaha NP during the dry season. In Katavi NP, it is commonly observed along the sand ridge running from Kavuu to Ngolima Plain.

of Mahale NP. The species is widespread throughout the Selous GR, Mikumi NP, the Selous–Niassa corridor and Muhuwesi FR, and is occasionally found in the Kilombero Valley. It may also occur in low numbers on community land to the south and southeast of the Selous GR. There are populations in the Wami–Mbiki WMA and Saadani NP, which are now probably isolated from the Selous population. A population of hartebeest, which is likely to be Lichtenstein's Hartebeest, has been reported from the Wembere Wetland, suggesting a possible extension of its northern miombo woodland range.

Population size and conservation status

The Selous GR is the main stronghold for Lichtenstein's Hartebeest in Africa, with approximately 17,000–18,000 individuals. They are now rare in the adjacent Kilombero Valley. Other important populations include the Ruaha–Rungwa ecosystem (1,300 animals), Saadani NP (1,500) and Ugalla GR (1,000). The Moyowosi–Kigosi GRs and the Katavi–Rukwa ecosystem both have smaller populations of around 700 animals. The species is now rare in Burigi–Biharamulo GR where only three animals were counted in 2000. Numbers have been declining outside protected areas, mainly due to illegal hunting and competition from cattle, as they share very similar diets; the main population in the Selous GR is probably stable.

Lichtenstein's Hartebeest
TOP: male, Selous GR (Tanzania); BOTTOM: female showing stains on her side from pre-orbital gland secretions (Zambia)

Common Wildebeest

Connochaetes taurinus

Brindled Gnu, Blue Wildebeest

SWAHILI: Nyumbu

A large antelope with a thick neck and shoulders and a slightly sloping back. Both sexes have horns (28–41 cm | 11–16" long) that curve sideways and then upwards, although males have a heavier boss. The face, muzzle and mane are black. The tail nearly reaches the ground and has long black hairs at the tip.

Subspecies

C. t. albojubatus: Eastern White-bearded Wildebeest, east of the East African Rift wall; light grey-brown body.

C. t. mearnsi: Western White-bearded Wildebeest, west of the East African Rift wall; dark blue-grey coat.

C. t. johnstoni: Nyassa Wildebeest, southern Tanzania; grey-brown body, black beard. Often with inverted white chevron across the nose, particularly south of Rufiji River.

Similar species

Unlikely to be mistaken for any other mammal.

Ecology and social behaviour

Wildebeests inhabit short grassland and open bushland, seldom far from water. They are mainly diurnal and strictly grazers, preferring short grasses (10–15 cm | 4–6" high). Wildebeests are social animals with highly dynamic social systems that range from permanently sedentary to highly migratory populations. Males monopolize harems of 6–30 females and their young in small territories of less than 2 ha (5 acres). Territories may be held year-round or for as little as a few hours. In the Serengeti ecosystem, large herds of Common Wildebeest migrate annually in search of optimal forage. They typically congregate on the short-grass plains of the Serengeti NP and Ngorongoro CA in the wet season (December–May), migrating to the woodlands of western Serengeti in June–July, and then moving to northern Serengeti and the Masai Mara (Kenya) in the dry season (August–November).

Least Concern	
HB:	170–240 cm (67–94")
Ht:	107–135 cm (42–53")
Tail:	60–75 cm (24–30")
Wt:	M 170–240 kg (370–530 lb)
	F 140–210 kg (310–460 lb)

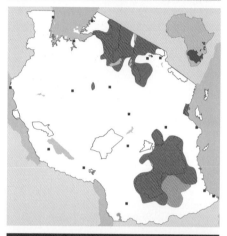

Where to look

The Serengeti NP is famous for its large Common Wildebeest concentrations; vast herds can be seen from December–May on the short-grass plains around Ndutu and the southern Serengeti. Wildebeest are commonly seen in the north of Tarangire during the dry season (July–November), while the Nyassa Wildebeest subspecies can be seen all year in the northern Selous GR, particularly around Lake Manze.

Distribution in Tanzania

The Eastern White-bearded Wildebeest occurs throughout the Tarangire ecosystem and from Lake Natron to West Kilimanjaro. There is also an introduced herd in Saadani NP. The Western White-bearded Wildebeest ranges throughout the Serengeti–Mara ecosystem; there is also a small population in the Lake Eyasi plains. The Nyassa Wildebeest is found south of the Wami River throughout the Selous ecosystem as far south as Muhuwesi FR, and may still occur in Liparamba GR on the border with Mozambique. Wildebeest also occur in the Wembere Wetland, but the subspecies is unclear.

Population size and conservation status
Tanzania has approximately 80% of the world's population of Common Wildebeest. The population in the Serengeti ecosystem increased substantially in number from 220,000 in 1961 to around 1·4 million in the 1970s following the elimination of the Rinderpest disease through a cattle vaccination programme. The population in the Serengeti has now stablilized at 1·0–1·3 million animals. Common Wildebeest numbers in the Tarangire ecosystem have decreased substantially from 25,000 in the mid-1980s to approximately 8,000 in 2012 due to heavy poaching in their dispersal areas, particularly during the late 1990s. This population spends at least part of the year outside protected areas, making it vulnerable both to poaching and loss of migration routes due to agricultural expansion. There are approximately 2,000–2,500 animals in Sadaani NP, where numbers are stable or increasing. Numbers in the West Kilimanjaro–Amboseli (Kenya) ecosystem declined precipitously from 10,000 to 800 individuals following a severe drought in 2008–10. The Nyassa Wildebeest subpopulation, which is concentrated in the Selous GR, has declined in the past decade from about 50,000 to 35,000 individuals for reasons that are unclear.

Common Wildebeest
TOP: male ssp. *mearnsi*, Ngorongoro CA ;
ABOVE: ssp. *johnstoni*, Selous ecosystem – note prominent white chevron across nose;
RIGHT: ssp. *albojubatus*, Tarangire NP

Roan Antelope

Hippotragus equinus

SWAHILI: Korongo

Least Concern	
HB:	190–240 cm (75–94")
Ht:	126–145 cm (50–57")
Tail:	48–54 cm (19–21")
Wt:	M 240–300 kg (530–660 lb)
	F 215–280 kg (470–620 lb)

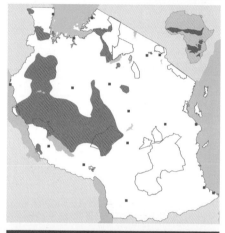

The second largest antelope in Tanzania after the Common Eland (*page 186*). Males are slightly larger than females. The upper body is a light sandy-brown and the underparts are yellowish or white; the legs are the same colour as the upper body. Both sexes have a black-tipped mane that runs from the back of the head to the shoulders. The face has a distinctive black-and-white pattern, with an all-white muzzle. The tail is long, mostly black, with a tassel at the tip. Both sexes have long, heavily ringed horns (56–81 cm | 22–32" long) that curve backwards in an arc.

Subspecies

H. e. langheldi: only subspecies found in Tanzania.

Similar species

Female Sable Antelopes (*page 242*) are smaller, have a reddish (rather than tan) coat, longer horns, and less black on the side of the face (see comparative photographs, *page 268*).

Ecology and social behaviour

The Roan Antelope's preferred habitat is open woodland–savanna, typically with medium to tall grasses, close to permanent water sources. In Tanzania, it is associated with *Brachystegia–Isoberlinia* miombo woodland, which is the dominant vegetation in the west of the country. This antelope is predominantly a grazer, although it will occasionally eat browse during the dry season. It is water-dependent and must drink at least once every two days. Females and young live in small herds of 5–20 animals led by a single territorial bull, or may range across the territories of several males. Herd home ranges are 60–120 km² (20–50 mi²). Young bachelors may form small herds but are generally solitary when they are adult and not with a breeding group.

Distribution in Tanzania

Roan Antelopes are concentrated in the central and western parts of Tanzania, with small populations in Maswa GR and Singida District in the north. They are found

Where to look

Katavi NP provides the best opportunities for seeing Roan Antelopes in Tanzania. Good places to try are around the Katuma River where it leaves the Katisunga floodplain, and the series of springs between there and Ikuu Ranger Post, where they drink from mid-morning to early afternoon during the dry season.
The Ngolima floodplain is also worth a try.
In Ruaha NP, small herds can be seen in the Lunda area in the eastern corner of the National Park, in the vicinity of Malindi springs, and on the road between the National Park entrance and Msembe. Two or more days of searching may be necessary to encounter this species.

in Swagaswaga GR, the Ruaha–Rungwa ecosystem, the Katavi ecosystem, across Ugalla GR, the Malagarasi swamp and Moyowosi and Kigosi GRs. There are small populations in the miombo woodland of Mahale NP, in Burigi–Biharamulo GRs, and in Ibanda– Rumanyika GRs, although it has disappeared from large parts of Tabora District. In the Serengeti ecosystem, the loss of *Combretum*-dominated woodland has greatly reduced the range of this antelope, and it is now restricted mainly to the Maswa and Grumeti GRs, and occasionally the western corridor in the Serengeti NP. Small groups sometimes pass through the Yaeda Valley. It is extinct in Tarangire NP, where it was last recorded in 1960. There are still small pockets of Roan Antelopes in the Kondoa Open Area and in the woodland bordering the Wembere Wetland.

Population size and conservation status
The largest concentration of Roan Antelopes is in the Ruaha–Rungwa ecosystem, with

approximately 1,000–1,500 individuals, with a further 1,200 animals spread across Ugalla and Moyowosi GRs and around Lake Sagara. There were approximately 450 individuals in the Katavi–Rungwa ecosystem in 2009. They are rare in the Serengeti ecosystem and Burigi–Biharamulo GR. This species occurs at low densities throughout its range and is particularly vulnerable to human disturbance and habitat change; local extinctions are not easily reversed by immigration from neighbouring areas. Overall, numbers are slowly declining.

Roan Antelope
TOP: male (Zambia);
BOTTOM: females, Grumeti GR
(Tanzania)

Sable Antelope

Hippotragus niger

SWAHILI: Mbarapi, Palahala

Least Concern	
HB:	175–195 cm (68–77")
Ht:	120–140 cm (47–55")
Tail:	40–75 cm (16–30")
Wt:	M 215–265 kg (470–580 lb)
	F 205–230 kg (450–500 lb)

A very large antelope with a thick neck and huge, curved horns. Both sexes have horns, although they are generally larger in males (95–122 cm | 37–48" long) than in females (70 cm | 28" long). It is sexually dimorphic, with adult male colouration typically black, while females and juveniles are russet-brown. Both sexes have an upright mane, a white belly and distinctive white facial markings. The tail is long and black with a short tassel at the tip.

Subspecies
H. n. roosevelti: coastal and southern Tanzania.

H. n. kirkii: west of Eastern Arc Mountains.

Similar species
Female Roan Antelopes (*page 240*) are a paler brown and have shorter horns than female Sable Antelopes (see comparative photographs, *page 268*).

Ecology and social behaviour
Typically found in miombo woodland, Sable Antelopes often move into valley-bottom grasslands to access permanent water during the dry season. They are primarily grazers but sometimes eat browse during the dry season. They are gregarious and territorial, often observed in herds of 15–25 females and their young, although groups of up to 75 individuals may gather during the dry season. These groups have stable, age-based hierarchies that are led by the top-ranking female. Males defend territories and will often walk at the rear of female groups to try to prevent them from leaving. Home ranges vary from less than 1 km² to 25 km² (0·5–10 mi²).

Distribution in Tanzania
Sable Antelopes are distributed across much of the south and west of the country. They are widespread in the Selous ecosystem, occurring in Mikumi NP, the Selous GR, the Kilombero Valley, the Selous–Niassa corridor, Muhuwesi FR and in the miombo woodland east of Liwale town. They are also found in the Ruaha–Rungwa ecosystem, Katavi NP, Rukwa,

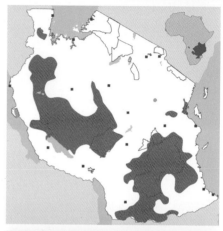

Where to look
Sable Antelopes are not easy to see in Tanzania. The best chance is in Ruaha NP in the dry season (August–November) when they frequently come down from the miombo escarpment to drink at the Makindi springs in the middle of the day. The same pattern occurs at permanent water sources in the Lunda area. It may take several visits to see this species in Ruaha. In the Selous GR it can occasionally be sighted on the main road between Sable Lodge and Matambwe during the wet season (November–May). It may also be seen in the north of Saadani NP.

Ugalla, Moyowosi, Kizigo, Burigi and Kimisi GRs, and in the Wembere Wetland. There are no recent reports from eastern Mahale NP, although they may still occur there. They were formerly distributed throughout the coastal areas from the Kenya border as far south as Lindi, but are now restricted to small pockets in Sadaani NP, Wami–Mbiki WMA and Msumbugwe FR near Pangani, where a small herd was sighted in 1998.

Population size and conservation status

The largest concentrations of Sable Antelopes are in the Selous GR and Selous–Niassa corridor, with an estimated 3,400–5,500 individuals. They are uncommon in Mikumi NP and are now very rare in the Kilombero Valley. There are approximately 2,400 individuals in the Ruaha–Rungwa ecosystem. They are common in Ugalla GR where 900 individuals were counted in 1996, and numbers in the Moyowosi GR have remained relatively constant over the past 30 years at around 1,000 individuals. They are uncommon in Katavi NP but are reported to be relatively common in Rungwa and Rukwa GRs and the adjacent areas of Piti, Lukwati and Chunya. Other populations include 200–400 in Sadaani NP, 40 in the Wami–Mbiki WMA, and less than 100 in the Burigi–Biharamulo GRs; the latter two populations are increasingly vulnerable to local extinction. Illegal hunting is the principle threat, although these antelope are well represented in protected areas and are not currently threatened in Tanzania.

Sable Antelope
TOP: adult male and juvenile ssp. *kirkii* (Zambia);
BOTTOM: females ssp. *kirkii,* Ugalla GR (Tanzania)

Fringe-eared Oryx

Oryx beisa

SWAHILI: Choroa

A large, thick-necked antelope with magnificent straight, pointed horns. Horn length is similar in both sexes (71–86 cm | 28–34"). The coat is a light tan-brown, separated from the white belly by a black side-stripe. The face has black and white markings running longitudinally from the forehead to the muzzle and the ears have black tufts at the tip. There are black stripes on the forelegs, down the front of the neck and on the rump. The tail is tan-coloured at the base and has a long black tassel at the tip.

Near Threatened	
HB:	150–170 cm (59–67")
Ht:	115–125 cm (45–49")
Tail:	40–50 cm (16–20")
Wt:	M 165–210 kg (370–460 lb| F 116–190 kg (255–415 lb)

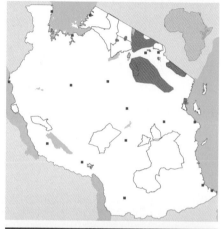

Subspecies
O. b. callotis: only subspecies found in Tanzania.

Similar species
Unlikely to be mistaken for any other mammal.

Ecology and social behaviour
Fringe-eared Oryx inhabit arid grassland, *Acacia–Commiphora* bushland and open woodland. They feed mainly on grasses, with some browse consumed during the dry season. Oryx can go for long periods without water, but will drink regularly if water is available. Mixed sex herds of 15–50 individuals, and occasionally up to 250 animals, move together, although older males often become more sedentary. In Tarangire NP, Fringe-eared Oryx utilize small areas of open grassland during the dry season and disperse widely during the wet season. Home ranges are 400 km² (155 mi²) or larger.

Distribution in Tanzania
Fringe-eared Oryx are closely associated with arid areas in northern Tanzania. In the Tarangire ecosystem, they are found around Lake Burungi, south Lolkisale Game Controlled Area and Makame WMA, as far south as the Kitwai plains. They occur on the eastern shores of Lake Natron, concentrated around Gelai and northern Lolsimongori Mountains, in parts of West Kilimanjaro and in Mkomazi NP. They occasionally migrate into the eastern Serengeti NP, to around Gol and Barafu kopjes, and to the Salei plains in

Where to look
In Tarangire NP, Fringe-eared Oryx are frequently seen on the road between Silale Swamp and Loiboserit Ranger Post, and a small herd is occasionally seen on the open grass plains around Lake Burungi during the dry season. In Mkomazi NP, a herd is regularly seen around Kavateta, and small groups can be seen on the short-grass plains south of Lake Natron.

Loliondo. They are now extinct in the Yaeda Valley and Manyara NP. A small herd was reported in 1988 on Mkwaja Ranch, now part of Sadaani NP, and another small group was seen regularly just north of Sadaani NP between 1995–97.

Population size and conservation status
Fringe-eared Oryx numbers have declined in the Tarangire ecosystem in recent years, dropping from 2,500 animals in 1994 to roughly 300 in 2011. They are now uncommon in Tarangire NP, although groups of over 20 individuals are seen regularly in

Loiboserit village (east of the National Park). A herd of 147 animals was observed in the Kitwai plains in the southern Masai Steppe in 2009. In Mkomazi NP, numbers are increasing and there were an estimated 250 animals in 2007. The largest population now occurs around Lake Natron, although these animals probably spend part of the year in southern Kenya. A herd of 75 individuals was recorded there in 2008, and there are reports of 250 animals being seen in one day. Fifteen animals were recorded on the Salei plains in Loliondo in 2011. The population on West Kilimanjaro is now very small, with only eight individuals counted in 2010. Fringe-eared Oryx is typically associated with dry, open grasslands, which makes them particularly vulnerable to illegal hunting by vehicle. The large majority of the population spends part of the year outside protected areas and numbers have been declining steadily. This species is now highly threatened in Tanzania.

Fringe-eared Oryx
TOP: male (Kenya)
BOTTOM: female (in front) with male (Kenya)

Dugong

Dugong dugon

SWAHILI: Nguva

Dugongs have large, rounded bodies, with two small, paddle-like flippers and a fluke-shaped tail. They have smooth, nearly naked skin, which is slate-grey above and paler below. The head is small and pig-like with a broad, flat muzzle and sensitive bristles covering the upper lip. The nostrils are positioned at the top of the nose and have flaps that close when the animal is submerged. Females are usually larger than males.

Similar species
Unlikely to be mistaken for any other mammal.

Ecology and social behaviour
Dugongs are found along the coastline in shallow marine waters, usually at depths of 1–12m (3–40 ft). They mostly avoid freshwater and deep seawater, although they will feed in deeper waters when winds are not strong and there is some evidence that they migrate across deep water. Dugongs are the only herbivorous marine mammal in Africa. Their preferred habitat is sheltered bays that are rich in seagrass, which forms their staple food. When Dugongs feed, they frequently cut long swathes through the seagrass, known as feeding trails. These trails, which are the width of a Dugong's mouth (20–25 cm | 8–10"), are created by the animal ripping up seagrass plants from the sea bed. They may travel l ong distances in response to availability of suitable seagrass beds. Dugongs are gregarious and can congregate in herds of over 300 individuals, although sightings of single individuals or mother-calf pairs are now more common as a result of population declines. They swim slowly below the surface of the water, rising every 2–3 minutes to breathe by lifting the tip of their nose out of the water. Although Dugongs are typically diurnal, they have resorted to feeding mostly at night due to heavy hunting pressure. Mating strategies vary by location, with males in some areas competing directly for sexually available females, and in other

Vulnerable	
HB:	2·2–3·0 m (7–10 ft)
Wt:	300–550 kg (660–1,200 lb)

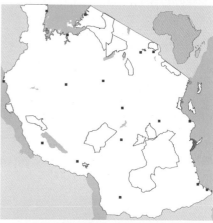

Where to look
The Rufiji Delta is the only place to see this species in Tanzania, although the chances of observing one are extremely slim.

areas adopting a lek system. They reproduce slowly and may live to over 70 years of age.

Distribution in Tanzania
Dugongs were once widespread along much of the Tanzanian coast, but they are now mainly restricted to the Rufiji Delta as far south as Somanga village, near Kilwa. Fishermen from Moa and Kwale villages, north of Tanga, claim that a small population of Dugongs existed some 15 km (10 miles) south of the Kenya border in 2003, although this population is now believed extinct. Dugongs are now extinct around the islands of Zanzibar and Pemba, and at Pangani, where they were last recorded in 2000; they are probably also extinct at Lindi and Mtwara. A single individual was reportedly sighted several times near Tumbuju on the west coast of Mafia Island in 2009 and 2012.

Population size and conservation status

Dugongs were formerly abundant in Tanzanian waters, although the population has declined rapidly since the mid-1970s to the point where it is now critically endangered. In a 2000–03 study, extensive interviews with fisherman along the coast in 57 villages produced just 32 records of Dugongs, of which eight were live animals and 24 were accidental net captures. Twenty-two of the sightings (69%) came from the Rufiji Delta, which has the largest remaining resident population in Tanzania. Most of these animals occurred in the southern part of the Delta, particularly around Mohoro Bay, where small groups of 3–4 individuals were occasionally seen during July and August. There are continued sightings from this area, with 12 sightings reported by fisherman in the southern Delta in 2011, suggesting the presence of a small breeding population. In the past, Dugongs were extensively hunted for their meat, and they are still often killed opportunistically if encountered. With the species now so rare, there is little active hunting and the greater threat is entanglement in fishing nets. Capture records indicate that 8–10 Dugongs were killed each year between 2000 and 2003, which is an unsustainable rate of loss given the very small population size. Other threats include the loss of seagrass habitat, particularly as a result of commercial prawn trawling, and direct disturbance. Without concerted conservation action, including the establishment of a Dugong Reserve, this species is likely to go extinct in Tanzania in the near future.

Dugong
(Republic of Vanuatu)

Humpback Whale

Megaptera novaeangliae

SWAHILI: Chongowi Kibyongo, Salesale

Least Concern	
HB:	15–17 m (50–60 ft)
Wt:	40,000 kg (88,000 lb)

A large whale, black-grey above and varying from dark to white below. The long flippers are almost one third of the body length and usually all white or dark above and white below. The tail flukes, which have an irregular trailing edge, are dark on the upper side and patterned black-and-white on the underside. The dorsal fin is small and stubby and set two-thirds of the way along the back on a small hump. It often shows its back, dorsal fin, and fluke when it dives. The bushy blow is highly visible, up to 3 m (10 ft) tall.

Where to look

Some tour operators offer whale watching boat trips off Mafia Island during the migration season. Sightings occur all along the coast including Tanga, Pangani, Pemba, Zanzibar, the Zanzibar channel, Mafia, Dar es Salaam, Mnazi Bay (Mtwara) and around Lindi. Other areas with frequent sightings are Ras Dege, south of Dar es Salaam, Mikindani Bay in Mtwara, and off the east coast of Zanzibar.

Similar species

Sperm Whales are similar in size but differ in their head shape, dark flippers, and dark, smooth-edged tail flukes. Its low, angled blow is distinctly different to the wide, vertical blow of the Humpback Whale.

Ecology and social behaviour

Humpback Whales off the East African coast migrate annually between their breeding grounds in the tropical and subtropical Indian Ocean and their feeding areas in the Antarctic Ocean. Along the coast of Tanzania, they are most often seen either alone or in mother–calf pairs, but groups of up to 15 can be encountered when breeding.

Population size and conservation status

This species migrates through Tanzanian waters between July and December, moving south through the Mozambique Channel to Antarctic waters. Most sightings in Tanzania are between September and October, with the peak in August. There are few records of Humpback Whales moving north, suggesting the return migration takes place farther offshore. In 2011, 572 whales were counted in Tanzania during the migration season. This is likely to be a small sample of the total population. The main threat to this species is entanglement in gill nets.

Humpback Whale TOP: tail fluke; BOTTOM: blow, head and back

248

Sperm Whale

Physeter macrocephalus

SWAHILI: Nyangumi Spamu

A very large, dark grey whale with an enormous square-shaped head. The upper and lower 'lips' are white. It lacks a proper dorsal fin, having only a small, triangular or round 'hump', behind which there may be a series of bumps running down to the tail. The skin is often lightly wrinkled. The single blowhole is offset to the left at the very front of the head. The low (usually less than 2 m (6 ft) tall) is projected forward and to the left. The dark tail flukes (usually raised prior to a deep dive) are broad and triangular, with a smooth trailing edge that has a deep, central notch.

Vulnerable	
HB:	M 13–18 m (40–60ft) | F 10–12 m (30–40ft)
Wt:	M 30,000–57,000 kg (66,000–125,400 lb)
	F 13,000–24,000 kg (28,600–52,800 lb)

Humpback Whale

Sperm Whale

Similar species
The Humpback Whale has much larger flippers that are partially white, and a small, stubby dorsal fin. Humpback Whales also have a series of small knobs on their forehead, a blow that is usually vertical, and tail flukes with an irregular trailing edge and white underside.

Ecology and social behaviour
This is a deep sea species, seldom found in waters less than 200 m (650 ft) deep. Sperm Whales live in relatively stable groups of 10–20 females and their young, while males are either solitary or form bachelor groups of up to 50 individuals.

Population size and conservation status
Sperm Whales can be found in East African waters year-round, although animals probably migrate to feeding areas in the south from

October–April and return to the warmer tropical waters in May–September. There are records for this species from Zanzibar and Mafia Island, where a 16m (50 ft) individual was washed onto the shore in 2008. The main threat is entanglement in fishing nets and collisions with ships.

Sperm Whale TOP: tail fluke; BOTTOM: blow, head and back

Cuvier's Beaked Whale
Longman's Beaked Whale

Ziphius cavirostris

Indopacetus pacificus

Adult **Cuvier's Beaked Whales** usually have a light brown to dark grey body and a white head; there is a white or lighter area on the back that can extend from the head to the small sickle-shaped dorsal fin located two-thirds of the way along the back. The forehead slopes gently down to a short, distinct beak. Adult males have two large teeth that visibly protrude upward from the tip of the lower jaw, and they are often heavily scarred on the body; females generally have little or no scarring. **Longman's Beaked Whales** are a similar size and body shape with a grey-brown or tan back and paler underside but have a very different head shape with a large, light-coloured melon and prominent beak.

Similar species

Risso's Dolphins (*page 254*) may also have white on the head and dorsal part of the body, but are much smaller and have a larger dorsal fin. **Longman's Beaked Whales** closely resemble the Southern Bottlenose Whale *Hyperoodon planifrons*, although this species has not been recorded from Tanzania.

Cuvier's Beaked Whale

Least Concern	
HB:	6–7 m (20–23 ft)
Wt:	2,000–3,000 kg (4,400–6,600 lb)

Longman's Beaked Whale

Data Deficient	
HB:	6–7 m (20–23 ft)
Wt:	unknown

Ecology and social behaviour

The **Cuvier's Beaked Whale** is a deep water species and is usually seen alone or in small groups (typically 3–12 individuals). This species seldom breaches and sightings are usually brief. The **Longman's Beaked Whale** has been recorded in groups of 1–100 individuals (with an average of 20 animals), although little is known about its behaviour.

Population size and conservation status

Specimens of both species were sighted during aerial surveys in February 2000. These are the only known records from Tanzania.

TOP: **Cuvier's Beaked Whale**; BOTTOM: **Longman's Beaked Whale**

Pygmy Sperm Whale

Kogia breviceps

SWAHILI: Nyangumi Spamu Ndogo

Pygmy Sperm Whales are a dark blue-grey above and white, tinged with pink, below. The head is square-shaped and has a very small lower jaw, and a dark-and-white, bracket-shaped marking running down behind the eye that resembles the gill slits of a fish (known as 'false gills'). The body shape and 'false gills' gives the Pygmy Sperm Whale a shark-like appearance. The dorsal fin is small and slightly hook-shaped and located more than halfway along the back.

Similar species
The very similar Dwarf Sperm Whale *Kogia sima* is not known from Tanzanian waters.

Ecology and social behaviour
This species is usually found far offshore and is rarely seen. It often lies motionless on the surface, where it is easily approached, and its movements are generally slow and sluggish, usually sinking (rather than rolling) below the surface when diving. There is no visible blow. Most sightings are of single individuals, although groups of up to six animals have been recorded.

Data Deficient	
HB:	3·0–3·5 m (10–11 ft)
Wt:	300–450 kg (660–990 lb)

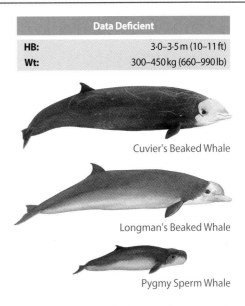

Cuvier's Beaked Whale

Longman's Beaked Whale

Pygmy Sperm Whale

Population size and conservation status
Little is known about this species in Tanzania, with the only records coming from strandings on Zanzibar. They can become entangled in fishing nets, and several stranded whales were found to have ingested plastic bags.

Pygmy Sperm Whale

251

False Killer Whale

Pseudorca crassidens

A long, slender-bodied whale with a tall, erect, sickle-shaped dorsal fin located midway along the back. The small, rounded head has a forehead that tapers gently to a rounded jaw that lacks a beak. Body colour is black or dark grey with a light patch on the throat and chest. The flippers have a bulge halfway down the front edge (diagnostic of this species). Males are significantly larger (10–15%) than females.

Data Deficient	
HB:	5–6m (16–20ft)
Wt:	1,000–2,300 kg (2,200–5,100 lb)

False Killer Whale

Killer Whale (female)

Short-finned Pilot Whale (male)

Similar species
Risso's Dolphins (*page 254*) are smaller, usually paler, and have scars on the body. Short-finned Pilot Whales have a bulbous head and a forward-located dorsal fin.

Ecology and social behaviour
Group size is usually 10–30 animals, although pods of several hundred have been reported. When moving, they often show much of their body above the surface and occasionally breach in a low, flat arc. Individuals travelling in groups often move in a wide front. They are frequently seen moving with other cetaceans, particularly bottlenose dolphins. False Killer Whales often strand in large numbers.

Population size and conservation status
Little is known about this species in Tanzanian waters. There is a record of 44 individuals being stranded near Stone Town, Zanzibar in December 1933.

Killer Whale (Orca)

Orcinus orca

SWAHILI: Oka

The largest of the dolphins, both sexes have very large dorsal fins, which may grow up to 1·8 m (6ft) tall in some males. The back and sides are mostly black, with white along the underside, the rear flanks, and a distinctive patch behind the eye. Most individuals have a grey 'saddle' patch behind the dorsal fin. The beak is short and blunt.

Data Deficient	
HB:	M 7–9m (23–30ft) | F 4·5–8m (15–26ft)
Wt:	2,500–5,500 kg (5,500–12,100 lb)

Similar species
Their distinctive colouration, large size and dorsal fin make Killer Whales unlikely to be confused with other species, although young animals could be mistaken for False Killer Whales or Short-finned Pilot Whales.

Ecology and social behaviour
Killer Whales live in multi-sex family units of 2–25 individuals which usually remain together for life. Adult males are sometimes solitary. Several closely related pods form clans that often develop their own cultural characteristics, such as call 'dialects' and hunting practices. Some clans, for instance, specialize in feeding on fish, while others eat primarily marine mammals. Prey as large as adult baleen whales may be taken.

Population size and conservation status
There is a single stranding record of a Killer Whale on Zanzibar in 1993. This is currently the only known record of the species from Tanzanian waters.

Short-finned Pilot Whale *Globicephala macrorhynchus*

A medium-sized, mostly black, whale. Specimens in the northern hemisphere have a grey 'saddle', although this is typically absent in African specimens. It has a bulbous melon on the head that extends forwards of the mouth. The dorsal fin has a very broad base and a backward-pointing tip and is located one-third of the way along the back. The flippers are short and sickle-shaped.

Similar species
Most likely to be confused with the False Killer Whale, but this differs in its tapered head shape and centrally located dorsal fin.

Ecology and social behaviour
This species lives in groups, ranging in size

Data Deficient	
HB:	3–6 m (10–20 ft)
Wt:	2,000–3,000 kg (4,400–6,600 lb)

from 15–30 individuals, although large aggregations of as many as 200 individuals have been recorded. Females usually remain in their family groups for life. Generally slow swimmers, groups may float motionless at the surface of the water. This species frequently travels with other cetaceans, including bottlenose dolphins (*pages 256–257*).

Population size and conservation status
The only record from Tanzanian waters is a single stranding off Zanzibar in 2006.

TOP: **Short-finned Pilot Whale**; MIDDLE: **False Killer Whale**; BOTTOM: **Killer Whale**

Risso's Dolphin

Grampus griseus

Least Concern	
HB:	3·0–3·5 m (10–12 ft)
Wt:	300–450 kg (660–990 lb)

A robust dolphin with a bulbous head and indistinct beak. The tall, sickle-shaped dorsal fin is located midway along the back. Individual colouration ranges from pale brown to dark grey, with light grey to white underparts. Most adults have heavy scarring on their back and flank. Scarring is heaviest in older animals, particularly in males, and can make some appear almost white. These scars are most likely the result of fights, but are possibly also caused by squid.

Similar species

False Killer Whales (*page 252*) are larger and darker, lack scars on the body and have a tapered, rather than bulbous, head. Risso's Dolphins often associate with Common Bottlenose Dolphins (*page 257*), which are easily distinguished by their beaks and lack of any significant scarring on the back.

Ecology and social behaviour

Typically found in water deeper than 180 m (600 ft), Risso's Dolphins generally occur in groups of 1–50 individuals, with groups of less than 12 being the most common. They feed predominantly at night, usually spending much of the day resting or moving slowly, although they can be quite active, often breaching and tail-slapping. On rare occasions they will ride the bow waves of boats.

Population size and conservation status

Little is known about this species in Tanzanian waters and the only records are from Zanzibar, where it is uncommon. It is not known whether Risso's Dolphin is a seasonal visitor or permanent resident. Twelve individuals were recorded as by-catch in fishing nets around Mnemba and Nungwi Islands on the east coast of Zanzibar between 2000 and 2003. Fishermen have also reported this species from the south and north coasts of Zanzibar.

Risso's Dolphin

Indo-Pacific Humpback Dolphin *Sousa chinensis*

SWAHILI: Pomboo Kibyongo

This beaked dolphin has a characteristic hump midway along the back, which is topped by a small, hooked dorsal fin. The size of the hump varies between individuals, but is generally larger in older animals. They are pale to dark grey above and pale white below. The beak is relatively long and slender.

Near Threatened	
HB:	2·0–2·8 m (6–9 ft)
Wt:	170–285 kg (375–630 lb)

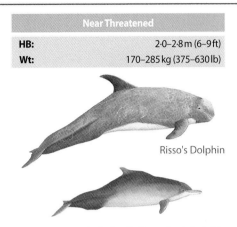

Risso's Dolphin

Indo-Pacific Humpback Dolphin

Similar species
The distinctive hump on the back of this species makes it relatively easy to identify.

Ecology and social behaviour
The group size of Indo-Pacific Humpback Dolphins on Zanzibar ranged from 1–8 individuals in one study carried out north of Stone Town, and 3–22 in another study off the south coast of Zanzibar. They often travel in multi-species groups with Indo-Pacific Bottlenose Dolphins (*page 256*) off the coast of Zanzibar. This species seldom bow-rides.

Population size and conservation status
Found in shallow waters less than 50 m (165 ft) deep on the south, west and northwest coast of Zanzibar, including around Stone Town, the Zanzibar channel and at Ushongo beach near Pangani. A study of this dolphin on the south coast of Zanzibar suggested a resident population of 71 individuals in 2001. This population is threatened by accidental capture in gillnets, which causes unsustainable annual mortality losses of up to 6% of the population. They are also hunted for shark bait. Sightings on Ushongo beach are rare.

Indo-Pacific Humpback Dolphin

255

Indo-Pacific Bottlenose Dolphin

Tursiops aduncus

SWAHILI: Pomboo Domonene / Pua ya Chupa

Data Deficient	
HB:	2·5 m (8 ft)
Wt:	180–230 kg (400–500 lb)

A large dolphin with a dark grey back and pale grey or off-white underside. Older individuals usually, but not always, have dark spots or flecks on the belly, although these markings are often absent in juveniles. The beak is relatively short and the tall, sickle-shaped dorsal fin is located midway along the back.

Similar species

The Common Bottlenose Dolphin is larger, darker and lacks spots on the underside. It has a more robust melon, a comparatively shorter, thicker beak and a proportionately taller dorsal fin. This species seldom comes close to shore in Tanzania, unlike the Indo-Pacific Bottlenose Dolphin. The Indo-Pacific Humpback Dolphin (*page 255*) is generally seen in smaller groups and can be distinguished by the distinctive hump at the base of the fin.

Ecology and social behaviour

This species is usually found in shallow water, less than 20 m (70 ft) deep and within 1 km (0·6 miles) of the shore. Off Zanzibar, group size ranges from 1–65 individuals, with groups of 8–21 being most common.

Indo-Pacific Bottlenose Dolphins and Indo-Pacific Humpback Dolphins often travel together.

Population size and conservation status

Indo-Pacific Bottlenose Dolphins probably range all along the coast of Tanzania, although there are currently records only from Zanzibar, Maziwe Island near Pangani, and offshore of Saadani NP. Records from diving boats at Maziwe Island indicate that they are seldom seen January–June, and are encountered 5–6 times a month in July–December. Population estimates suggest that there are 136–179 individuals off the south coast of Zanzibar, which forms the basis for dolphin tourism based at Kizimkazi. However, this population suffers incidental by-catch from local fisheries that may kill nearly 10% of the population each year. Unregulated dolphin watching activities in Tanzania have also been shown to have a negative effect on dolphin behaviour and movement patterns, which may impact on their reproductive success.

Indo-Pacific Bottlenose Dolphin

Common Bottlenose Dolphin   *Tursiops truncatus*

SWAHILI: Pomboo Pua ya Chupa

A large, grey dolphin with a subtle three-toned colour pattern. It has a dark grey cape that extends from the top of the head (sometimes from the top of the beak) to halfway between the dorsal fin and the fluke. The flanks are usually a paler grey and the underside is off-white or even pinkish-white. The beak is relatively short. The tall, sickle-shaped dorsal fin is located midway along the back.

Least Concern	
HB:	2·4–3·8 m (8–12 ft)
Wt:	150–430 kg (330–950 lb)

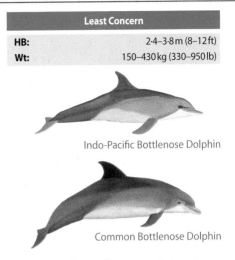

Indo-Pacific Bottlenose Dolphin

Common Bottlenose Dolphin

Similar species
Indo-Pacific Bottlenose Dolphins look very similar, and the two species are difficult to differentiate unless seen extremely well. Adult Indo-Pacific Bottlenose Dolphins often have spotted underparts, and are slightly smaller with a less pronounced melon and a proportionately longer beak. They are also usually found closer to the shore than Common Bottlenose Dolphins.

Ecology and social behaviour
There are both inshore and offshore forms of the Common Bottlenose Dolphin that differ in behaviour and ecology. It is unclear which form is found in Tanzania, although this species is generally associated with deep water off the East African coast. The average group size is 15 animals, but ranges from 1–1,000+.

Population size and conservation status
The similarity between this species and the Indo-Pacific Bottlenose Dolphin means that there is little accurate information on the status of the Common Bottlenose Dolphin in Tanzania. Most valid records are from strandings or accidental captures. Single juveniles of this species were trapped in gill nets off both the northwest and east coast of Zanzibar between 2000 and 2003, and in 2006 approximately 600 individuals were stranded on the northwest coast of Zanzibar.

Common Bottlenose Dolphin

Spinner Dolphin

Stenella longirostris

SWAHILI: Pomboo Mizunguko

Data Deficient	
HB:	1·3–2·3 m (4–8 ft)
Wt:	25–80 kg (55–170 lb)

A medium-sized dolphin with a distinctive three-toned body pattern: dark grey that extends from the forehead, along the top of the head and back, to midway along the tail stock; light grey that extends from the top of the beak, through the eye and along the flanks to the tail flukes; and a white (to pinkish) lower jaw, chin and belly. The beak is long and slender; the dorsal fin varies in shape, mainly depending on age and gender, from tall, upright and triangular to slightly hooked.

Similar species
Spinner Dolphins and Pantropical Spotted Dolphins have been recorded moving in mixed-species groups off Nungwe on the north coast of Zanzibar. Pantropical Spotted Dolphins have spots on the back and side of the body, although these may be very faint and difficult to see; they also tend to be darker on the belly. This species does not spin when leaping. Common Bottlenose Dolphins (*page 257*) and Indo-Pacific Bottlenose Dolphins (*page 256*) move in smaller groups and leap out of the water less frequently.

Ecology and social behaviour
Spinner Dolphins typically occur in large groups of 100 or more individuals. They are named after their habit of leaping up to 3m (10 ft) clear of the water and spinning longitudinally, like a corkscrew.

Population size and conservation status
There are many records from around Zanzibar, particularly in the northeast around Matemwe and Nungwe. They are also occasionally recorded in deeper water around the outer reefs off Maziwe Island near Pangani. In Zanzibar, between 2000 and 2003, 44 Spinner Dolphin deaths were recorded in gillnet traps, with most captures from the northeast of the Island.

Spinner Dolphin TOP: spinning; BOTTOM: travelling

Pantropical Spotted Dolphin

Stenella attenuata

SWAHILI: Pomboo

Least Concern	
HB:	2·4–2·6 m (8–9 ft)
Wt:	90–120 kg (200–260 lb)

A slender dolphin with a forehead that slopes gently down to a long, narrow beak. The tip of the beak and the 'lips' are often white. The sickle-shaped dorsal fin is relatively narrow and pointed compared to other similar-sized dolphins. Adults usually have a dark back, paler grey flanks and a pale grey belly, although they may appear all black. Adults are usually heavily spotted on the back, sides and underside, but the extent of spotting varies between individuals, and spots may not be visible from a distance. Juveniles may be unspotted or have black spots just on the belly.

Spinner Dolphin

Pantropical Spotted Dolphin

Rough-toothed Dolphin (*p.260*)

Fraser's Dolphin (*p.260*)

Similar species
Both Common Bottlenose Dolphin (*page 257*) Indo-Pacific Bottlenose Dolphin (*page 256*) are larger and stockier and have a taller dorsal fin. Indo-Pacific Bottlenose Dolphins have spotting confined to the underside and are usually found closer to shore than the Pantropical Spotted Dolphin. Spinner Dolphins are usually white below and have a unique spinning behaviour.

Ecology and social behaviour
There are both inshore and offshore forms of Pantropical Spotted Dolphin but only the offshore form is known from Tanzanian waters, usually in water deeper than 200 m (650 ft). This species travels in pods of 20–300 animals (average approximately 100 animals), and occasionally travels in mixed-species groups with Spinner Dolphins.

Population size and conservation status
Pantropical Spotted Dolphins are uncommon in Tanzanian waters. Six individuals were killed in drift nets set by fisherman off the northern coast of Zanzibar between 2000 and 2003.

Pantropical Spotted Dolphin

259

Rough-toothed Dolphin

Steno bredanensis

SWAHILI: Pomboo Meno Mabaya

Least Concern	
HB:	2·4–2·8 m (8–9 ft)
Wt:	145–155 kg (320–340 lb)

A large dolphin with a dark grey dorsal 'cape', light grey sides, and white or pinkish-white underparts. There are often whitish scars on the back and sides. The large dorsal fin, located midway along the back, is pointed and less hook-shaped than in other larger dolphins of the region. The head lacks the prominent melon that is a distinctive feature of most other oceanic dolphins and is instead conical, with no distinct differentiation between the forehead and the beak. The beak has 'lips' that are often white or pinkish white.

Similar species
Although somewhat similar to bottlenose dolphins (*pages 256–257*) the conical head shape, large dorsal fin and white 'lips' of the Rough-toothed Dolphin are distinctive.

Ecology and social behaviour
Little is known about this open ocean species, which is seldom seen close to shore. It is mostly found in groups of 10–12 animals, although pods of up to 50 have been recorded. Groups tend to swim shoulder-to-shoulder in synchrony, often 'skimming' along with their heads and beaks out of the water. They regularly accompany other species of dolphin.

Population size and conservation status
The only known sighting in Tanzanian waters comes from an aerial survey around Zanzibar during 2000. There are, however, confirmed records from neighbouring countries.

Fraser's Dolphin

Lagenodelphis hosei

SWAHILI: Pomboo

Least Concern	
HB:	2·1–2·7 m (7–9 ft)
Wt:	160–210 kg (350–460 lb)

A stocky dolphin with a very short beak and short flippers. It has a blue-grey back, pale grey sides, and a distinctive black band that extends from the upper part of the beak, past the eye, to the anus. This black band becomes wider and darker with age, being most striking in adult males and least defined or absent in juveniles. The belly is white or pink. The relatively small dorsal fin is almost triangular.

Similar species
This species' distinct colour pattern, very short beak and large group size make identification relatively straightforward.

Ecology and social behaviour
Fraser's Dolphin is typically found in deep tropical seas and is seldom found in shallow water or close to shore. It occurs in large groups of 50–1,000 animals that produce much splashing and a distinctive frothy wake when travelling. They often mix with other dolphin species, including False Killer Whales (*page 252*).

Population size and conservation status
In Tanzania, this species is known only from Zanzibar where it has been recorded as by-catch in fishing nets.

see *page 259* for comparative illustrations of these two species

Subantarctic Fur Seal   *Arctocephalus tropicalis*

Least Concern	
HB:	M 1·8 m (6 ft) | F 1·5m (5 ft)
Wt:	M 130–165 kg (290–360 lb)
	F 50–55 kg (110–120 lb)

A large seal with a short snout. Adults are dark brown on the back and sides and have a creamy-yellow chest and face. The top of the head is dark brown, contrasting with the yellow face and creating a mask-like effect. Pups are black and moult to the same colour as the adults when approximately three months old.

Similar species
No other species of seal has been positively identified from Tanzania. However, it is possible that vagrant **Afro-Australian Fur Seals** *Arctocephalus pusillus* and **Antarctic Fur Seals** *Arctocephalus gazella* may also occasionally occur. The former have a longer snout than the Subantarctic Fur Seal and the females and juveniles are a pale brown-grey, rather than yellow on their undersides. Antarctic Fur Seals are more silvery in appearance.

Ecology and social behaviour
Mostly found in subantarctic waters, the nearest colonies of Subantarctic Fur Seal are on Amsterdam Island and Prince Edward Island in the Antarctic Ocean some 4,500–5,300 km (2,800–3,300 miles) south of Zanzibar. Breeding sites are populated by breeding bulls and females with newborn pups. Occupants of non-breeding haul-out sites generally consist mostly of subadult males, with a few adult males and females.

Population size and conservation status
The Subantarctic Fur Seal is a rare vagrant to Tanzanian waters. In June 2008, local fishermen captured a juvenile at Gwede beach near Matemwe on the west coast of Zanzibar. The animal was in very poor condition and died two days later. The stuffed specimen is now at the local zoo in Stone Town. In July 2002, another fur seal was seen and killed by fishermen at Chokocho village on Pemba Island. However, the body was not preserved, and the specimen was not identified to species level.

Subantarctic Fur Seal (Amsterdam Island)

Genets and civets

page 142

African Civet
HB 67–84 cm | 26–33"
Ht 35–40 cm | 14–16"

page 142

Small Indian Civet
HB 49–68 cm | 19–26"
Ht: no data

Black feet,
stripes on back

page 136

Servaline Genet
HB 45–50 cm | 18–20"
Ht 18–20 cm | 7–8"

Tight, uniformly
coloured spots

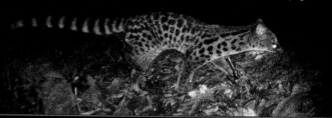

page 134

Common Genet
HB 46–51 cm | 18–20"
Ht 15–20 cm | 6–8"

Long tail, white tail tip,
black on rear part
of hind legs,
small spots

page 138

Large Spotted Genet
HB 42–52 cm | 17–20"
Ht 16–18 cm | 6–7"

Rosette spots,
black tail tip,
white on inner
side of legs

page 140

Miombo Genet
HB 44–48 cm | 17–19"
Ht 18–20 cm | 7–8"

Black 'socks' on
rear legs, bushy tail

Mongooses

page 156

Egyptian Mongoose
HB 50–60 cm | 20–24"
Ht 19–20 cm | 7"

Large, black face and legs,
runs with body low to ground

page 158

Slender Mongoose
HB 27–34 cm | 11–13"
Ht 10–12 cm | 4–5"

Small, uniform body colour,
tail tip usually raised

page 152

Bushy-tailed Mongoose
HB 39–42 cm | 16–17"
Ht 18–20 cam | 7–8"

Tail usually bushy,
dark lower lip

page 162

Meller's Mongoose
HB 44–50 cm | 17–20"
Ht 15–18 cm | 6–7"

Large, long legs,
shaggy tail with
white undercoat.

page 150

Marsh Mongoose
HB 48–64 cm | 19–25"
Ht 18–20 cm | 7–8"

Tail tapered,
light coloured
lower lip

Zorilla
HB 28–38 cm | 11–15"
Ht 10–13 | 4–5"

Long coat, bushy tail

page 110

African Striped Weasel
HB 27–33 cm | 11–13"
Ht 7–8 cm | 3"

Solid white crown,
distinct stripes
on back

page 112

Hyraxes

Bush Hyrax HB 38–47 cm | 15–19"

Pointed nose, white below, clear white markings above eye

page 34

Rock Hyrax HB 40–58 cm | 16–23"

Short nose, cream below, less distinct white above eyes

page 32

page 36

page 36

Southern Tree Hyrax
HB 35–60 cm | 14–24"

White on cheeks and lips, short nose

Eastern Tree Hyrax
HB 35–60 cm | 14–24"

Very dark, uniform colour

Striped Hyaena and Aardwolf

Aardwolf
HB 65--80 cm | 26–31"
Ht 45–50 cm | 18–20"

White throat, distal half of tail black

page 148

Striped Hyaena
HB 100–120 cm | 39–47"
Ht 65–80 cm | 25–31"

Black throat, white tail

page 146

Small antelope

Bush Duiker
HB 70–115 cm | 28–45"
Ht 45–70 cm | 18–28"

Black ridge on nose,
black stripe down
tail, long body

page 196

Steenbok
HB 72–87 cm | 28–34"
Ht 45–60 cm | 18–24"

Large ears,
very small
tail

page 206

Sharpe's Grysbok
page 204

HB 60–85cm | 24–33"
Ht 50 cm | 20"

White flecks in coat

Natal Red Duiker
page 200

HB 80–95 cm | 31–37"
Ht 38–47 cm | 15–19"

Curved back,
black on
neck

Blue Duiker
page 194

HB 55–66 cm | 22–26"
Ht 31–38 cm | 12–15"

Dark blue-grey coat, black stripe
flanked with white on tail

Kirk's Dik-dik
page 208

HB 54–71 cm | 21–28"
Ht 30–44 cm | 12–17"

Long snout,
very short tail,
grey neck
and rump

Suni
page 192

HB 55–61 cm | 22–24"
Ht 33–35 cm | 13–14"

Brown coat, tail uniform
brown above, white below

265

Medium-sized antelope

Thomson's Gazelle   *page 212*
HB 92–107 cm | 36–42"
Ht 58–70 cm | 23–28"

Brown rump above tail,
tail black, prominent
black stripe on flanks

Grant's Gazelle   *page 214*
HB 135–160 cm | 53–63"
Ht 85–94 cm | 33–37"

White rump above tail,
tail mostly white, females
sometime have black stripe

Bushbuck male   *page 188*
HB 117–142 cm | 51–67"
Ht 64–87 cm | 25–34"

Grey collar

Bushbuck female   *page 188*
HB 114–132 cm | 51–63"
Ht 60–71 cm | 24–28"

Grey collar on neck

Sitatunga male   *page 190*
HB 150–170 cm | 59–67"
Ht 88–125 cm | 35–49"

Shaggy coat,
splayed hooves

Sitatunga female   *page 190*
HB 135–145 cm | 53–57"
Ht 75–90 cm | 30–35"

Shaggy coat,
splayed hooves

Impala *page 206*
HB 120–150 cm | 47–59"
Ht 80–93 cm | 31–37"

Black stripes on
either side of rump
and on tail

Mountain Reedbuck *page 220*
HB120–145 cm | 47–57"
Ht 72–84 cm | 28–33"

Grey body

Puku *page 226*
HB 126–146 | 50–57"
Ht 73–83 cm | 29–33"

Lyre-shaped horns,
stocky build

Southern Reedbuck *page 222*
HB 120–160 cm | 47–63"
Ht 80–95 cm | 31–37"

Long tail, gently arcing horns

Oribi *page 218*
HB 93–112 cm | 38–45"
Ht 60–69 cm | 23–29"

Straight horns,
sharp contrast between
coat and underbelly

Bohor Reedbuck *page 224*
HB 100–135 cm | 39–53"
Ht 75–89 cm | 30–35"

Sharply curved horns

Large antelope

Greater Kudu male

page 184

HB 186–217 cm | 73–85"
Ht 120–130 cm | 47–51"

Mane along underside
of neck

Lesser Kudu male

page 182

HB 150–170 cm | 59–67"
Ht 95–105 cm | 37–41"

Slate grey colour,
two white marks on
underside of neck,
small chevron

Greater Kudu female

page 184

HB 150–170 cm | 59–67"
Ht 95–105 cm | 37–41"

Large chevron on forehead
meets / almost
meets.

Lesser Kudu female

page 182

HB 110–130 cm | 43–51"
Ht 90–100 cm | 35–39"

Two white marks on
underside of neck

Sable Antelope female

page 242

HB 175–195cm | 68–77"
Ht 120–140cm | 47–55"

Reddish body,
distinct white belly,
long horns

Roan Antelope female

page 240

HB 190–240 cm | 75–94"
HT 126–145 cm | 50–57"

Light brown body,
short horns

National Parks and major protected areas of Tanzania

The following pages provide summary information and species lists for the major protected areas in Tanzania. These fall under the jurisdiction of several different agencies, and are managed for different purposes. The mainland **National Parks** are operated by Tanzania National Parks (TANAPA), and are designated exclusively for wildlife conservation and photographic tourism. **Jozani Chwaka Bay National Park** in Zanzibar (Unguja Island) has similar status to the mainland national parks but is administered by the Zanzibar Department of Forestry and Nonrenewable Natural Resources. The **Ngorongoro Conservation Area** operates under the jurisdiction of the Ngorongoro Conservation Area Authority (NCAA), and allows multiple land uses, including pastoral activities, settlement, and agriculture. **Game Reserves** are managed by the Wildlife Division of the Ministry of Natural Resources and Tourism, and are designated for sport hunting, with the exception of the northern Selous Game Reserve, which is used for photographic tourism.

The species lists are coded as follows:

Status within the protected area:

C	Common	P	Possible: Not recorded in the National Park although suitable habitat exists.
U	Uncommon	E	Extinct: Formerly reported in the National Park, but no records for over 20 years.
R	Rare	[I]	Introduced: Species introduced although not historically native to the area.
V	Vagrant (passes through occasionally)	[RI]	Re-introduced: Species formerly reported in the National Park and re-introduced following local extinction.

Likelihood of seeing a species within the protected area:

Likely to be seen during a 2-day trip
Likely to be seen during a 5-day trip or multiple visits
Low chance of being seen by visitor

Arusha National Park

Size: 542 km² (210 mi²)   **Established**: 1960

Main habitats: Montane forest, lakeshore and altimontane shrubland on upperslopes of Mount Meru

Seasons: DRY: June–October   WET: November–May
Very little seasonal variation in wildlife.

Activities: Game drives, guided forest walks, canoeing

Mammal Highlights: Guereza Black-and-white Colobus, Mitis Monkey, Natal Red Duiker, Suni

Aardvark	U	African Wild Dog	R	Dwarf Mongoose	U
Eastern Tree Hyrax	C	Bat-eared Fox	U	Black Rhinoceros	E
Savanna Elephant	U	Zorilla	U	Plains Zebra	C
Guereza Black-and-white Colobus	C	African Clawless Otter	U	Bushpig	U
Olive Baboon	C	Honey Badger	U	Common Warthog	C
Vervet Monkey	C	African Palm Civet	R	Common Hippopotamus	C
Mitis Monkey	C	Serval	P	Giraffe	C
Large-eared Greater Galago	C	Wild Cat	U	African Buffalo	C
Small-eared Greater Galago	C	Lion	V	Common Eland	V
Senegal Lesser Galago	C	Leopard	C	Bushbuck	C
East African Springhare	U	Common Genet	U	Suni	C
Crested Porcupine	C	Large-spotted Genet	C	Bush Duiker	R
Cape Hare	P	African Civet	C	Natal Red Duiker (Harvey's)	C
African Savanna Hare	C	Spotted Hyaena	C	Steenbok	R
White-bellied Hedgehog	C	Marsh Mongoose	U	Kirk's Dik-dik	C
Ground Pangolin	P	Bushy-tailed Mongoose	C	Klipspringer	R
Side-striped Jackal	P	Egyptian Mongoose	P	Mountain Reedbuck	E
Golden Jackal	V	Slender Mongoose	C	Bohor Reedbuck	R
Black-backed Jackal	U	White-tailed Mongoose	U	Waterbuck (Common)	C
		Banded Mongoose	U		

Gombe Stream National Park

Size: 52 km² (20 mi²)   **Established:** 1968

Main habitats: Wet miombo woodland

Seasons: DRY: May–October   WET: November–May
Chimpanzees are generally easier to find in the dry season.

Activities: Guided forest walks

See page 269 for a key to the species codes

Mammal Highlights: Chimpanzee, Red-tailed Monkey, Eastern Red Colobus

Chequered Elephant-shrew	C	African Wild Dog	E	Egyptian Mongoose	U
Bush Hyrax	E	African Clawless Otter	R	Slender Mongoose	U
Chimpanzee	C	Spotted-necked Otter	E	White-tailed Mongoose	C
Eastern Red Colobus	C	Honey Badger	U	Banded Mongoose	U
Olive Baboon	C	African Palm Civet	U	Bushpig	C
Vervet Monkey	U	Serval	R	Common Hippopotamus	R
Red-tailed Monkey	C	Wild Cat	P	African Buffalo	E
Mitis Monkey	C	Lion	E	Bushbuck	C
Large-eared Greater Galago	U	Leopard	E?	Blue Duiker	P
Senegal Lesser Galago	U	Large-spotted Genet	U	Bush Duiker	U
Cape Porcupine	C	African Civet	C	Oribi	P
Ground Pangolin	U	Spotted Hyaena	E	Waterbuck (Defassa)	E
Side-striped Jackal	R	Marsh Mongoose	U	Roan Antelope	E

Jozani Chwaka Bay National Park

Size: 50 km² (19 mi²)   **Established**: 2004
Currently the only National Park on Zanzibar

Main habitats: Coastal forest, groundwater forest, mangrove forest

Seasons: DRY: June–October WET: November–May
Very little seasonal variation in wildlife.

Activities: Guided walks

Mammal Highlights: Zanzibar Red Colobus, Ader's Duiker (rare)

* This species list is the same for Zanzibar (Unguja Island)

√ = present

Jozani Chwaka Bay*	
Black-and-rufous Elephant-shrew	C
Four-toed Elephant-shrew	C
Eastern Tree Hyrax	C
Zanzibar Red Colobus	C
Vervet Monkey	C
Mitis Monkey	C
Small-eared Greater Galago	C
Zanzibar Dwarf Galago	C
Crested Porcupine	P
African Palm Civet	R
Leopard	E
Servaline Genet	U
African Civet	U
Small Indian Civet	U
Bushy-tailed Mongoose	C
Slender Mongoose	C
Banded Mongoose	U
Bushpig	C
Suni	C
Blue Duiker	U
Ader's Duiker	U

Pemba Island	
Eastern Tree Hyrax	√
Zanzibar Red Colobus	√
Vervet Monkey	√
Mitis Monkey	√
Small-eared Greater Galago	√
Small Indian Civet	√
Slender Mongoose	P
Banded Mongoose	P
Marsh Mongoose	√
Blue Duiker	√

Mafia Island	
Black-and-rufous Elephant-shrew	√
Four-toed Elephant-shrew	√
Eastern Tree Hyrax	√
Vervet Monkey	√
Mitis Monkey	√
Small-eared Greater Galago	√
Small Indian Civet	√
Egyptian Mongoose	√
Small Indian Mongoose	√
Bushpig	√
Common Hippopotamus	√
Suni	√
Blue Duiker	√
Dugong	V

Katavi National Park

Size: 4,470 km² (1,725 mi²)   **Established**: 1974

Main habitats: Wet miombo woodland, floodplain grasslands

Seasons: DRY: June–October   WET: November–May
Wildlife viewing better in the dry season.

Activities: Game drives, night drives, guided bush walks

Mammal Highlights: Lion, Roan Antelope, large herds of African Buffalo and Common Hippopotamus

Aardvark	U	Honey Badger	C	Bushpig	C
Chequered Elephant-shrew	P	African Palm Civet	P	Common Warthog	C
Four-toed Elephant-shrew	C	Cheetah	R	Common Hippopotamus	C
Bush Hyrax	P	Caracal	R	Giraffe	C
Southern Tree Hyrax	P	Serval	R	African Buffalo	C
Savanna Elephant	C	Wild Cat	R	Greater Kudu	U
Yellow Baboon	C	Lion	C	Common Eland	U
Vervet Monkey	C	Leopard	C	Bushbuck	C
Mitis Monkey	R	Large-spotted Genet	U	Bush Duiker	C
Large-eared Greater Galago	C	Miombo Genet	C	Sharpe's Grysbok	U
Senegal Lesser Galago	C	African Civet	C	Kirk's Dik-dik	P
East African Springhare	R	Spotted Hyaena	C	Klipspringer	U
Cape Porcupine	U	Aardwolf	P	Oribi	R
African Savanna Hare	U	Marsh Mongoose	C	Southern Reedbuck	U
Ground Pangolin	R	Bushy-tailed Mongoose	U	Bohor Reedbuck	C
Side-striped Jackal	U	Egyptian Mongoose	U	Waterbuck (Defassa)	C
Black-backed Jackal	R	Slender Mongoose	C	Impala	C
African Wild Dog	U	White-tailed Mongoose	U	Topi	C
Zorilla	R	Banded Mongoose	C	Lichtenstein's Hartebeest	C
		Dwarf Mongoose	C	Roan Antelope	C
		Plains Zebra	C	Sable Antelope	R

277

Kitulo National Park

Size: 413 km² (160 mi²)   **Established**: 2002

Main habitats: Afromontane grassland, bamboo forest

Seasons: DRY: June–October   WET: November–May
Little seasonal variation in wildlife; wet season is best
for flowering plants.

Activities: Guided walks

Mammal Highlights: Angola Black-and-white Colobus, Kipunji, Striped Weasel, Abbott's Duiker (rare)

Aardvark	R	Side-striped Jackal	U	Egyptian Mongoose	R
Chequered Elephant-shrew	C	Zorilla	C	Slender Mongoose	C
Bush Hyrax	U	African Striped Weasel	U	Banded Mongoose	R
Southern Tree Hyrax	U	African Clawless Otter	R	Bushpig	U
Savanna Elephant	E	Honey Badger	R	African Buffalo	E
Angola Black-and-white Colobus	C	African Palm Civet	U	Common Eland	E
Kipunji	R	Serval	C	Bushbuck	U
Mitis Monkey	C	Wild Cat	R	Blue Duiker	R
Rungwe Dwarf Galago	U	Lion	V	Bush Duiker	U
Cape Porcupine	U	Leopard	U	Abbott's Duiker	R
African Savanna Hare	C	Large-spotted Genet	C	Klipspringer	U
Smith's Red Rock Hare	U	African Civet	U	Oribi	U
White-bellied Hedgehog	R	Spotted Hyaena	E	Southern Reedbuck	R
		Marsh Mongoose	U	Impala	E

Lake Manyara National Park

Size: 330 km² (127 mi²)
30% is land and 70% is
Lake Manyara

Established: 1960
UNESCO Biosphere
Reserve

Main habitats: Mature groundwater forest, lake and lakeshore

Seasons: DRY: June–October   WET: November–May
Very little seasonal variation in wildlife.

Activities: Game drives, canoeing and night drives

Mammal Highlights: Savanna Elephant, Common Hippopotamus, Klipspringer, Bushy-tailed Mongoose

Aardvark	U	African Clawless Otter	U	Banded Mongoose	C
Bush Hyrax	C	Spotted-necked Otter	P	Dwarf Mongoose	C
Southern Tree Hyrax	P	Honey Badger	R	Black Rhinoceros	E
Savanna Elephant	C	Cheetah	R	Plains Zebra	C
Olive Baboon	C	Caracal	R	Bushpig	U
Vervet Monkey	C	Serval	C	Common Warthog	C
Mitis Monkey	C	Wild Cat	U	Common Hippopotamus	C
Large-eared Greater Galago	P	Lion	C	Giraffe	C
Small-eared Greater Galago	C	Leopard	C	African Buffalo	C
Senegal Lesser Galago	C	Common Genet	U	Bushbuck	C
Ground Pangolin	P	Large-spotted Genet	C	Natal Red Duiker (Harvey's)	R
Crested Porcupine	U	African Civet	C	Kirk's Dik-dik	C
Cape Hare	P	Spotted Hyaena	C	Klipspringer	C
African Savanna Hare	C	Aardwolf	P	Thomson's Gazelle	C
White-bellied Hedgehog	C	Marsh Mongoose	C	Mountain Reedbuck	E
Golden Jackal	R	Bushy-tailed Mongoose	C	Bohor Reedbuck	R
Black-backed Jackal	C	Egyptian Mongoose	P	Waterbuck (Common)	C
African Wild Dog	V	Slender Mongoose	C	Impala	C
Zorilla	R	White-tailed Mongoose	C	Common Wildebeest	U

Mahale Mountains National Park

Size: 1,613 km² (623 mi²)   **Established**: 1985
National Park includes 50 km
(31 mi) of lake shore, and
extends 1·6 km (1 mi) into
Lake Tanganyika

Main habitats: Afromontane forest, wet miombo
woodland

Seasons: DRY: May–October   WET: November–May
Little seasonal variation in wildlife, although
Chimpanzees are harder to find in May and June.

Activities: Guided forest walks

Mammal Highlights: Chimpanzee, Red-tailed Monkey, Eastern Red Colobus

Aardvark	C	Giant Pangolin	C	Banded Mongoose	C
Chequered Elephant-shrew	C	Side-striped Jackal	U	Dwarf Mongoose	U
Four-toed Elephant-shrew	P	African Wild Dog	V	Plains Zebra	U
Bush Hyrax	C	Zorilla	R	Bushpig	C
Southern Tree Hyrax	C	African Clawless Otter	U	Common Warthog	C
Savanna Elephant	C	Spotted-necked Otter	U	Common Hippopotamus	U
Chimpanzee	C	Honey Badger	U	Giraffe	U
Angola Black-and-white Colobus	U	African Palm Civet	R	African Buffalo	U
Eastern Red Colobus	C	Serval	R	Greater Kudu	P
Yellow Baboon	C	Wild Cat	R	Common Eland	R
Vervet Monkey	C	Lion	R	Bushbuck	C
Red-tailed Monkey	C	Leopard	C	Blue Duiker	C
Mitis Monkey	C	Large-spotted Genet	C	Bush Duiker	C
Large-eared Greater Galago	U	Miombo Genet	P	Weyns's Duiker	E?
Senegal Lesser Galago	U	African Civet	C	Sharpe's Grysbok	U
Grant's Dwarf Galago	U	Spotted Hyaena	U	Klipspringer	U
Cape Porcupine	C	Marsh Mongoose	P	Waterbuck (Defassa)	U
African Savanna Hare	C	Bushy-tailed Mongoose	C	Topi	R
Smith's Red Rock Hare	P	Slender Mongoose	U	Lichtenstein's Hartebeest	U
Ground Pangolin	P	White-tailed Mongoose	U	Roan Antelope	R
				Sable Antelope	R

283

Mikumi National Park

Size: 3,320 km² (1,282 mi²)   **Established**: 1964

Main habitats: Dry miombo woodland, flood-plain grassland.

Seasons: DRY: June–November WET: December–May
Little seasonal variation in wildlife.

Activities: Game drives

Mammal Highlights: Many large savanna species, Honey Badger

Aardvark	U	Black-backed Jackal	C	Dwarf Mongoose	C
Chequered Elephant-shrew	U	African Wild Dog	R	Black Rhinoceros	E
Four-toed Elephant-shrew	C	Zorilla	P	Plains Zebra	C
Southern Tree Hyrax	P	African Clawless Otter	C	Bushpig	C
Eastern Tree Hyrax	P	Honey Badger	C	Common Warthog	C
Savanna Elephant	C	African Palm Civet	R	Common Hippopotamus	C
Angola Black-and-white Colobus	C	Cheetah	P	Giraffe	C
Yellow Baboon	C	Serval	U	African Buffalo	C
Vervet Monkey	C	Wild Cat	P	Greater Kudu	U
Mitis Monkey	C	Lion	C	Common Eland	C
Large-eared Greater Galago	C	Leopard	C	Bushbuck	C
Small-eared Greater Galago	C	Large-spotted Genet	C	Suni	U
Senegal Lesser Galago	C	Miombo Genet	P	Bush Duiker	C
Zanzibar Dwarf Galago	C	African Civet	C	Natal Red Duiker	U
East African Springhare	R	Spotted Hyaena	C	Sharpe's Grysbok	P
Crested Porcupine	C	Marsh Mongoose	U	Bohor Reedbuck	C
Cape Porcupine	P	Bushy-tailed Mongoose	U	Waterbuck (Common)	U
African Savanna Hare	C	Slender Mongoose	C	Impala	C
White-bellied Hedgehog	P	White-tailed Mongoose	U	Lichtenstein's Hartebeest	U
Ground Pangolin	R	Banded Mongoose	C	Common Wildebeest	C
Side-striped Jackal	P	Meller's Mongoose	P	Sable Antelope	U

Mkomazi National Park

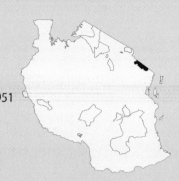

Size: 3,245 km² (1,253 mi²)

Established: 2008
Upgraded from a Game
Reserve established in 1951

Main habitats: Semi-arid *Acacia* bushland

Seasons: DRY: June–October WET: November–May
Best visited in the dry season.

Activities: Game drives, guided bush walks, night drives

See page 269 for a key to the species codes

Mammal Highlights: Dry country ungulates, Lesser Kudu, Gerenuk, Fringe-eared Oryx

Aardvark	U	Bat-eared Fox	C	Plains Zebra	C
Black-and-rufous Elephant-shrew	P	Zorilla	R	Bushpig	R
Rock Hyrax	R	Honey Badger	C	Common Warthog	C
Bush Hyrax	C	Cheetah	U	Giraffe	C
Southern Tree Hyrax	U	Caracal	C	African Buffalo	U
Savanna Elephant	U	Serval	C	Lesser Kudu	C
Angola Black-and-white Colobus	R	Wild Cat	C	Common Eland	C
Yellow Baboon (+ hybrid)	C	Lion	U	Bushbuck	U
Vervet Monkey	C	Leopard	C	Suni	U
Mitis Monkey	U	Common Genet	C	Bush Duiker	C
Large-eared Greater Galago	P	Large-spotted Genet	C	Natal Red Duiker (Harvey's)	C
Small-eared Greater Galago	U	African Civet	C	Steenbok	C
Senegal Lesser Galago	C	Spotted Hyaena	U	Kirk's Dik-dik	C
Crested Porcupine	C	Striped Hyaena	R	Klipspringer	U
Cape Hare	C	Aardwolf	C	Grant's Gazelle	U
African Savanna Hare	C	Marsh Mongoose	R	Gerenuk	C
White-bellied Hedgehog	P	Egyptian Mongoose	U	Bohor Reedbuck	U
Ground Pangolin	R	Slender Mongoose	U	Waterbuck (Common)	U
Side-striped Jackal	R	White-tailed Mongoose	C	Impala	U
Black-backed Jackal	C	Banded Mongoose	C	Coke's Hartebeest	C
African Wild Dog [RI]	R	Dwarf Mongoose	C	Fringe-eared Oryx	U
		Black Rhinoceros [RI]	R		

287

Mount Kilimanjaro National Park

Size: 1,668 km² (644 mi²)

Established: 1973
UNESCO World Heritage
Site

Main habitats: Dormant volcano with afromontane forest, altimontane shrubland, and glaciers near the summit

Seasons: DRY: June–October   WET: November–May
Little to no seasonal variation in wildlife.

Activities: Guided mountain trekking

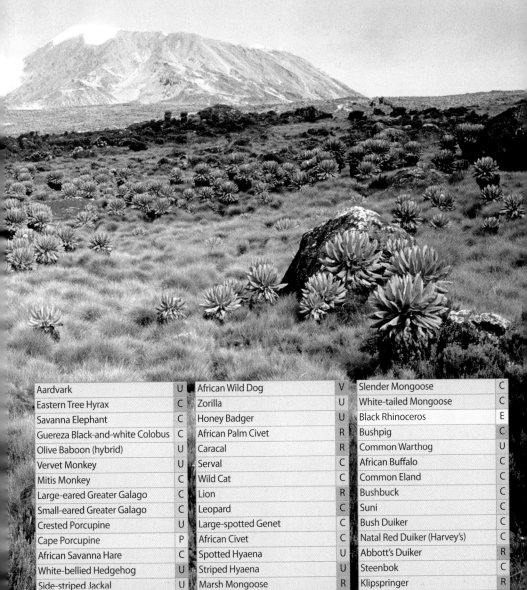

Mammal Highlights: Guereza Black-and-white Colobus, Mitis Monkey, Abbott's Duiker (rare)
The National Park boundary begins at the forest edge and very few lowland species are found in the National Park.

Aardvark	U	African Wild Dog	V	Slender Mongoose	C
Eastern Tree Hyrax	C	Zorilla	U	White-tailed Mongoose	C
Savanna Elephant	C	Honey Badger	U	Black Rhinoceros	E
Guereza Black-and-white Colobus	C	African Palm Civet	R	Bushpig	C
Olive Baboon (hybrid)	U	Caracal	R	Common Warthog	U
Vervet Monkey	U	Serval	C	African Buffalo	C
Mitis Monkey	C	Wild Cat	C	Common Eland	C
Large-eared Greater Galago	C	Lion	R	Bushbuck	C
Small-eared Greater Galago	C	Leopard	C	Suni	C
Crested Porcupine	U	Large-spotted Genet	C	Bush Duiker	C
Cape Porcupine	P	African Civet	C	Natal Red Duiker (Harvey's)	C
African Savanna Hare	C	Spotted Hyaena	U	Abbott's Duiker	R
White-bellied Hedgehog	U	Striped Hyaena	U	Steenbok	C
Side-striped Jackal	U	Marsh Mongoose	R	Klipspringer	R
Black-backed Jackal	U	Egyptian Mongoose	C	Bohor Reedbuck	U
				Waterbuck (Common)	U

Ngorongoro Conservation Area

Size: 8,292 km² (3,200 mi²)
Ngorongoro Crater is
304 km² (117 mi²)

Established: 1959
UNESCO World Heritage
Site & Biosphere Reserve

Main habitats: Montane forest, short-grass plains, *Acacia* woodland

Seasons: DRY: June–October WET: November–May
Best time for the wildebeest migration on the plains is January–April. Very little seasonal variation of wildlife in the Crater.

Activities: Game drives, guided bush walks

Mammal Highlights: Spectacular wildebeest and zebra migration, many large predators and large ungulates, including Black Rhinoceros

Aardvark	U	African Striped Weasel	R	Common Warthog	C
Rock Hyrax	P	African Clawless Otter	R	Common Hippopotamus	U
Bush Hyrax	C	Honey Badger	U	Giraffe	C
Southern Tree Hyrax	C	Cheetah	C	African Buffalo	C
Savanna Elephant	C	Caracal	U	Lesser Kudu	R
Olive Baboon	C	Serval	C	Greater Kudu	U
Vervet Monkey	C	Wild Cat	C	Common Eland	C
Mitis Monkey	C	Lion	C	Bushbuck	C
Large-eared Greater Galago	C	Leopard	C	Suni	C
Small-eared Greater Galago	C	Common Genet	C	Bush Duiker	R
Senegal Lesser Galago	C	Large-spotted Genet	C	Steenbok	C
East African Springhare	C	African Civet	C	Kirk's Dik-dik	C
Crested Porcupine	C	Spotted Hyaena	C	Klipspringer	U
Cape Hare	U	Striped Hyaena	U	Thomson's Gazelle	C
African Savanna Hare	C	Aardwolf	U	Grant's Gazelle	C
Smith's Red Rock Hare	P	Marsh Mongoose	U	Mountain Reedbuck	R
White-bellied Hedgehog	R	Bushy-tailed Mongoose	C	Bohor Reedbuck	C
Ground Pangolin	R	Egyptian Mongoose	U	Waterbuck (Defassa)	C
Side-striped Jackal	U	Slender Mongoose	C	Impala	C
Golden Jackal	C	White-tailed Mongoose	C	Topi	V
Black-backed Jackal	C	Banded Mongoose	C	Coke's Hartebeest	C
African Wild Dog	V	Dwarf Mongoose	C	Common Wildebeest	C
Bat-eared Fox	C	Black Rhinoceros	R	Roan Antelope	V
Zorilla	C	Plains Zebra	C	Fringe-eared Oryx	V
		Bushpig	C		

Ruaha National Park

Size: 20,225 km² (7,800 mi²)   **Established**: 1964
Largest National Park in
Tanzania

Main habitats: *Acacia–Commiphora* bushland, dry
miombo woodland, riverine forest, flood-plain grasslands

Seasons: DRY: May–October   WET: November–April
Wildlife viewing better in the dry season.

Activities: Game drives, guided bush walks, night drives

See page 269 for a key to the species codes

Mammal Highlights: Big cats, many large ungulate species, including Sable Antelope, Roan Antelope, Savanna Elephant

Aardvark	U	African Palm Civet	R	Bushpig	U
Four-toed Elephant-shrew	U	Cheetah	U	Common Warthog	C
Bush Hyrax	C	Caracal	R	Common Hippopotamus	C
Southern Tree Hyrax	R	Serval	U	Giraffe	C
Savanna Elephant	C	Wild Cat	U	African Buffalo	C
Yellow Baboon	C	Lion	C	Lesser Kudu	U
Vervet Monkey	C	Leopard	C	Greater Kudu	C
Mitis Monkey	U	Common Genet	C	Common Eland	U
Large-eared Greater Galago	U	Large-spotted Genet	C	Bushbuck	U
Senegal Lesser Galago	U	Miombo Genet	P	Bush Duiker	U
East African Springhare	U	African Civet	C	Natal Red Duiker (Harvey's)	R
Crested Porcupine	U	Spotted Hyaena	C	Sharpe's Grysbok	U
Cape Porcupine	P	Striped Hyaena	U	Steenbok	U
African Savanna Hare	U	Aardwolf	C	Kirk's Dik-dik	C
Smith's Red Rock Hare	P	Marsh Mongoose	R	Klipspringer	C
White-bellied Hedgehog	R	Bushy-tailed Mongoose	U	Grant's Gazelle	U
Ground Pangolin	R	Egyptian Mongoose	U	Oribi	U
Side-striped Jackal	U	Slender Mongoose	C	Southern Reedbuck	U
Black-backed Jackal	C	White-tailed Mongoose	C	Bohor Reedbuck	U
African Wild Dog	U	Meller's Mongoose	R	Waterbuck (Defassa)	C
Bat-eared Fox	C	Banded Mongoose	C	Impala	C
Zorilla	R	Dwarf Mongoose	C	Topi	U
African Clawless Otter	R	Black Rhinoceros	E	Lichtenstein's Hartebeest	U
Honey Badger	U	Plains Zebra	C	Roan Antelope	U
				Sable Antelope	U

Rubondo Island National Park

Size: 457 km² (176 mi²)   **Established**: 1977
Half of the National Park
extends into the lake
surrounding the Island

Main habitats: Lowland rainforest, papyrus swamp

Seasons: DRY: June–October WET: November–May
Virtually no seasonal variation in wildlife.

Activities: Guided forest walks, boat trips

Mammal Highlights: Sitatunga, Spotted-necked Otter

Savanna Elephant	C	Marsh Mongoose	U
Chimpanzee [I]	U	Bushpig	C
Guereza Black-and-white Colobus [I]	U	Common Hippopotamus	C
Vervet Monkey	C	Giraffe [I]	C
African Clawless Otter	U	Bushbuck	C
Spotted-necked Otter	C	Sitatunga	C
Large-spotted Genet	U	Suni [I]	U

Saadani National Park

Size: 1,100 km² (425 mi²)

Established: 2005
Upgraded from a
Game Reserve that was
established in 1962

Main habitats: Coastal forest, mangrove forest,
savanna-grassland

Seasons: DRY: June–October WET: November–May
Little seasonal variation in wildlife.

Activities: Game drives, riverboat trips

Mammal Highlights: Angola Black-and-white Colobus, Miombo Genet, Natal Red Duiker, Rondo Dwarf Galago (rare)

Aardvark	R	Zorilla	P	Bushpig	C
Black-and-rufous Elephant-shrew	C	African Clawless Otter	U	Common Warthog	C
Four-toed Elephant-shrew	C	Honey Badger	U	Common Hippopotamus	C
Savanna Elephant	C	Caracal	R	Giraffe	C
Angola Black-and-white Colobus	C	Serval	R	African Buffalo	C
Yellow Baboon	C	Lion	C	Greater Kudu	U
Vervet Monkey	C	Leopard	C	Common Eland	U
Mitis Monkey	C	Large-spotted Genet	C	Bushbuck	C
Large-eared Greater Galago	C	Miombo Genet	C	Suni	C
Small-eared Greater Galago	C	African Civet	C	Blue Duiker	C
Zanzibar Dwarf Galago	C	Spotted Hyaena	U	Bush Duiker	C
Rondo Dwarf Galago	R	Marsh Mongoose	U	Natal Red Duiker (Harvey's)	C
Crested Porcupine	C	Bushy-tailed Mongoose	U	Bohor Reedbuck	C
Cape Porcupine	P	Slender Mongoose	C	Waterbuck (Common)	C
African Savanna Hare	C	White-tailed Mongoose	U	Lichtenstein's Hartebeest	C
Ground Pangolin	R	Banded Mongoose	C	Common Wildebeest	C
Black-backed Jackal	R	Dwarf Mongoose	C	Sable Antelope	U
African Wild Dog	R	Plains Zebra	U	Fringe-eared Oryx	V

Selous Game Reserve

Size: 50,000 km² (19,300 mi²)
The oldest and largest
reserve in Africa

Established: 1896
UNESCO World Heritage
Site

Main habitats: Dry miombo woodland, coastal forest,
riverine forest, flood-plain grassland

Seasons: DRY: June–October WET: November–May
Little seasonal variation in wildlife.

Activities: Game drives, guided bush walks, riverboat trips

Mammal Highlights: Many large ungulates, African Wild Dog

Aardvark	R	Zorilla	U	Black Rhinoceros	R
Chequered Elephant-shrew	U	African Clawless Otter	U	Plains Zebra	C
Black-and-rufous Elephant-shrew	U	Honey Badger	U	Bushpig	C
Four-toed Elephant-shrew	C	Cheetah	P	Common Warthog	C
Bush Hyrax	C	Caracal	R	Common Hippopotamus	C
Southern Tree Hyrax	U	Serval	C	Giraffe	C
Savanna Elephant	C	Wild Cat	P	African Buffalo	C
Angola Black-and-white Colobus	C	Lion	C	Greater Kudu	U
Yellow Baboon	C	Leopard	C	Common Eland	C
Vervet Monkey	C	Large-spotted Genet	C	Bushbuck	C
Mitis Monkey	C	Miombo Genet	U	Suni	U
Large-eared Greater Galago	C	African Civet	C	Bush Duiker	C
Small-eared Greater Galago	C	Spotted Hyaena	C	Natal Red Duiker (+ hybrid)	U
Senegal Lesser Galago	C	Aardwolf	R	Sharpe's Grysbok	U
Crested Porcupine	C	Marsh Mongoose	U	Klipspringer	U
Cape Porcupine	C	Bushy-tailed Mongoose	P	Southern Reedbuck	P
African Savanna Hare	C	Egyptian Mongoose	R	Bohor Reedbuck	R
White-bellied Hedgehog	R	Slender Mongoose	C	Puku	R
Ground Pangolin	R	White-tailed Mongoose	U	Waterbuck (Common)	C
Side-striped Jackal	U	Meller's Mongoose	P	Impala	C
Black-backed Jackal	R	Banded Mongoose	C	Lichtenstein's Hartebeest	C
African Wild Dog	C	Dwarf Mongoose	C	Common Wildebeest	C
				Sable Antelope	U

Serengeti National Park

Size: 14,763 km² (5,700 mi²)
Oldest and second-largest
National Park in Tanzania

Established: 1951
UNESCO World Heritage
SIte & Biosphere Reserve

Main habitats: Vast short-grass plains, *Acacia* woodland,
kopjes (rocky outcrops)

Seasons: DRY: June–October   WET: November–May
Best time to see wildebeest calving on short grass plains
is January–April.

Activities: Game drives, guided bush walks

Mammal Highlights: The largest mammal migration in Africa.
Many large ungulates and large predators.

Aardvark	U	African Clawless Otter	R	Common Warthog	C
Rock Hyrax	C	Honey Badger	U	Common Hippopotamus	C
Bush Hyrax	C	African Palm Civet	R	Giraffe	C
Southern Tree Hyrax	C	Cheetah	C	African Buffalo	C
Savanna Elephant	C	Caracal	U	Lesser Kudu	R
Guereza Black-and-white Colobus	U	Serval	C	Greater Kudu	R
Olive Baboon	C	Wild Cat	C	Common Eland	C
Patas Monkey	R	Lion	C	Bushbuck	C
Vervet Monkey	C	Leopard	C	Bush Duiker	R
Large-eared Greater Galago	C	Common Genet	C	Steenbok	C
Senegal Lesser Galago	C	Large-spotted Genet	C	Kirk's Dik-dik	C
East African Springhare	C	African Civet	C	Klipspringer	C
Crested Porcupine	C	Spotted Hyaena	C	Thomson's Gazelle	C
Cape Hare	U	Striped Hyaena	U	Grant's Gazelle	C
African Savanna Hare	C	Aardwolf	U	Oribi	C
Smith's Red Rock Hare	R	Marsh Mongoose	U	Mountain Reedbuck	U
White-bellied Hedgehog	R	Egyptian Mongoose	U	Bohor Reedbuck	C
Ground Pangolin	R	Slender Mongoose	C	Waterbuck (Defassa)	C
Side-striped Jackal	U	White-tailed Mongoose	C	Impala	C
Golden Jackal	C	Banded Mongoose	C	Topi	C
Black-backed Jackal	C	Dwarf Mongoose	C	Coke's Hartebeest	C
African Wild Dog [RI]	V	Black Rhinoceros [RI]	R	Common Wildebeest	C
Bat-eared Fox	C	Plains Zebra	C	Roan Antelope	R
Zorilla	U	Bushpig	C	Fringe-eared Oryx	V

Tarangire National Park

Size: 2,850 km² (1,100 mi²)   **Established**: 1970

Main habitats: *Acacia–Commiphora* bushland with scattered Baobabs, riverine bushland, dry bushland in the south

Seasons: DRY: June–October WET: November–May
Best time for large concentrations of ungulates along the Tarangire River is July–October. Large gatherings of elephants in January–February.

Activities: Game drives, guided bush walks and night drives

See page 269 for a key to the species codes

Mammal Highlights: Large groups of Savanna Elephant and African Buffalo, Fringe-eared Oryx, Greater and Lesser Kudu, Lion

Aardvark	R	Cheetah	U	Common Hippopotamus	U
Bush Hyrax	C	Caracal	R	Giraffe	C
Southern Tree Hyrax	C	Serval	U	African Buffalo	C
Savanna Elephant	C	Wild Cat	C	Lesser Kudu	U
Olive Baboon	C	Lion	C	Greater Kudu	U
Yellow Baboon	V	Leopard	C	Common Eland	C
Vervet Monkey	C	Common Genet	C	Bushbuck	U
Large-eared Greater Galago	P	Large-spotted Genet	U	Bush Duiker	U
Small-eared Greater Galago	P	African Civet	C	Steenbok	C
Senegal Lesser Galago	C	Spotted Hyaena	C	Kirk's Dik-dik	C
East African Springhare	C	Striped Hyaena	U	Klipspringer	U
Crested Porcupine	C	Aardwolf	U	Thomson's Gazelle	V
Cape Hare	P	Marsh Mongoose	R	Grant's Gazelle	C
African Savanna Hare	C	Egyptian Mongoose	U	Gerenuk	U
Smith's Red Rock Hare	U	Slender Mongoose	C	Mountain Reedbuck	V
White-bellied Hedgehog	R	White-tailed Mongoose	C	Bohor Reedbuck	C
Ground Pangolin	R	Banded Mongoose	C	Waterbuck (Common)	C
Black-backed Jackal	C	Dwarf Mongoose	C	Impala	C
African Wild Dog	R	Black Rhinoceros	E	Coke's Hartebeest	C
Bat-eared Fox	U	Plains Zebra	C	Common Wildebeest	C
Zorilla	U	Bushpig	U	Roan Antelope	E
Honey Badger	U	Common Warthog	C	Fringe-eared Oryx	R

Udzungwa Mountains National Park

Size: 1,990 km² (768 mi²)   **Established**: 1992

Main habitats: Afromontane forest, miombo woodland, lowland rainforest

Seasons: DRY: June–October WET: November–May
Little seasonal variation in wildlife.

Activities: Guided forest walks

Mammal Highlights: Udzungwa Red Colobus, Sanje Mangabey, Abbott's Duiker

Aardvark	C	Smith's Red Rock Hare	P	Bushy-tailed Mongoose	C
Chequered Elephant-shrew	U	White-bellied Hedgehog	P	Jackson's Mongoose	R
Grey-faced Elephant-shrew	U	Ground Pangolin	R	Slender Mongoose	U
Four-toed Elephant-shrew	C	Side-striped Jackal	R	White-tailed Mongoose	U
Bush Hyrax	R	African Wild Dog	R	Meller's Mongoose	R
Southern Tree Hyrax	P	Zorilla	R	Banded Mongoose	U
Eastern Tree Hyrax	C	African Striped Weasel	R	Bushpig	C
Savanna Elephant	C	African Clawless Otter	U	Common Hippopotamus	U
Angola Black-and-white Colobus	C	Honey Badger	C	African Buffalo	U
Udzungwa Red Colobus	C	African Palm Civet	C	Lesser Kudu	R
Sanje Mangabey	U	Caracal	R	Greater Kudu	R
Yellow Baboon	C	Serval	R	Common Eland	R
Vervet Monkey	C	Wild Cat	P	Bushbuck	U
Mitis Monkey	C	Lion	R	Suni	C
Large-eared Greater Galago	U	Leopard	C	Blue Duiker	U
Small-eared Greater Galago	R	Servaline Genet	C	Bush Duiker	R
Zanzibar Dwarf Galago	C	Large-spotted Genet	U	Natal Red Duiker (Harvey's)	C
Mountain Dwarf Galago	U	African Civet	C	Abbott's Duiker	U
Crested Porcupine	U	Spotted Hyaena	U	Kirk's Dik-dik	U
Cape Porcupine	P	Aardwolf	R	Klipspringer	P
African Savanna Hare	P	Marsh Mongoose	U	Waterbuck (Common)	U
				Sable Antelope	R

Glossary

aestivate	to become dormant or have greatly reduced activity levels during a prolonged hot or dry period.
aquatic	living in or near fresh water.
basal	situated at, or arising from, the base.
arboreal	living or active in trees.
Biosphere Reserve	areas recognized by UNESCO as biologically and culturally significant and which promote sustainable development based on community efforts and sound science.
boss	a knob-like swelling at the base of an animal's horn.
breach	the act of a cetacean leaping fully or partially out of the water.
browse	a type of food or foraging behaviour: eating branches, shoots, and leaves of bushes and trees.
browser	an animal that feeds on branches and foliage.
CA (abbrev.)	(Ngorongoro) Conservation Area; a multiple use protected area.
camera trap nights	the number of days a camera trap is operational in the field, multiplied by the number of cameras used in a survey.
carrion	decaying flesh of dead animals.
chevron	a 'V'-shaped line or stripe across an animal's nose.
CITES (abbrev.)	the Convention on International Trade in Endangered Species of Wild Fauna and Flora
cm (abbrev.)	centimetre(s) (unit of length)
coral rag forest or thicket	coastal scrub forest with shallow soils overlying coral limestone.
crepuscular	active at sunrise and sunset.
cryptic	secretive and inconspicuous.
dewlap	a fold of loose skin that hangs beneath the neck.
distal	situated away from the centre of the body or point of attachment.
diurnal	active during the day.
dorsal	on, or referring to, the upper side or back of an animal.
ecosystem	a community of organisms and their physical environment. Used in this text to describe the geographical range of migrating mammals.
endemic	native or restricted to an area.
flank	the side of an animal's body.
FR (abbrev.)	Forest Reserve; an area of forest protected for multi-purpose use.
ft (abbrev.)	feet (unit of length)
g (abbrev.)	gramme(s) / gram(s) (unit of mass)
GR (abbrev.)	Game Reserve; a protected area used for sport hunting.
grazer	an animal that feeds on grass.
Guinea-Congo lowland forest	moist tropical broadleaf forest typical of the lowands near the Congo River basin and Central Africa.

ha *(abbrev.)*	hectare(s) (unit of area)
harem	a group of female animals, typically defended by a male.
HB *(abbrev.)*	head and body measurement: the length of the body from the tip of the nose to the base of the tail.
Ht *(abbrev.)*	height at shoulder measurement: length from the top of the shoulder blade to the foot in a standing animal.
herbivorous	feeds on plant material.
hindgut fermentation	digestive process occurring in animals with a single-chambered stomach.
hock	the backwards-pointing joint in the hind leg of a quadrupal animal between the knee and the hoof.
home range	an area routinely occupied by an individual or group.
hybrid	the offspring of parents of different species.
insectivorous	feeds on invertebrates.
IUCN *(abbrev.)*	the International Union for Conservation of Nature
kg *(abbrev.)*	kilogram(s) (unit of mass)
km / km^2 *(abbrev.)*	kilometre(s) / square kilometre(s) (unit of length / area)
kopje	a group of large rocks in an otherwise open area.
lb *(abbrev.)*	pound(s) (unit of mass)
lek	a site where males gather to attract females, and females go to select and mate with males.
lyre-shaped / lyrate	having or suggesting the shape of a lyre, or 'U'-shaped.
m *(abbrev.)*	metre(s) (unit of length)
mi / mi^2 *(abbrev.)*	mile(s) / square mile(s) (unit of length / area)
mm *(abbrev.)*	millimetre(s) (unit of length)
melanistic	a black or darker colour form caused by the excessive production of melanin pigment.
melon	the bulbous forehead of a toothed whale or dolphin containing a mass of fatty tissue that is believed to be used for echolocation.
midden	a pile of dung droppings, deposited regularly to mark an individual's territory.
morphology	the form and structure of an animal.
niche	an animal's role in its community.
nocturnal	active during the night.
NP *(abbrev.)*	National Park; a protected area used for photographic tourism.
omnivorous	feeds on both plant and animal matter.
ossified	tissue or cartilage that has turned into bone.
oz *(abbrev.)*	ounce(s) (unit of mass)
pelage	an animal's coat of fur or hair.
perianal	the area around the anus.
prehensile	the ability of an appendage to grasp or hold (*e.g.* a tail, tongue, trunk, feet).

preorbital	in front of or near the eye.
proboscis	an elongated nose (*e.g.* an elephant's trunk).
quadrupedal	walks on all four feet.
Ramsar site	a critically important wetland that is recognized under the Convention on Wetlands of International Importance, the Ramsar Convention.
rinderpest	an infectious disease in ruminants that causes fever, diarrhea, and inflammation of the mucous membrane. May be fatal in epidemics.
riparian	occurring on the banks of a river, stream, or wetland.
rut	an annual period of heightened sexual activity where males fight for access to females.
sp. *(abbrev.)*	species
species	the basic unit of taxonomic classification that describes a group of similar organisms that share similar genes and are capable of interbreeding and producing viable offspring.
species complex	a group of closely related species, where the exact demarcation between species is unclear due to recent or incomplete reproductive isolation.
ssp. *(abbrev.)*	subspecies
sp./ssp. nov. *(abbrev.)*	a species/subspecies that is yet to receive a scientific name.
subspecies	a sub-unit of taxonomic classification of a species; individuals of a subspecies are capable of interbreeding and producing viable offspring but are generally restricted by geographic isolation.
stochastic	a random event or pattern.
taxonomy	the science of defining groups of biological organisms on the basis of shared characteristics and organizing them into a classification system.
termitaria	A group of termite mounds.
terrestrial	living or active on the ground.
UNESCO *(abbrev.)*	the United Nations Educational, Scientific and Cultural Organization
ventral	on, or referring to, the underside or belly of an animal.
vestigial claw	a remnant claw that has become functionless through evolution.
World Heritage Site	an area recognized by UNESCO as having special cultural or physical significance.
Wt *(abbrev.)*	weight (unit of mass)
WMA *(abbrev.)*	Wildlife Management Area; a protected area that allows communities to manage and benefit from wildlife on their land.

Photographic credits

The production of this book would not have been possible without the help and co-operation of the many photographers who have kindly allowed their images to be reproduced. We therefore extend our gratitude and acknowledge the skill and patience involved. Every photograph published in this book is acknowledged in this section.

97 **Tree Pangolin**: TOP: Michael Gore/FLPA; BOTTOM: Philippe Hoogstoel

99 **Giant Pangolin**: BOTH IMAGES: TMAP

101 **Side-striped Jackal**: TOP: Sarah Durant; BOTTOM: Brian Scott

103 **Golden Jackal**: TOP: Charles and Lara Foley; BOTTOM: Jo Anderson

105 **Black-backed Jackal**: TOP: Tony Murtagh; BOTTOM: Jason Woolgar

107 **African Wild Dog**: BOTH IMAGES: Grégoire Bouguereau

109 **Bat-eared Fox**: TOP: Tui De Roy/Minden Pictures/FLPA; BOTTOM: Sarah Durant

111 **Zorilla**: TOP: Ian Beames/ardea.com; BOTTOM: W.T. Miller/Minden Pictures/FLPA

113 **African Striped Weasel**: Utah's Hogle Zoo

115 **African Clawless Otter**: TOP: Pat De La Harpe/naturepl.com; BOTTOM: Frans Vandewalle

117 **Spotted-necked Otter**: TOP: Don Roberson; BOTTOM: Luis Casiano/Biosphoto/FLPA

119 **Honey Badger**: TOP: Nick Garbutt / naturepl.com; BOTTOM: Grégoire Bouguereau

121 **African Palm Civet**: ssp. *arborea*: Michele Menegon; ssp. *gerrardi*: Francesco Rovero

123 **Cheetah**: TOP: Charles and Lara Foley; BOTTOM: Sarah Durant

125 **Caracal**: TOP: Greg & Yvonne Dean (WorldWildlifeImages.com); BOTTOM: Grégoire Bouguereau

127 **Serval**: TOP: Greg & Yvonne Dean (WorldWildlifeImages.com); BOTTOM: TMAP

129 **Wild Cat**: TOP: Grégoire Bouguereau; BOTTOM: Jason Woolgar

131 **Lion**: Kenneth K. Coe

133 **Leopard**: TOP: Donald Winspear; BOTTOM: Gian Schachenmann

135 **Common Genet**: Sultana Bashir

137 **Servaline Genet**: TOP: TMAP; BOTTOM: Francesco Rovero

139 **Large-spotted Genet**: TOP: TMAP; BOTTOM: M. Watson/ardea.com

141 **Miombo Genet**: TOP: Arturo Caso (CKWRI); BOTTOM: Yves Hausser (ADAP) and Claude Fischer (UASWS)

143 **African Civet**: TOP: Nick Gordon/ardea.com; BOTTOM: Warwick Tarboton

Small Indian Civet: T.R.A. Arunthavaselvan

145 **Spotted Hyaena**: Andy & Gill Swash (WorldWildlifeImages.com)

147 **Striped Hyaena**: Grégoire Bouguereau

149 **Aardwolf**: TOP: Anup Shah / naturepl.com; BOTTOM LEFT: Jason Woolgar; BOTTOM RIGHT: TMAP

151 **Marsh Mongoose**: TOP: Charles and Lara Foley; BOTTOM: David Bygott

153 **Bushy-tailed Mongoose**: BOTH IMAGES: TMAP

155 **Jackson's Mongoose**: TOP: Daniela De Luca and Noah Mpunga; BOTTOM: Francesco Rovero

157 **Egyptian Mongoose**: TOP: Sian Brown and Richard Hoare; BOTTOM: Suzi Eszterhas/Minden Pictures/FLPA

159 **Slender Mongoose**: TOP: Charles and Lara Foley; BOTTOM: Anna Estes

Small Indian Mongoose: Martin Pelanek

161 **White-tailed Mongoose**: TOP: Philip Perry; BOTTOM: Warwick Tarboton

163 **Meller's Mongoose**: BOTH IMAGES: TMAP

165 **Banded Mongoose**: BOTH IMAGES: Charles and Lara Foley

167 **Dwarf Mongoose**: TOP: Philip Perry; BOTTOM: Andy & Gill Swash (WorldWildlifeImages.com)

169 **Black Rhinoceros**: TOP: Kenneth K. Coe; BOTTOM: Jerry Kent

171 **Plains Zebra**: ssp. *boehmi*: Andy & Gill Swash (WorldWildlifeImages.com); ssp. *crawshaii*: Jim Frost

173 **Bushpig**: male ssp. *koiropotamus*: Warwick Tarboton; male ssp. *hassama*; female ssp. *hassama*: TMAP

175 **Warthog**: male: Frans Lanting/FLPA; female with young: Tui De Roy/Minden Pictures/FLPA

177 **Comon Hippopotamus**: BOTH IMAGES: Andy & Gill Swash (WorldWildlifeImages.com)

179 **Giraffe**: female: Steven Garvie; male: Andy & Gill Swash (WorldWildlifeImages.com)

181 **African Buffalo**: male: Kenneth K. Coe; female with calf: Andy & Gill Swash (WorldWildlifeImages.com)

183 **Lesser Kudu**: male: Steven Garvie; female: Kenneth K. Coe

185 **Greater Kudu**: male: Kenneth K. Coe; female: Jason Woolgar

187 **Common Eland**: male: Charles and Lara Foley; female with calves: Andy & Gill Swash (WorldWildlifeImages.com)

189 **Bushbuck**: ssp. *dama*: Jason Woolgar; male ssp. *delamerei*: Colin Beale; female ssp. *delamerei*: TMAP

191 **Sitatunga**: male: Ariadne Van Zandbergen/africaimagelibrary; female: Jerry Kent

193 **Suni**: male ssp. *kirchenpaueri*: Daudi Peterson; female ssp. *moschatus*: Tim Davenport

195 **Blue Duiker**: ALL IMAGES: TMAP

197 **Bush Duiker**: male: Greg & Yvonne Dean (WorldWildlifeImages.com); male ssp. nov.; female ssp. *orbicularis*: TMAP

199 **Ader's Duiker**: female: Tim Davenport; male: Tom Struhsaker

201 **Natal Red Duiker**: TOP: male ssp. *harveyi*: Charles and Lara Foley; BOTTOM: male ssp. *robertsi*; male ssp. *harveyi*: TMAP

203 **Abbott's Duiker**: male: Francesco Rovero; female: Andrew Bowkett

205 **Sharpe's Grysbok**: TOP: Alan Weaving/ardea.com; BOTTOM LEFT: Yves Hausser (ADAP) and Claude Fischer (UASWS); BOTTOM RIGHT: TMAP

207 **Steenbok**: male: Charles and Lara Foley; female: Tui De Roy/Minden Pictures/FLPA

209 **Kirk's Dik-dik**: female ssp. *cavendishi*: Charles and Lara Foley; male ssp. *thomasi*: Tris Enticknap; male ssp. *kirkii*: TMAP

211 **Klipspringer**: male ssp. *schillingsii*: Kenneth K. Coe; female ssp. *schillingsii*: Jason Woolgar
213 **Thomson's Gazelle**: male: Greg & Yvonne Dean (WorldWildlifeImages.com); female with calf: Andy & Gill Swash (WorldWildlifeImages.com)
215 **Grant's Gazelle**: male ssp. *robertsi*: Charles and Lara Foley; male ssp. *granti*: Frank Husslage; female and calf ssp. *robertsi*: Andy & Gill Swash (WorldWildlifeImages.com)
217 **Gerenuk**: male; female: Kenneth K. Coe; feeding: Jason Woolgar
219 **Oribi**: male ssp. *hastata*; male ssp. *cottoni*: Kenneth K. Coe; female ssp. *cottoni*: Ron Eggert
221 **Mountain Reedbuck**: male: Kenneth K. Coe; female: Philip Perry
223 **Southern Reedbuck**: male: Kenneth K. Coe; female: Warwick Tarboton
225 **Bohor Reedbuck**: male: Ron Eggert; female: Charles and Lara Foley
227 **Puku**: BOTH IMAGES: Kenneth K. Coe
229 **Waterbuck**: male ssp. *ellipsiprymnus*: Andy & Gill Swash; female ssp. *defassa*: Jason Woolgar
231 **Impala**: male: Andy & Gill Swash (WorldWildlifeImages.com); female: Charles and Lara Foley
233 **Topi**: male: Kenneth K. Coe; female with calf: Philip Perry
235 **Coke's Hartebeest**: male: Kenneth K. Coe; female: Ron Eggert
237 **Lichtenstein's Hartebeest**: male: Kirsten Skinner; female: Kenneth K. Coe
239 **Common Wildebeest**: male ssp. *mearnsi*: Andy & Gill Swash (WorldWildlifeImages.com); ssp. *johnstoni*: TMAP; ssp. *albojubatus*: Charles and Lara Foley
241 **Roan Antelope**: male: Kenneth K. Coe; females: Jason Anderson
243 **Sable Antelope**: BOTH IMAGES: Kenneth K. Coe
245 **Fringe-eared Oryx**: BOTH IMAGES: Kenneth K. Coe
247 **Dugong**: Mike Parry/Minden Pictures/FLPA
248–260 *All cetacean illustrations*: Robert Still
248 **Humpback Whale**: Virt Kitty | Flickr Creative Commons Commercial; flukes: Hugh Harrop
249 **Sperm Whale**: Hugh Harrop; flukes: Erwin Winkelman | Flickr Creative Commons Commercial
250 **Cuvier's Beaked Whale**: Hugh Harrop; **Longman's Beaked Whale**: Anthony Pierce
251 **Pygmy Sperm Whale**: Robert Pitman
253 **Short-finned Pilot Whale**: Malcolm Schuyl/FLPA; **False Killer Whale**: Jeremy Kiszka; **Killer Whale**: Hugh Harrop
254 **Risso's Dolphin**: Graeme Cresswell
255 **Indo-Pacific Humpback Dolphin**: Martin Nicoll/Biosphoto/FLPA
256 **Indo-Pacific Bottlenose Dolphin**: Hugh Lansdown/FLPA
257 **Common Bottlenose Dolphin**: Hugh Harrop
258 **Spinner Dolphin**: Robert Pitman; spinning: Jeremy Kiszka

259 **Pantropical Spotted Dolphin**: Robert Pitman
260 **Rough-toothed Dolphin**: Graeme Cresswell; **Fraser's Dolphin**: Robert Pitman
261 **Subantarctic Fur Seal**: Clem Haagner/ardea.com
262 **African Civet**; **Servaline Genet**; **Common Genet**; **Large-spotted Genet**; **Miombo Genet**: TMAP; **Small Indian Civet**: T.R.A. Arunthavaselvan;
263 **Egyptian Mongoose**: Bill Stanley; **Slender Mongoose**; **Marsh Mongoose**: Charles and Lara Foley; **Bushy-tailed Mongoose**; **Meller's Mongoose**; **Zorilla**: TMAP; **African Striped Weasel**: Utah's Hogle Zoo
264 **Bush Hyrax**: Mustafa Hassanali; **Rock Hyrax**: Greg & Yvonne Dean (WorldWildlifeImages. com); **Southern Tree Hyrax**: Charles and Lara Foley; **Eastern Tree Hyrax**; **Aardwolf**: TMAP; **Striped Hyaena**: Grégoire Bouguereau
265 **Steenbok**; **Natal Red Duiker**; **Kirk's Dik-dik**: Charles and Lara Foley; **Bush Duiker**; **Blue Duiker**: TMAP; **Sharpe's Grysbok**: Alan Weaving/ardea.com; **Suni**: Mnemba Island Lodge
266 **Thomson's Gazelle**: Charles and Lara Foley; **Grant's Gazelle**: Frank Husslage; **Bushbuck**: male: Colin Beale; female: Ron Eggert; **Sitatunga**: male: Ariadne Van Zandbergen/africaimagelibrary; female: Jerry Kent
267 **Impala**: Charles and Lara Foley; **Mountain Reedbuck**: Philip Perry; **Puku**; **Oribi**: Kenneth K. Coe; **Southern Reedbuck**: Warwick Tarboton; **Bohor Reedbuck**: Ron Eggert
268 **Greater Kudu**: male: Kenneth K. Coe; female: Jason Woolgar; **Lesser Kudu**: male; female: Kenneth K. Coe; **Sable Antelope**: Kenneth K. Coe; **Roan Antelope**: Jason Anderson
269 Selous Game Reserve: Robert Ross/rjrossphoto.com
270 Arusha National Park: Olli Marttila
272 Gombe Stream National Park: Olli Marttila
274 Jozani Chwaka Bay National Park: Tim Davenport
276 Katavi National Park: Jason Woolgar
278 Kitulo National Park: Tim Davenport
280 Lake Manyara National Park: Janneke van den Bosch
282 Mahale Mountains National Park: Olli Marttila
284 Mikumi National Park: Peter Stanley
286 Mkomazi National Park: Olli Marttila
288 Mount Kilimanjaro National Park: Olli Marttila
290 Ngorongoro Conservation Area: Andy & Gill Swash (WorldWildlifeImages.com)
292 Ruaha National Park: Olli Marttila
294 Rubondo Island National Park: Olli Marttila
296 Saadani National Park: Olli Marttila
298 Selous Game Reserve: Robert Ross/rjrossphoto.com
300 Serengeti National Park: Olli Marttila
302 Tarangire National Park: Sophia Lenferna
304 Udzungwa Mountains National Park: Francesco Rovero

Recommended further reading

The following books are highly recommended to complement the information in this book:

Estes, R.D. 1991. *The Behavior Guide to African Mammals*. University of California Press, Berkley.

Kingdon, J. 1997. *The Kingdon Field Guide to African Mammals*. Academic Press, San Diego.

Marttila, O. 2011. *The Great Savanna: The national parks of Tanzania and other key conservation areas*. Auris Publishers, Finland.

The following are excellent reference books for African mammals:

Kingdon, J., Butynksi, T., Hoffmann, M., Happold, M. & Kalina, J. (eds.) 2013. *Mammals of Africa* (6 Vols). Bloomsbury, London.

Skinner, J. D. & Chimimba, C. T. (2005). *The Mammals of the Southern African Subregion*. Third Edition. Cambridge University Press, Cape Town.

References

The following is a selected list of the references that were used in writing this book:

Amir, O. A., Jiddawi, N. S., & Berggren, P. 2005. The Occurrence and Distribution of Dolphins in Zanzibar, Tanzania, with Comments on the Differences Between Two Species of *Tursiops*. *Western Indian Ocean Journal of Marine Science* 4(1): 83–93.

Amir, O.A., Berggren, P., Jiddawi, N.S. 2012. Recent records of marine mammals in Tanzanian waters. *Journal of Cetacean Research and Management* 12(2):249–253.

Apps, P. 2000. *Smither's Mammals of Southern Africa: A Field Guide*. Struik Publishers, Cape Town.

Berggren, P., Amir, O. A., Guissamulo, A., Jiddawi, N. S., Ngazy, S., Stensland, E., Särnblad, A. & Cockroft, V. G. 2007. Sustainable Dolphin Tourism in East Africa. MASMA Technical Report. WIOMSA Book Series No.7: 1–72.

Berggren, P. 2009. *Whales and Dolphins: A field guide to marine mammals of East Africa*. East Publishing, Norwich, UK.

Bertram, B. C. R. 1982. Leopard ecology as studied by radio tracking. *Symposium of the Zoological Society of London* 49: 341–352.

Bonnington, C., Steer, M. D., Lamontagne, J., Owen, N., & Grainger, M. 2010. Evidence for local declines in Tanzania's Puku antelope (*Kobus vardoni*) population between 1999 and 2003. *African Journal of Ecology* 48(4): 1139–1142.

Borner, M. 1988. The rehabilitated chimpanzees of Rubondo Island. *Oryx* 19(3): 151–154.

Brink, H., Smith, R. J., & Skinner, K. 2013. Methods for lion monitoring: a comparison from the Selous Game Reserve, Tanzania. *African Journal of Ecology* 51(2): 366–375

Burgess, N. D. & Clarke, P. G. 2000. *Coastal Forests of Eastern Africa*. IUCN – The World Conservation Union, Switzerland.

Butynski, T. M., De Jong, Y. A., Perkin, A. W., Bearder, S. K., & Honess, P. E. 2006. Taxonomy, Distribution, and Conservation Status of Three Species of Dwarf Galagos (*Galagoides*) in Eastern Africa. *Primate Conservation* 21: 63–79.

Butynski, T. M. & De Jong, Y. A. 2011. Zanzibar Red Colobus on Pemba Island, Tanzania: population status 38 years post-introduction. In: *Global Re-introduction Perspectives: 2011* (ed. Soorae, P.S.). IUCN/SSC Re-introduction Specialist Group, Abu Dhabi, UAE. 168–174.

Caro, T. M., Pelkey, N., Borner, M., Severre, E. L. M., Campbell, K. L. I., Huish, S. A., Ole Kuwai, J., Farm, B. P., Woodworth, B. L. 1998. The impact of tourist hunting on large mammals in Tanzania: an initial assessment. *African Journal of Ecology* 36: 321–346.

Caro, T. M. 2003. Umbrella species: critique and lessons from East Africa. *Animal Conservation* 6: 171–181.

Caro, T. 2008. Decline of large mammals in the Katavi–Rukwa ecosystem of western Tanzania. *African Zoology* 43 (1): 99–116.

Caso, M. S. A. 2002. *Leopard Pilot Population Study at Rungwa–Piti Ecosystem*. Report. Tanzania, East Africa.

Coe, M., McWilliam, N. M., Stone, G. & Packer, M. (eds.). 1999. *Mkomazi: The Ecology, Biodiversity and Conservation of a Tanzanian Savanna.* Royal Geographical Society, London.

Cordeiro, N. J, Seddon, N., Capper, D. R., Ekstrom, J. R. R., Howell, K. M., Isherwood, I. S., Msuya, C. A. M., Mushi, J. T., Perkin, A. W., Pople R. G. & Stanley, W. T. 2005. Notes on the ecology and status of some forest mammals in three Eastern Arc Mountains. *Journal of East African Natural History* 94: 175–189.

Coster, S. and Ribble, D. O. 2005. Density and cover preferences of Black-and-rufous Elephant-shrews (*Rhynchocyon petersi*) in Chome Forest Reserve, Tanzania. *Belgian Journal of Zoology* 135: 175–177.

Davenport, T.R.B., Stanley, W.T., Sargis, E.J., De Luca, D.W., Mpunga, N.E., Machaga, S.J., & Olson, L.E. 2006. A new genus of African monkey, Rungwecebus: morphology, ecology, and molecular phylogenetics. *Science*, 312: 1378–1381.

Davenport, T. R. B., De Luca, D. W., Jones, T., Mpunga, N. E., Machaga, S. J., Kitegile, A. & Phillipps, G. P. 2008. The Critically Endangered Kipunji *Rungwecebus kipunji* of southern Tanzania: first census and conservation status assessment. *Oryx*, 42(3): 352–359.

Davenport, T. R. B., Nowak, K., & Perkin, A. 2013. Primate Priority Areas in Tanzania. *Oryx*, 48(1): 39-51.

De Luca, D. W. & Mpunga, N.E. 2005. *Carnivores of the Udzungwa Mountains Presence, distributions and threats.* Wildlife Conservation Society Report.

De Luca, D. W. & Mpunga, N. E. 2013. Small carnivores of the Mt. Rungwe–Kitulo landscape, southwest Tanzania: presence, distributions and threats. *Small Carnivore Conservation.* 48: 67–82.

De Luca, D. W & Rovero, F. 2006. First records in Tanzania of the vulnerable Jackson's Mongoose *Bdeogale jacksoni (Herpestidae).* Oryx 40(4): 468–471.

De Jong, Y. A., Butynski, T. M., Isbell, L. A., & Lewis, C. 2009. Decline in the geographical range of the Southern Patas Monkey *Erythrocebus patas baumstarki* in Tanzania. *Oryx*, 43(2): 267–274.

De Jong, Y. A., Butynski, T. M. & Perkin, A. W. 2011. *List of the Primates of Tanzania.* Website: www.wildsolutions.nl

Doggart, B. N., Leonard, C., Perkin, A., Menegon, M., & Rovero, F. 2008a. TFCG Technical Paper 18. *The vertebrate biodiversity and forest condition of the North Pare mountains.* pp. 1–79. Dar es Salaam.

Doggart, B. N., Leonard, C., Perkin, A., Menegon, M., & Rovero, F. 2008b. TFCG Technical Paper 18. *The vertebrate biodiversity and forest condition of Udzungwa Mountains Forests in Mufindi District.* pp. 1–142. Dar es Salaam.

Dorst, J. & Dandelot, P. 1976. *A Field Guide to the Larger Mammals of Africa.* Collins, London.

Durant, S. M., Craft, M., Foley, C. A. H., Hampson, K., Lobora, A., Msuha, M., Eblate, E., Bukombe, J., Mchetto, J., Pettorelli, N. 2010. Does size matter? An investigation of habitat use across a carnivore assemblage in the Serengeti, Tanzania. *Journal of Animal Ecology* 79(5): 1012–1022.

Durant, S. M., Craft, M. E., Hilborn, R., Bashir, S., Hando, J. & Thomas, L. 2011. Long-term trends in carnivore abundance using distance sampling in Serengeti National Park, Tanzania. *Journal of Applied Ecology* 48: 1490–1500.

East, R. 1999. *African Antelope Database 1998.* IUCN, Gland, Switzerland.

Easton, E. R. 1978. Observations on the distribution of the hedgehog *(Erinaceus albiventris)* in Tanzania. *African Journal Ecology* 17: 175–176

Ehardt, C. L., Jones, T. P. and Butynski, T. M. 2005. The endangered Sanje Mangabey (*Cercocebus sanjei*) of the Udzungwa Mountains, Tanzania: Current protective status, ecology and strategies for improving conservation. *International Journal of Primatology* 26: 557–583.

Estes, R. D. 1991. *The Behavior Guide to African Mammals.* University of California Press.

Estes, R.D. Atwood, J. L. & Estes, A. B. 2006. Downward trends in Ngorongoro Crater ungulate populations 1986–2005: Conservation concerns and the need for ecological research. *Biological Conservation* 131: 106–120.

Estes, R. D. & East, R. 2009. Status of the Wildebeest *(Connochaetes taurinus)* in the wild 1967–2005. *WCS Working Papers* No. 37.

Folkens, P. A., Reeves, R. R., Stewart, B. S., Clapham, P. J. & Powell, J. A. 2002. *National Audubon Society Guide to Marine Mammals of the World.* Alfred A. Knopf, New York.

Goldman, H. V., & Winther-Hansen, J. 2003. *The Small Carnivores of Unguja Results of a Photo-Trapping Survey in Jozani Forest Reserve.* Zanzibar, Tanzania. Report.

Grimshaw, J. M., Cordeiro, N. J., Foley, C. A. H. 1995. The Mammals of Kilimanjaro. *Journal of East African Natural History* 84: 105–139.

Grimshaw, J. M. 1998. The Giant Forest Hog (*Hylocherus meinertzhageni*) in Tanzania – Records rejected. *Mammalia* 62(1): 123–125.

Groves, C. P. 2001. *Primate Taxonomy.* p. 350. Smithsonian Institution Press, Washington, D.C.

Groves, P. G. 2007. The endemic Uganda Mangabey, *Lophocebus ugandae*, and Other Members of the *albigena* Group (*Lophocebus*). *Primate Conservation* 22: 123–120.

Hall K.R.L. 1965. Behaviour and ecology of the wild Patas Monkey, *Erythrocebus patas. Uganda Journal of Zoology* 148: 15–87.

Haltenorth, T. & Diller, H. 1980. *A field guide to the mammals of Africa including Madagascar.* Collins, London.

Hoeck. H.N., Klein, H. & Hoeck, P. 1982. Flexible social organization in hyrax. *Zeitschrift fur Tierpsychologie* 59: 265–298

Hofmeyer, G. & Amir, O. 2010. Vagrant Subantarctic fur seal on the coast of Tanzania. *African Zoology* 45(1): 144–146.

Homewood, K. M. & Rodgers, W. A. 1981. A previously undescribed mangabey from southern Tanzania. *International Journal of Primatology* 2: 47–55.

Iida, E. G., Idani, G. & Ogawa, H. 2012. Mammalian Fauna of the Miombo Forest in the Ugalla Area, Western Tanzania. *African Study Monographs* 33(4): 253–270.

Ikanda, D. K. & Packer, C. 2006. *Lion abundance and distribution in Tanzania: a status report to the Wildlife Division.* Unpublished report, 1–14.

Jenkins, R. K. B., Maliti, H. T. & Corti, G. R. 2003. Conservation of the Puku Antelope (*Kobus vardoni*, Livingstone) in the Kilombero Valley, Tanzania. *Biodiversity and conservation* 12(4): 787–797.

Kingdon, J. 1974–1982. *East African Mammals. (7 Vols.)* The University of Chicago Press, Chicago.

Kingdon J. 1997. *The Kingdon Field Guide to African Mammals.* Academic Press, San Diego.

Kingdon, J., Butynksi, T., Hoffmann, M., Happold, M. & Kalina, J. (eds.). 2013. *Mammals of Africa (6 Vols.)* Bloomsbury, London.

Kissui, B. M. 2008. Livestock predation by lions, leopards, spotted hyenas and their vulnerability to retaliory killing in the Maasai Steppe, Tanzania. *Animal Conservation* 11(5): 422–432.

Kiszka, J., Muir, C., Poonian, C., Cox, T. M., Amir, O. A., Bourjea, J., Razafindrakoto, Y., Wambitji, N. & Bristol, N. 2009. Marine Mammal Bycatch in the Southwest Indian Ocean: Review and Need for a Comprehensive Status Assessment. *Western Indian Ocean Journal of Marine Science* 7 (2): 119–136.

Kruuk, H. 1972. *The Spotted Hyaena.* University of Chicago Press, Chicago.

Kruuk, H. & Goudswaard, P. C. 1990. Effects of changes in fish populations in Lake Victoria on the food of otters (*Lutra maculicollis* Schinz and *Aonyx capensis* Lichtenstein). *African Journal of Ecology* 28: 322–329.

Kock, D. & Howell, K. M. 1999. The enigma of the Giant Forest Hog: *Hylocherus meinertzhageni* (Mammalia: Suidae), in Tanzania reviewed. *Journal of East African Natural History* 88: 25–34.

Kock, D. & Stanley, W. T. 2009. Mammals of Mafia Island, Tanzania. *Mammalia* 73: 339–352.

Kundaeli, J. N. 1976. Distribution of tree hyrax (*Dendrohyrax validus validus* True) on Mt. Kilimanjaro, Tanzania. *East African Wildlife Journal* 14: 253–264.

Marshall, A. R. 2008. *Ecological Report on Magombera Forest.* World Wide Fund for Nature, Tanzania Programme Office.

Marshall, A.R. Aloyce, Z., Mariki, S., Jones, T.P., Burgess, N., Kilahama, R., Massao, J., Nashanda, E., Sawe, C., Rovero, R. & Watkin, J. 2007. Tanzania's second Nature Reserve: improving the conservation status of the Udzungwa Mountains? *Oryx* 41: 429–430.

Marttila, O. 2011. *The Great Savanna: the National Parks of Tanzania and other key conservation areas.* Auris Publishers, Finland.

Matzke, G. 1975. *Large mammals, small settlements and big problems: a study of overlapping space preferences in southern Tanzania.* PhD Dissertation. Syracuse University, New York.

Mduma, S. R., Lobora, A. L., Foley, C. A. H., & Jones, T. 2010. *Tanzania Elephant Management Plan 2010-2015.* Tanzania Wildlife Research Institute.

Mésochina, P., Mbangwa, O., Chardonnet, P., Mosha, R., Mtui, B., Drouet, N., Crosmary, W. & Kissui, B. 2010. *Conservation status of the lion (Panthera leo Linnaeus, 1758) in Tanzania.* Wildlife Division of Tanzania.

Moyer, D., Plumptre, A. J., Pintea, L., Moore, J., Stewart, F., Davenport, T. R. B., Piel, A. 2006. *Surveys of chimpanzees and other biodiversity in Western Tanzania.* Wildlife Conservation Society & Jane Goodall Institute.

Muir, C. E., Sallema, A., Abdallah, O., De Luca, D. W. & Davenport, T. R. B. 2003. The dugong (*Dugong dugon*) in Tanzania: A national assessment of status, distribution and threat. *Wildlife Conservation Society* 1–31.

Msuha, M. J. 2009. *Human impacts on carnivore biodiversity inside and outside protected areas in Tanzania.* PhD Dissertation. University College London.

Mutch. G. R. P. 1980. *The Larger Mammals of the Moyowosi.* Tanzania Notes and Records no. 84 and 85.

Nahonyo, C. L., Mwasumbi, L. B., Eliapenda, S., Msuya, C., Mwansasu, C., Suya, M. T., Mponda, B. O. & Kihaule, P. 2002. *Jozani–Chwaka Bay proposed National Park biodiversity inventory report.* Department of Zoology and Marine Biology, University of Dar es Salaam.

Nelson, F. 2000. West side story. Commanding physical presence: Kilimanjaro from Sinya Village in far northern Tanzania. *Swara* 23: 39–41.

Owen N., Wilkins V., Fanning E., & Howell K. M. (eds.). 2007. Frontier Tanzania. *Biodiversity Research and Awareness in the lesser-known Eastern Arc Mountains (BREAM) Volume I: Mahenge Mountains Report, Ulanga District.* Society for Environmental Exploration and the University of Dar es Salaam.

Pakenham, R.H.W. 1984. *The Mammals of Zanzibar and Pemba Islands.* Harpenden: privately printed.

Perkin, A., & Bearder, S. 2004. Minziro Forest reveals new galago and bat records for Tanzania. *The Arc Journal* 16.

Perkin, A. 2004. A new range record for the African Palm Civet *Nandina binotata* (Carnivora, Viverridae) from Unguja Island, Zanzibar. *African Journal of Ecology* 42: 232–234.

Perkin, A., Bearder, S. K., Davenport, T. R. B., & Butynski, T. M. 2005. Mt. Rungwe Galago, Galagoides sp. nov. In *Report to IUCN/SSC Primate Specialist Group (PSG), International Primatological Society (IPS) and Conservation International (CI)*, (eds.) Mittermeier, R.A., Valladares-Pádua, C, Rylands, A.B., Eudey, A.A., Butynski, T.M., Ganzhorn, J.U., Kormos, R., Aguiar, J.M., & Walker, S. Washington, DC. 1–15.

Pitra, C., Hansen, A. J., Lieckfeldt, D. & Arctander, P. 2002. An exceptional case of historical outbreeding in African Sable Antelope populations. *Molecular Ecology* 11(7): 1197–1208.

Plumptre, A. J., et al. 2010. *Eastern Chimpanzee (Pan troglodytes schweinfurthii): Status Survey and Conservation Action Plan 2010–2020.* IUCN/SSC Primate Specialist Group, Gland, Switzerland. 1–52.

Rathbun, G. B. 2013. Sengi distribution maps at http://www.sengis.org/distribution.php accessed on 4 January 2013.

Richmond, M. 2011. *Summary. Humpback Whale sightings for Kenya, Tanzania and Mozambique.* Whales Ahoy! Newsletter No.4.

Rodgers, W.A. 1982. The decline of large mammal populations on the Lake Rukwa grasslands, Tanzania. *African Journal of Ecology* 20: 13–22.

Rodgers, W.A & Swai, I. 1988. Country Report. Tanzania. In: East, R. (ed.). Antelopes. Global survey and Regional Action Plans. Part 1. East and Northeast Africa. IUCN, Gland, Switzerland.

Rovero, F., Jones, T., & Sanderson, J. 2005. Abbott's Duiker (*Cephalophus spadix* True 1890) and other forest antelopes of Mwanihana Forest, Udzungwa Mountains, Tanzania, as revealed by camera-trapping. *Tropical Zoology* 18(1): 13–23.

Rovero, F., Struhsaker, T. T., Marshall, A. R., Rinne, T. A., Pedersen, U. B., Butynski, T. M., Ehardt, C. L. & Mtui, A. S. 2006. Abundance of Diurnal Primates in Mwanihana Forest, Udzungwa Mountains, Tanzania. *International Journal of Primatology* 27(3): 675–697.

Rovero, F., Rathbun, G. B., Perkin, A., Jones, T., Ribble, D. O., Leonard, C., Mwakisoma, R. R. & Doggart, N. 2008. A new species of Giant Sengi or Elephant-shrew (genus *Rhynchocyon*) highlights the exceptional biodiversity of the Udzungwa Mountains of Tanzania. *Journal of Zoology* 274(2): 126–133.

Rovero, F., Marshall, A. R., Jones, T. & Perkin, A. 2009. The primates of the Udzungwa Mountains: diversity, ecology and conservation. *Journal of Anthropological Sciences* 87: 93–126.

Rovero, F., Mtui, A. S., Amani. S., Kitegile, A. S. & Nielsen, M. R. 2012. Hunting or habitat degradation? Decline of primate populations in Udzungwa Mountains, Tanzania: An analysis of threats. *Biological Conservation* 146: 89–96.

Rushby, G. G. & Swynnerton, G. H. 1946. Notes on Some Game Animals of Tanganyika Territory. *Tanganyika Notes and Records* 22: 14–26.

Safari Club International. 2008. *SCI Record Book of Trophy Animals.* Edition XII, Vols. 1 & 2. Safari Club International, Tucson.

Sale, J. B., Lamprey, H., Rodgers, A., Kingdon, J., Rathbun, G., Duff-McKay, A., Douglas-Hamilton, I., Gwynne, M.D., Swank, W., Myers, N., Western, D., Curry-Lindahl, K., Hillman, J.C. 1977. *Scientific and Technical Committee Report of the working group on the Status of East African Mammals Phase 1: Large Mammals.* East African Wildlife Society.

Salter, R. F. & Davenport, T. R. B. 2011. *Orchids and Wildflowers of Kitulo Plateau.* WILDGuides, Hampshire.

Shirihai, H. & Jarrett, B. 2006. *Whales, Dolphins and other Marine Mammals of the World.* Princeton Field Guides, Princeton.

Sinclair, A. R. E., Mduma, S., Hopcraft, J. G. C., Fryxell, J. M., Hilborn, R., & Thirgood, S. 2007. Long-term ecosystem dynamics in the Serengeti: lessons for conservation. *Conservation Biology* 21(3): 580–590.

Sinclair, A. R. E. 2012. *Serengeti Story: life and science in the world's greatest wildlife region.* Oxford University Press, Oxford.

Skinner, J. D. & Chimimba, C. T. 2005. *The Mammals of the Southern African Subregion.* Third Edition. Cambridge University Press, Cape Town.

Stensland, E., Carlén, I., Särnblad, A., Bignert, A., & Berggren, P. 2006. Population size, distribution, and behavior of Indo-Pacific Bottlenose *(Tursiops aduncus)* and Humpback *(Sousa chinensis)* Dolphins off the south coast of Zanzibar. *Marine Mammal Science* 22(3): 667–682.

Stuart, T. & Stuart, C. 2006. *Field guide to the mammals of Africa.* Struik Nature, South Africa.

Struhsaker, T. T. 2005. Conservation of Red Colobus and their habitats. *International Journal of Primatology* 26: 525–538.

Struhsaker, T. T. & Siex K. S. 1998. Translocation and introduction of the Zanzibar Red Colobus monkey: success and failure with an endangered island endemic. *Oryx* 32(4): 277–284.

Struhsaker, T. T. & Siex, K. S. 2008. *Procolobus kirkii.* In: IUCN 2010. IUCN Red List of Threatened Species. Version 2010.1. www.iucnredlist.org.

Swynnerton, G. H. & Hayman, R. W. 1951. A checklist of the land mammals of the Tanganyika territory and the Zanzibar protectorate. *Journal of the East Africa Natural History Society* 20: 274–392.

TAWIRI. 2009. *Tanzania Carnivore Conservation Action Plan.* TAWIRI, Arusha, Tanzania. Available from **www.tanzaniacarnivores.org/information/publications**

Taylor, M. E. 1970. The distribution of the genets, *Genetta genetta, G. servalina* and *G. tigrina* in East Africa. *Journal of the East African Natural History Society* 28: 7–9.

Uehara, S. 2003. Population densities of diurnal mammals sympatric with the chimpanzees of the Mahale Mountains, Tanzania: comparison between the census data of 1996 and 2000. *African Study Monographs* 24(3): 169–179.

Van Vuuren, B. J., & Robinson, T. J. 2001. Retrieval of four adaptive lineages in duiker antelope: evidence from mitochondrial DNA sequences and fluorescence in situ hybridization. *Molecular Phylogenetics and Evolution* 20(3): 409–425.

Vesey-FitzGerald, D. F. 1964. Mammals of the Rukwa Valley. *Tanganyika Notes and Records* 62: 61–72.

Walsh, M. T. 2007. Island Subsistence: Hunting, Trapping and the Translocation of Wildlife in the Western Indian Ocean. *Azania* 42: 83–113.

Waltert, M., Chuwa, M., & Kiffner, C. 2009. An assessment of the Puku (*Kobus vardonii* Livingstone 1857) population at Lake Rukwa, Tanzania. *African Journal of Ecology* 47(4): 688–692.

West, L. 2011. *Sea Sense Annual Report 2011*

West, L. 2010. *Sea Sense Annual Report January – December 2010*

West, L. 2011. *Sea Sense Newsletter July – December 2011*

White, F. 1983. *The Vegetation of Africa – a descriptive memoir to accompany the Unesco/AETFAT/UNSO vegetation map of Africa*; Natural Resources Research Report; United Nations, Paris. 1–356.

Wildlife Conservation Society (WCS). 2005. Last of the Wild Data (Human Footprint) Version 2, (LTW-2): Global Human Footprint Dataset (Geographic). Wildlife Conservation Society (WCS) and Center for International Earth Science Information Network (CIESIN).

Wilson, D. E. & Reeder, D. M. 2005. *Mammal Species of the World. A Taxonomic and Geographical Reference.* Third Edition. Vols. 1 and 2. Johns Hopkins University Press, Baltimore.

Wilson, D. E. & Mittermeier, R. A. (eds.) 2009. *Handbook of the Mammals of the World.* Vol. 1. Carnivores. Lynx Edicions, Barcelona.

Wilson, D. E. & Mittermeier, R. A. (eds.) 2011. *Handbook of the Mammals of the World.* Vol. 2. Hoofed Mammals. Lynx Edicions, Barcelona.

Wilson, V. J. 2001. *Duikers of Africa: Masters of the African Forest Floor.* Chipangali Wildlife Trust, Zimbabwe.

World Wide Fund for Nature (WWF). 2004. *Towards a Western Indian Ocean Dugong Conservation Strategy: The status of Dugongs in the Western Indian Ocean Region and Priority Conservation Actions.* Dar es Salaam, Tanzania: WWF. 1–68.

Zachos, F. E., Apollonio, M., Bärmann, E. V., Festa-Bianchet, M., Göhlich, U., Christian, J., Haring, E., et al. 2013. Species inflation and taxonomic artefacts — A critical comment on recent trends in mammalian classification. *Mammalian Biology*, 78: 1–6.

Zinner, D., Groeneveld, L. F., Keller, C., & Roos, C. 2009. Mitochondrial phylogeography of baboons (*Papio spp.)*: indication for introgressive hybridization? *BMC evolutionary biology* 9: 83.

Index

This index includes the common English and *scientific* names of all the mammals included in this book. The names in **bold** indicate the preferred English names. The index also lists the main National Park and protected area pages.

Bold numbers refer to the page on which the main text for the species or major protected area can be found.
Italicized numbers indicate other page(s) on which a photograph may be found.
Non-bold numbers are used to refer to species that do not have their own account but are referred to in the text.